THE DISENCHANTMENT OF
SECULAR DISCOURSE

THE DISENCHANTMENT

OF

SECULAR DISCOURSE

Steven D. Smith

HARVARD UNIVERSITY PRESS

Cambridge, Massachusetts, and London, England

2010

Library of Congress Cataloging-in-Publication Data

Smith, Steven D. (Steven Douglas), 1952–
The disenchantment of secular discourse / Steven D. Smith.
    p.   cm.
Includes bibliographical references and index.
ISBN 978-0-674-05087-7 (alk. paper)
1. Secularism.   2. Discussion.   I. Title.
BL2747.S645 2010
211'.6—dc22   2009041104

To my mother

Contents

THE DISENCHANTMENT OF
SECULAR DISCOURSE

I

THE WAY WE TALK NOW

From time to time, we all find ourselves on that treacherous terrain where law and politics confront morality and justice. So we consider some controversial political decision or program or practice and ask whether it is moral or immoral, just or unjust, acceptable or unacceptable. Is torture always intolerable, or are there occasions when it is a necessary evil? Should "partial birth" abortions be prohibited? Is there a workable distinction between just and unjust wars, and if so, how should some particular conflict (such as the war in Iraq) be regarded? Should same-sex marriages be legalized? Do people have a right to end their lives, and to receive a doctor's assistance in doing so? What should we think about affirmative action? What are our responsibilities, if any, to people who want to immigrate to this country, or who are already here illegally? And so on, and so forth.

Sometimes we discuss such questions in private, or in congregations of people with whom we share a lot in how we think and talk. At other times, by contrast, we speak in a more public way with and to larger and more diverse audiences. We write an op-ed for a newspaper or listen to a call-in talk show on the radio. Or, in a class at a public university, we participate in a discussion involving students and faculty of various backgrounds, races, and political persuasions, and also of various religions (or lack thereof, or opposition thereto). Granting that the distinction is one of degree, let us describe the kind of talk about issues of political morality that goes on in these larger, more mixed settings as "public discourse."

And how illuminating, or how helpful or edifying or cogent, is public discourse these days? A mayor of New York famously used to ask his constituents from time to time, "How am I doing?" We might ask a similar question about public discourse today, in America: how is it doing? To be sure, in each case a full answer would be complex: a mayor and our public discourse no doubt perform better on some days and in some areas than others. Still, it may be worth posing the question in its raw simplicity. How efficacious is our public discourse today?

In the abstract, we might suppose that public discourse today ought to be rich and edifying, at least in comparison to its condition in earlier times. For one thing, technology is light-years beyond what it was: with not only telephones and television, but now word processing and the Internet and blogs of all shapes and sorts, the accessible means of research and communication are exponentially greater today than in earlier eras. And whereas public discourse was once largely an affair for educated white males, the diversity of voices today is much greater. A wider range of voices, one might suppose, should make for a greater variety of perspectives, and hence for a richer discourse.

In addition, basic literacy in the general population is surely higher today than it was, say, two or three centuries ago. Opportunities for more specialized education are greater as well. In the country's founding era, intellectual leaders like Benjamin Franklin and Thomas Jefferson were the country's equivalent of scientists, entrepreneurs, moralists, philosophers, and politicians all rolled into one: "Jack-of-all-trades; master of none," as the saying goes. Today there is still room for jacks-of-all-trades, but we also have the luxury, in our universities and think tanks and research institutions, of training and supporting people who devote their lives to specialized research and reflection on almost every conceivable issue and sub-issue. Such specialization, one might think, ought to contribute to a more refined and illuminating public discourse.

For these and related reasons, we might expect the general quality of public discourse on matters of political morality to be more probing and cogent today than it was in ages past. So, does the reality match these hopeful expectations?

Looking for an Argument?

Sadly, it does not. On the contrary. Or at least that complaint has been widely voiced of late.

Thus, in a recent book, Susan Jacoby laments the current "age of American unreason."[1] Over the past half century, Jacoby argues, we have experienced a "conscious degradation of standards for political self-presentation and discourse." "[T]he scales of American history have shifted heavily against the vibrant and varied intellectual life so essential to functional democracy," Jacoby insists, and public discourse today is characterized by "a new species of anti-rationalism, feeding on and fed by an ignorant popular culture of video images and unremitting noise that leaves no room for contemplation or logic."[2]

Ronald Dworkin's assessment is, if possible, even gloomier. Dworkin deplores "the lack of any decent argument in American political life."[3] "[M]ost people," he laments, "now have no interest in discussion or debate with those they regard as belonging to an entirely alien religious or political culture."[4] Nor is it only ordinary folks (a word I use with apologies to Jacoby, who cringes at the term[5]) who have lost interest in serious deliberation or debate, Dworkin declares. "[T]he news is not much better when we look . . . to the contributions of public intellectuals and other commentators. Intellectuals on each side set out their own convictions," but rarely do they make any effort to engage in "genuine argument."[6]

As a result, our political discourse is in an "appalling state."[7] "[W]e have not managed to construct even the beginnings of a decent public argument about these matters [of human rights, religious freedom, taxes, and other public issues]."[8] Indeed, "our politics are now so debased that they threaten our standing as a genuine democracy."[9]

Reviewing Dworkin's book, Danny Priel finds irony in this indictment. That is because in Priel's view, Dworkin's own book "is almost entirely lacking in, well, serious argument with the challenges to the views it expresses."[10] Priel comments that Dworkin purports to promote public debate "not so much to engage in serious discussion for the sake of discovering the truth, for Dworkin is confident that he already knows it. Rather, the point of having the debate is to give Dworkin the stage upon which he could explain to his political opponents where they go wrong."[11]

To Dworkin, this criticism no doubt seems unfair, even perverse. Dworkin insists that debate is crucially important and that he is trying earnestly, even desperately, to promote "genuine argument." But then, of course, many of the people Dworkin criticizes would doubtless say the same thing: they think, or they certainly act as if, they are engaging in argument. Indeed, a certain kind of observer might read Dworkin's book and wonder what world he is living in. "Take a good look around you!" the observer might implore. "Everywhere you look, people are arguing—passionately, often bitterly. Democratic presidential candidates against other Democratic candidates (and their spouses), and Republican candidates against Republicans. Democrats against Republicans. Creationists against evolutionists. Pro-life and pro-choice people. Evangelicals and Catholic bishops against secularists. The 'new atheists' against the traditional theists. Bill O'Reilly and Keith Olbermann. The problem today, in this country at least, is hardly a paucity of argument; on the contrary, there is far, far *too much* arguing!"

The previous paragraph was written, as you may have surmised, in the midst of the 2008 presidential primaries. As times change, you can change the specific examples, but you may not really need to change them, yet. In any case, the prevalence of arguing—of bitter contention—seems unlikely to diminish any time soon.

This observation, however, need not invalidate Dworkin's lament over the absence of "genuine argument." There is indeed a good deal of contention, Dworkin might respond—a good deal of sound and fury, or noisy clash of opinions. Even so, there is precious little real *argument*, strictly speaking—little genuine *debate*. Because if you look closely at what people say, they do not really engage their opponents, or even reveal the real bases for their own positions; they merely dress up their preestablished conclusions in verbiage. People may look like they are engaged in debate. They may even think they are engaged in debate. But in reality, they aren't.

So it seems to Dworkin, anyway, and so Dworkin's own pronouncements appear to Priel. And Dworkin and Priel may both be right.

Indeed, it seems to me (and my discussion will proceed from this judgment) that their criticism *is* right, *for the most part*. Perhaps Jacoby and Dworkin and like-minded critics exaggerate. Most of us can point to some pundit or poet or theorist—some *living* sage—whom we find to be wise and insightful, and to whom we turn for analysis or guidance. It is not as if public discourse today is utterly devoid of intelligent, sensible, even inspired contributors. Still, on so many matters of importance, the general quality of discussion does indeed seem disappointingly shallow. A few people may be saying wise things, but the other participants in the discourse often seem unwilling to listen to or actually to engage this wisdom. There can be clever comments and even profound insights, but these may nonetheless not converge to create a meaningful *discourse*. And so there is not, as Dworkin complains, "genuine argument."

Diagnosing the Deficiencies

How might we find ourselves in this peculiar and unhappy situation? How could this condition—of noisy, passionate contention but no "genuine argument"—arise?

Critics like Jacoby and Dworkin offer familiar diagnoses. Our schools have failed to provide citizens with a decent education.[12] The media are more interested in making a profit, and hence in entertaining, than in providing substantial and challenging news coverage and commentary.[13] The combination of television and other modern technologies—the Internet, video games, text-messaging—has created a public and especially a younger generation eager only to browse and skim, but without the patience actually to read and think.[14] Politicians and the media have pandered to such debased tastes by offering sound bites instead of serious discussion.[15] And on top of (or because of) these contributions to a "dumbing down" of public discourse, religion, and in particular evangelical or fundamentalist religion, once thought to have retreated into the private sphere, has once again invaded the public domain, with baneful effect.[16]

There may well be a measure of truth in these claims. But they seem to be descriptions more of symptoms than of underlying causes. For one thing, at least some of the developments that so depress critics like Jacoby and Dworkin—television, mass public education, new communication technologies such as the Internet—do not seem intrinsically associated with shallow or debased discourse: indeed, they might well be viewed (and often *have* been viewed) as potential contributors to a richer and deeper public conversation. So if these institutions have indeed become the scenes of a degraded discourse, it seems more plausible to view this development as a further and related *consequence* of whatever it is that has produced our current degradation, not as a basic *cause* of that condition.

In addition, if poor schooling, a sound-bite media culture, and evangelical religion were principal causes of the unsatisfactory condition of public discourse, then we might expect to find a more vibrant and illuminating discourse in other contexts that are not as much influenced by these factors, such as . . . law, maybe? In law, after all, highly trained (and well-paid) lawyers spend countless (billable) hours doing research, preparing briefs, and presenting sometimes mind-numbingly elaborate or technical arguments. The adversary system is designed to ensure that opposing viewpoints are vigorously presented. Seasoned judges listen to the arguments in a leisurely, structured format, and then deliberate about their conclusions, and then set forth and defend those conclusions in published and often lengthy opinions that they know will be subjected to close critical scrutiny by lawyers, legislators, and public interest or advocacy groups. Could there be a context more conducive to "genuine argument"?

And indeed, law *is* sometimes held out as a sort of oasis within the arid desert of public discourse—a small enclave in which a truly reasoned public discourse flourishes. Yale professor Owen Fiss, for example, has long been an enthusiast for this view.[17] As a student in one of Fiss's classes, I listened to many a homily on the theme. The closing sentence of a book by Harvard professor Mary Ann Glendon conveys a similar notion: "'Reason,' say the ancient voices. 'Reason, now and always, the life of the law.'"[18] In a similar vein, the Supreme Court has sometimes been held up as the exemplar of "public reason";[19] in fact, generations of constitutional theorists have defended the Court's authority to strike down democratically enacted legislation by asserting that the Court is more attuned to sober, dispassionate reasoning than legislators are.[20]

Dworkin himself has been a leading advocate of this viewpoint,[21] and he reiterates it in his recent book. "I have retained my enthusiasm for trusting important matters of political morality to constitutional judges," he declares, because the judicial forum "allows us to conduct an important part of the argument I said we need in the disciplined language of legal and hence political principle."[22]

Unfortunately, the reality in this respect falls desperately short of the promotions put out by enthusiasts of the judiciary like Dworkin and Fiss. To be sure, the Supreme Court's agenda often prompts the justices to pronounce upon not only the narrowly legal but also the prudential and moral dimensions of matters such as abortion, the "right to die," and affirmative action. And the resulting opinions can be ponderous and intimidating (to nonlawyers and students, anyway). But the actual quality of reasoning is almost invariably thin, conclusory, and disappointing. Assigned to write an essay on a similar issue for a freshman English course, a thoughtful student could usually produce something that, although of course lacking in authority and gravitas, would be as searching in its substance. Thus, I think Daniel Farber was accurate when he observed that Supreme Court opinions are "increasingly arid, formalistic, and lacking in intellectual value." The Court's opinions, Farber comments, "almost seem designed to wear the reader into submission as much as actually to persuade."[23]

Indeed, Farber may have given the Court too much credit. Typically, judicial decisions invalidating challenged laws ultimately boil down to peremptory assertions by the judges that the law in question has no "rational basis" or is the product of prejudice or "animus." Thus, citing "a substantial number of Supreme Court decisions, involving a range of legal subjects, that condemn public enactments as being expressions of prejudice or irrationality or invidiousness," Robert Nagel shows how "to a remarkable extent our courts have become places where the name-calling and exaggeration that mark the lower depths of our political debate are simply given a more acceptable, authoritative form."[24]

Farber's and Nagel's assessments are a few years old, to be sure, but nothing in more recent jurisprudence calls for a drastically different conclusion: indeed, Dworkin himself indicates that Supreme Court decisions in recent years have taken a turn for the worse.[25] A week or so ago (as of the time I write), a precocious younger colleague of mine remarked, following a workshop on constitutional issues, that Supreme Court opinions in general are "garbage." The judgment was overstated, no doubt—one that would be tempered and hedged in a more official or polite setting. And this particular colleague happens to be encumbered by not only a J.D. but also a Ph.D. in political science; political scientists are known to be disdainful of legal reasoning. Even so, I suspect that many or even most constitutional scholars have ventured similar if milder judgments in off-the-record contexts conducive to candor.

Dworkin's NYU colleague Jeremy Waldron offers a pointed assessment:

> [T]he alleged reason-giving advantage associated with courts is a sham. What courts call "giving reasons" is an attempt to connect the decision they are facing with some piece of abstract and ill-thought-through eighteenth-century prose. Or it is an attempt to construct desperate analogies between the present decision they face and other decisions that happen to have come before them (in which they were engaged in similar contortions). . . . And all the time, the real issues at stake in the good-faith disagreement . . . get pushed to the margins. They usually take up a paragraph or two of the twenty pages or more devoted to an opinion, and even then the issues are seldom addressed directly.[26]

"By making political questions into judicial questions," Waldron continues, "American constitutional practice tends to degrade the process of the open consideration of the reasons that are relevant to the justification of the decisions we face." And he concludes that "[John] Rawls's view of public reason—his position that the Supreme Court is the exemplar of public reason—seems to suggest that it would be a good idea to extend this degradation into public discourse generally."[27]

If judicial opinions are unsatisfying, though, it might be that legal *scholarship* is more searching and efficacious. It should be, shouldn't it? After all, scholars have the luxury of taking as long as they like (subject, to be sure, to concerns such as careerism, tenure decisions, and merit raises) to research and ponder the issues they engage, and the freedom to follow the arguments and evidence wherever those guides may lead. Nor are they required, as judges usually are, to reach some definite, binary conclusion ("Plaintiff wins" or "Plaintiff loses"). So legal scholarship might naturally run deeper than the more practice-oriented discourse of judges and lawyers. And (here I can only offer a peremptory, and perhaps self-serving, assessment) by and large it does. Even so, Stanford law professor Deborah Rhode reports a consensus that "too much [legal scholarship] is trivial, ephemeral, unoriginal, insular, pretentious or simply irrelevant."[28] For support, Rhode cites judge and professor Richard Posner's judgment that a great deal of legal scholarship is "trivial, ephemeral, and soon forgotten," Berkeley professor Dan Farber's description of the "intellectual aridity" of legal scholarship, and Yale professor Robert Gordon's opinion that much legal scholarship is "horribly pretentious and vacuous."[29]

In sum, if our public discourse on matters of political morality seems degraded, that lamentable condition is not limited to the sort of "sound bite" talk that we encounter in a presidential campaign or on Fox News or MSNBC. The problem runs deeper, it seems—and thus calls for a more searching assessment of its likely causes. Without rejecting the diagnoses offered by Jacoby, Dworkin, and like-minded critics, therefore, this book investigates an alternative explanation.

From Reason to Reasonableness

I will need to present that explanation in stages. In the first place, it seems evident that there is a general loss of faith in the capacity of reasoned discourse to provide cogent resolutions of controversial moral and political issues. If people come to believe astrology is bunk, they predictably will waste little time poring over the daily horoscope. By the same token, if people lose faith in the efficacy of reasoning, it is hardly surprising that they will expend little effort engaging in it.

In this respect, the current intellectual climate is strikingly unlike the one that prevailed during the time in which the American republic (and, some might say, the modern world) were born—the so-called Enlightenment. *Then* thinkers were confident that, as the eminent historian Henry Steele Commager wrote, "with Reason as their guide they could penetrate to the truth about the Universe and about Man, and thus solve all of those problems that pressed upon them so insistently."[30] Commager, immersed in and seemingly intoxicated by the eighteenth-century writings, exudes as much as describes the scope and the audacity of that mind-set, or that mood:

> Everything discussed and disputed! What a din of controversy and debate, what a clashing of minds. . . . What is the nature of the universe and of the celestial mechanics that God imposed upon it? How does Man fit into the cosmic system? Is religion necessary? . . . What is the end and the object of life? Is it happiness, and if so, what is happiness? . . . What is the origin of government, what the basis and the limits of government? What are the rights of Man—that cuts close to the bone!

These are the great questions that sent pens scratching across an infinity of pages, that launched a thousand Essays, Discourses, Considerations, Inquiries, and Histories. How they speculated, how they probed, how they wrote![31]

From our current vantage point, that enthusiasm, and that confidence in the capacity of "Reason" (notice that Commager uses the upper case) to "solve all of those problems that pressed upon [us] so insistently," may look quaint, almost childlike. The era of so-called Enlightenment was, James Q. Whitman observes, "an odd and often overblown age." And the thinkers of that period—the Voltaires, Jeffersons, Franklins—"remained fallible, and often comically fallible, human beings. The thrill of using one's free reason for the first time, it seems, often clouded the senses."[32]

By now, that particular cloud has been at least partially dispersed, and expectations regarding what "reason" can deliver have come coldly down to earth.

These deflated expectations for reason are reflected in the "political liberalism" of the most celebrated political philosopher of our time, John Rawls. An earnest insistence that important public decisions be justified by something called "public reason" remains conspicuous in Rawls's work.[33] But the term is apt to mislead. Upon inspection, it becomes apparent that Rawls's "public reason" is not the "Reason" of Commager's Enlightened thinkers; indeed, it comes closer in crucial respects to being Reason's nemesis—or at least its nanny, whose task is to keep Reason under control and out of sight when the important public functions occur.

Thus, for the thinkers described by Commager, Reason's function was to explore such matters as "the nature of the universe," "the end and the object of life," and the meaning of "happiness," and to bring the truths discovered in such inquiries to bear on practical matters such as "the basis and the limits of government" and "the rights of Man." Moreover, the Enlightened thinkers supposed that the uninhibited exercise of reason would lead people to recognize truth; and this supposition in turn implied an eventual convergence on truth.

In this spirit, Jefferson confidently predicted that "there is not a young man now living who will not die a Unitarian."[34] In retrospect, and in view of Unitarianism's comparatively meager numbers today, the prediction seems a bit bizarre. But there was a logic to it: if you have great confidence in the powers of reason (as Jefferson seems to have had), and if Unitarianism is the position recommended by reason (as Jefferson evidently supposed), then it would seem likely enough that under reason's benign tutelage people would eventually converge on that position.

Today any similar expectation seems utterly naïve with respect to religion, morality, politics, or political philosophy. On the contrary, clear thinking today must begin, Rawls maintains, by acknowledging that a pervasive pluralism in such matters is and will continue to be our condition.[35] No one expects that anything called "reason" will dispel such pluralism by leading people to converge on a unified truth—certainly not about ultimate or cosmic matters such as "the nature of the universe" or "the end and the object of life." Indeed, unity on such matters could be achieved only by state coercion: Rawls calls this the "fact of oppression."[36] So a central function of "public reason" today is precisely to keep such matters *out of* public deliberation (subject to various qualifications and exceptions that Rawls conceded as his thinking developed). And citizens practice Rawlsian public reason when they *refrain from* invoking or acting on their "comprehensive doctrines"—that is, their deepest convictions about what is really true—and consent to work only with a scaled-down set of beliefs or methods that claim the support of an ostensible "overlapping consensus."[37]

But why would someone agree to bracket her most fundamental convictions about what is true in "reasoning" about important public matters? She would do this, Rawls explains, if and because she is "reasonable"—meaning that in a situation of pluralism she understands that no one's truth is going to prevail over its rivals, and so rather than seeking to ground public decisions in truth she is "ready to propose principles and standards as fair terms of cooperation and to abide by them willingly, given the assurance that others will likewise do so."[38] To be reasonable is thus not the same as to be rational, and indeed "there is no thought of deriving the reasonable from the rational."[39] Far from being an exercise of Reason, "reasonableness" reflects a willingness, in the interest of civil peace, to rein in that potentially disruptive faculty.

In short, in the eighteenth century, a commitment to reason denoted a willingness to pursue the truth and to follow the argument wherever it leads, with the confidence that reason will ultimately lead people to converge on the truth. In contemporary political liberalism, in stark contrast, "reasonableness" denotes a willingness *not* to pursue or invoke for vital public purposes what one believes to be the ultimate truth—a willingness based on the judgment that reason will *not* lead to convergence but will instead subvert a civic peace that can be maintained only if people agree not to make important public decisions on the basis of arguing about what is ultimately true.

In this way, Reason is displaced by "reasonableness"—which in effect amounts to a willingness *not* to ask too much of, or to assign too much responsibility to, reason. Jeremy Waldron observes that "the constraints Rawls imposes on civic discourse so diminish our ability to grasp the true weight and implications of reasons in political argument as to deprive the practices they are supposed to govern of any entitlement to be called 'justificatory' in the true sense of the word."[40]

Suppose, though, that we set aside that larger criticism for the moment: an urgent practical question still presses. What if the truncated discursive resources available within the downsized domain of "public reason" are insufficient to yield any definite answer to a difficult issue—abortion, say, or same-sex marriage, or the permissibility of torture under emergency circumstances? What if these limited resources fail to provide a satisfying justification for a decision on such issues? This worry is hardly academic. On the contrary, it seems apparent that at least for such hotly disputed controversies, the limited scope of beliefs and methods that actually can claim an "overlapping consensus" in a radically pluralistic society are insufficient to provide a generally persuasive basis for decision and justification.[41]

Rawls attempts to finesse this daunting problem by simply stipulating that an "essential feature of public reason is that its political conceptions should be complete." Under this stipulation, "public reason" is *by definition* adequate to "give a reasonable answer to all, or to nearly all, questions involving constitutional essentials and matters of basic justice":[42] a discourse lacking such completeness, it seems, would not qualify as a form of "public reason."

But this stipulation does nothing to address the real-world problem. Instead, it merely prompts a reformulation of the objection: not "Public reason will leave many vital questions unresolved" (because by stipulation, it seems, "public reason" cannot fail in that way), but rather "Public reason (so defined) does not exist." Which would in fact be a very plausible conclusion to draw—and one that brings us back to our current lamentable condition as described by critics like Susan Jacoby and Ronald Dworkin.

Now, though, instead of laying principal blame on poor schools or profit-driven media or evangelical religion, we can notice the way in which shallowness in discourse is actually *prescribed by* some of the most influential political thought of our time. (Because Rawls was only the most prominent in a whole family of like-minded theorists.) It is hardly an exaggeration to say that the very point of "public reason" is to keep public discourse shallow—to keep it from drowning in the perilous depths of questions about "the nature of the universe," or "the end and the object of life," or other tenets of our comprehensive doctrines. And that prescription, as we have seen, is in turn the product of a general loss of confidence in the capacity of reason to actually lead people to truth in such matters. "You have your opinions and I have mine," we are wont to think, "and nothing in our so-called 'reasoning' is likely to change our minds."

Given this lack of confidence in the efficacy of reason, is it any wonder that fewer people actually make the effort to engage in genuine reasoning in public discourse? Why *should* anyone invest time and effort in such a predictably futile project? The Enlightenment program of reason—of Reason—seems to be a sinking ship (with respect to matters of political morality, anyway), as even the champions of "public reason" quietly but effectively concede; and people and rats usually scurry to get off, not on, such a ship.

But this conclusion prompts another question: how did people come to lose confidence in the capacity of reason to lead people to truth? What happened to cause the Enlightenment's faith in reason—the faith portrayed in Commager's giddy description—to fade?

Different people will answer that question differently, obviously. And as usual, a full historical account, if such were even possible, would be dauntingly complex, and would include not just intellectual influences but also cultural, political, and military events and developments—the horrors of World War I trench warfare, Auschwitz, and the Gulag, for example. Still, for present purposes, the core of the most eligible answers can be conveyed in two contrasting stories. (These stories are of course simplifications of a much more convoluted history.) The first story is familiar, and is easily discernible in the writing of critics like Jacoby and Dworkin and like-minded thinkers. The second, though hardly original with me, is less familiar. But it is, I believe, ultimately more illuminating—I might say, with trepidation and with apologies to Rawls and Rorty, that it is ultimately more *true*—than the first one.

How the Enlightenment Went Out: The Standard Story

In the standard depiction, the Enlightenment reflected a struggle by the partisans of reason against the dark forces of religion, tradition, and superstition.[43] In Europe, Christianity in particular was viewed as an "infection," Peter Gay says, and as a form of "disease."[44] American proponents of Enlightenment, like Jefferson, were generally more moderate in their opinions,[45] but they also insisted on the superiority of reason over tradition, and an Enlightened figure like Jefferson ridiculed what he perceived as the ignorance and irrationality of more traditional or orthodox forms of religion.[46] The commitment to reason manifested itself, among other places, in the crafting of the American Constitution which, because it was a product of rational deliberation, was held out as (in Jefferson's sanguine description) "unquestionably the wisest ever yet presented to men."[47]

In believing that life and government could be brought under the dominion of reason, however, the Enlightened thinkers acted on what seems to be a recklessly optimistic estimate of what human beings are capable of—reckless on their own premises, at least. People have often found security, comfort, and consolation in tradition and religion; or at least so hold the partisans of secular reason (who often find religion to be largely inexplicable *except* in such terms). So the Enlightenment project was a "lively experiment,"[48] or perhaps an enactment of the parable of Plato's cave. The project gambled on the hope that human beings, once brought into the light of reason, could be persuaded to live in that unblinking glare rather than retreating back into the dark, warm, womb-like cave of religion and tradition. As civilization progressed, religion would dwindle and largely disappear—or at least would retreat to the private domain, leaving a public sphere governed by secular reason.[49]

So the project was a gamble based on an optimistic view of human potential. Sadly, that view was *too* optimistic. (I am still summarizing the first or standard story). Thus, in a narrow sense the Enlightenment in America was already finished by the early years of the nineteenth century, as the wave of revivalistic and sometimes grotesque religiosity often called the "Second Great Awakening" swept across the country. The commitment to reason did not disappear, however, and in this country it has persisted in an unstable détente with traditional religion ever since. There have been occasional embarrassments (the Scopes "monkey trial," for example), but there have also been advances. Universities, for example, once heavily religious in character, are by now almost exclusively secular.[50] And at least if taken at face value (as it may not deserve to be), constitutional doctrine now officially confines government to the domain of the secular.[51]

Still, particularly in times of heightened fear and confusion, people feel a greater need for security and reassurance,[52] and they tend to retreat from reason, reverting to their religious traditions. The 1960s, with the Vietnam War, the Kennedy and King assassinations, and the countercultures of antiwar, drugs, and the "hippie" movement, were one such time of confusion. In the wake of the 1960s, a conservative religious reaction gained force and made itself increasingly intrusive in political discourse.[53] The shock of September 11 inaugurated another such period of fear and confusion, and not surprisingly, religion has pushed back the discourse of reason in the ensuing years. Thus, the reelection of George W. Bush was, as Garry Wills dramatically put it, "The Day the Enlightenment Went Out."[54] Whether the election of Barack Obama has persuaded observers like Wills that the Enlightenment has been turned on again remains unclear, but it seems early to be unduly sanguine.

In one version or another, I think, this story is familiar—wearyingly so, for those of us who inhabit the academy. It is so familiar that many may regard it as virtually axiomatic. But there is a different story—one that is less familiar but, in my view, more compelling.

How the Enlightenment Went Out: A Revisionist Account

The alternative story agrees with much of the standard story in its broad outlines, but it assigns different valences and evaluations to some of the key components and developments, and thus issues in a diagnosis of our situation that is in some respects directly contrary to that of the standard story. The alternative story can agree that the Enlightenment was a movement away from a more pervasively religious and traditional world and in the direction of a more secular one. And while denying that religion is merely a manifestation of fear and insecurity, or that there is any necessary conflict between reason and religion, the alternative story can acknowledge that the self-styled champions of "Enlightenment" have often viewed the world in just these terms. But insofar as Enlightenment has faded, the alternative story does not rely primarily on fear and insecurity (or even on poor schools, profit-driven media, or the Internet) to explain that decline. Instead, it proposes a different explanation.

The explanation would go something like this: In the cultures of classical and premodern times, Western peoples inhabited a world that they understood (sometimes on theistic grounds, as in Jewish and Christian thought, and sometimes in a nontheistic way, as in Aristotle's philosophy) to be intrinsically normative or purposeful. Louis Dupre describes the classical Greek view that the universe was a "cosmos" or "ontotheological synthesis." In this conception,

> [n]ature teleologically directs organic processes to their destined perfection. It establishes the norms that things developing in time must follow if they are to attain their projected end. The more comprehensive term *kosmos* constitutes the ordered totality of being that coordinates those processes as well as the laws that rule them. *Kosmos* includes, next to the *physis* of organic being, the *ethos* of personal conduct and social structures, the *nomos* of normative custom and law, and the *logos,* the rational foundation that normatively rules all aspects of the cosmic development.[55]

In a similar vein, Remi Brague explains that in the premodern thought of the West, whether Christian, Jewish, or Islamic, "human action had been conceived of as being in phase with cosmological realities that were presumed to furnish humankind with a model, a metaphor, or at least a guarantee, of right conduct."[56]

The transition to the modern world occurred when it came to be accepted that progress in knowledge and control would be enhanced by leaving behind this metaphysically profuse (or perhaps promiscuous) cosmos in favor of a leaner world viewed as complete in its empirically observable, naturalistic, or physical dimension. Aristotelian "teloses" and "final causes" (an internal "oakness" pulling the acorn to grow into a tree) would be phased out; only "efficient causes" (one billiard ball striking and moving another) would remain. God would be, not denied, exactly, but excluded from scientific explanations and, later, from public political justifications. Instead of a purposeful, intrinsically moral cosmos brought into existence by a biblical deity or a Platonic demiurge according to an intelligent and normative design, the world would now be conceived to be composed of atomic particles randomly colliding and combining in intricate ways, and over the course of eons sometimes evolving into more and more complicated systems and entities, including ourselves.

The preceding paragraph is, of course, a gross simplification. Paradigm shifts of this type and magnitude do not occur all at once, or in any orderly or linear fashion, or as a result of some sort of agreement that they should occur. In fact, and sometimes to the consternation of contemporary partisans of Enlightenment, Jefferson and his colleagues did not banish deity from their explanations; in fact, they pervasively invoked Providence and the providential scheme in their accounts of everything from natural rights to the continued existence (as Jefferson supposed) of mammoths in North America.[57] Even today, the classical view, or offshoots or vestiges of it, persist and flourish in some cultural neighborhoods. Nonetheless, the story serves to convey an overall change that began in the early modern period and that has largely been completed by now, at least in much public discourse and especially in the discourse of the academy.

The historical developments that have led to this change are, of course, complex:[58] typical accounts emphasize nominalistic philosophical and voluntaristic theological developments of the late Middle Ages and early modern period,[59] the Protestant Reformation and the political reaction to the ensuing wars of religion,[60] and the spectacular achievements of science.[61] Other scholars call attention to the organized efforts of thinkers and movements of the nineteenth and twentieth centuries.[62] Under such influences, countless social thinkers predicted the advent of a world in which religion would have largely withered away.[63] And although those predictions have by now been to a significant extent discredited or at least seriously revised, it does appear that a "secular" worldview has come to dominate some areas of life. Peter Berger points out that although predictions of the decline of religion have largely proven to be mistaken, "[t]here exists an international subculture composed of people with Western-type education, especially in the humanities and social sciences, that is indeed secularized."[64]

Max Weber famously described the change as the "disenchantment of the world";[65] he sometimes spoke of modernity as an "iron cage," in which life is lived and discourse is conducted according to the stern constraints of secular rationalism.[66] It is that cage—the cage of secular discourse—within which public conversation and especially judicial and academic discourse occurs today.

Life in the Cage

And how has the exchange of a purposeful, normatively laden cosmos for a more stripped-down, secular universe worked out? Here the alternative story draws a distinction. In disciplines and fields of inquiry devoted to understanding the physical or natural world—in the natural sciences, in other words—the shift to a secular framework has been associated with a spectacular growth of knowledge, both theoretical and applied. This success is hardly surprising: regarding the world as a physical, naturalistic system is nicely congenial to inquiries interested in the physical, naturalistic dimension of the world. As a result, science has flourished, and conspicuously so: we now have genetic engineering, space exploration, and instant worldwide communication that would have astonished even our Enlightened ancestors.

In more normative domains, by contrast, it has turned out—I am still presenting the alternative story—that the secular vocabulary is too truncated to express the full range of our values, intuitions, commitments, or convictions. To be sure, some normative perspectives and disciplines (or at least disciplines with normative implications) are more compatible with the newer framework than others are; unsurprisingly, those are the perspectives and disciplines that have tended to prosper. Thus, economics, concerned with people's empirically measurable preferences as manifested in willingness to buy and sell, has achieved the reputation of being perhaps the most solid and rigorous of the so-called social sciences. The reputation may well be deserved. (These sentences were initially written before the economic meltdown of 2008; perhaps they need to be revised.)

Still, many of us have the sense that economics, for all of its power and insight, captures only a subset of the normative commitments we in fact have. And we perceive that the effort to convert noneconomic values into the currency of economics has the consequence of effectively negating or denaturing those values.[67]

More generally, utilitarianism (of which economics seems at least a close relation) is more at home in the secular world than some other normative positions are. But once again, many people find that utilitarianism simply does not adequately grasp or express their deeper normative commitments.[68]

In short, it may be that we can do science well enough within the iron cage of secular discourse, but when we try to address normative matters, we run up against a dilemma. We can try to treat all of our normative commitments as if they were the sorts of commitments that secularly congenial disciplines like economics or rational choice theory can recognize (and, again unsurprisingly, many academics are powerfully attracted to this approach); but then we may perceive that we have done violence to many of our deepest convictions. Or we can refuse to attempt that translation; but then it is awkward finding within secular discourse the words and concepts to say what we really want to say and to articulate what we really believe.

And so, the alternative story continues, when we attempt to engage in reasoning about vital normative concerns, our performances turn out to be a pretty shabby and unsatisfactory affair. So unsatisfactory, in fact, that many people eventually conclude that there is little point in pretending to participate in the enterprise at all—an enterprise that often looks like an exercise in inventing, as F. H. Bradley put it," bad reasons for what [we] believe on instinct."[69] And the result is predictable: a public discourse that is sometimes, as Dworkin says, "appalling."

Smugglers' Blues

This alternative story may seem altogether too gloomy, just as the accounts of current public discourse given by critics like Susan Jacoby and Ronald Dworkin may seem excessively glum. Such grim descriptions may prompt a challenge: if our discourse is so deficient—so "appalling"—then how is it that our world continues to go on, and not so badly? Political discourse may be shallow and politics may be an unedifying spectacle, but Americans still enjoy relatively high levels of freedom and economic prosperity. (A comparison to other times and places suggests that this statement remains true even in the midst of a serious economic recession.) Let us suppose that the constitutional reasoning of lawyers and judges *is* spectacularly unpersuasive, as I have suggested: even so, and acknowledging that particular decisions or legal doctrines will seem wrong and even iniquitous to some of us, our legal system still works relatively well compared to other systems we might observe in history or in other places in the world. If discourse is so bad, how can life still be, in many respects, so good?

Once again, any attempt at a complete answer to that question would be imposingly complex. For present purposes, though, there is a short and simple explanation for how things continue to work. And that explanation is . . . smuggling. Our modern secular vocabulary purports to render inadmissible notions such as those that animated premodern moral discourse—notions about a purposive cosmos, or a teleological nature stocked with Aristotelian "final causes," or a providential design. But if our deepest convictions rely on such notions, and if these convictions lose their sense and substance when divorced from such notions, then perhaps we have little choice except to smuggle such notions into the conversation—to introduce them incognito under some sort of secular disguise.

Such smuggling is, I happen to think, ubiquitous in modern public discourse. Some of it is small scale and idiosyncratic—the work of random discursive privateers (like, say, Ayn Rand). Much of it occurs under the auspices of large and powerful families of terms, concepts, and rhetorical tropes. As it happens, in the public discourse of present-day America, we have two dominant normative families—not the Corleone and Tattaglia families, but rather the autonomy-liberty-freedom family and the equality-neutrality-reciprocity family. These powerful and eminently respectable normative families do a good deal of legitimate business, for which we may all be grateful—I certainly am—but they also run extensive smuggling operations. (Sometimes the two families team up for these purposes, as in the Eisgruber-Sager "Equal Liberty" principle, which we will bump into in Chapter 4.)

I am far from the first to observe the workings of these operations. Take the autonomy-liberty-freedom family. "Freedom" is a term that inspires respect, even reverence. In the abstract, everyone admires it: who goes around proclaiming, "I'm against freedom"? (Not me, certainly.) And no doubt a vast amount of good has been accomplished under the banner of freedom. Consequently, there is ample scope for advocates to wrap their favored agendas in the flag of freedom. But, of course, there are different kinds or conceptions of freedom: "negative" versus "positive" freedom, "individual" versus "civic" or "political" freedom. Moreover, an expansion of one person's freedom often means a contraction of other people's freedom: if we recognize and protect the freedom of the pornographer to market pornographic materials, we simultaneously reduce the freedom of people to live and raise their children in a pornography-free community. Hence, appeals to "freedom" can easily be—and often are—question-begging: freedom becomes an honorable label used to smuggle in an advocate's particular agenda or conception of what is good and valuable.

In this vein, reviewing a history by Eric Foner of the various uses of "freedom" in American politics, Michael Klarman comments that "by demonstrating the infinite contestability and malleability of freedom, Foner has proven that the concept does no serious work in the various debates in which it is invoked."

> This is not to say, of course, that all arguments about freedom are equally convincing. It is to say that the reason some such arguments are more persuasive than others has nothing to do with their merit as arguments about freedom, but rather is attributable to the attractiveness of the substantive cause on behalf of which they are mustered.[70]

And Klarman concludes that

> [f]reedom . . . is an empty concept. To say that one favors freedom is really to say nothing at all. As is so often the case in constitutional law, one ultimately cannot avoid taking a position on the merits. Whether freedom is good or bad depends entirely on the particular substantive cause on behalf of which freedom is invoked.[71]

To be sure, theorists and advocates attempt to supply substantive criteria to fill in this emptiness. Probably the most powerful and pervasive such filler, at least in Anglo-American discourse, has been the famous "harm principle" proposed by John Stuart Mill. We will look at that principle more closely in a later chapter, and we will see that to a large extent, the principle has served as an immensely effective vehicle for . . . smuggling.

Or consider the equality family, which in recent decades seems to have muscled aside even the venerable freedom family at the center of American public discourse. More than a quarter century ago, Peter Westen published an article called "The Empty Idea of Equality" in the *Harvard Law Review*.[72] Westen's basic point was simple: as a normative value, equality is a formal notion, meaning simply that "like cases should be treated alike" and "unlike cases should not be treated alike." Those propositions are hardly controversial; what *is* controversial is whether particular instances actually *are* alike in relevant respects. *That* question cannot be answered by invoking equality, however, but only by reflecting on the substantive values or criteria that apply or should apply to a particular issue. Blind people are like those who are not blind for some purposes (voting, for example) because blindness is not relevant to the substantive criteria governing voting. But blind people are unlike those who are not blind for other purposes (for example, driving a car) because ability to see *is* relevant to the substantive criteria that govern the ability to drive.

Westen suggested that if we know what the relevant substantive criteria are, we do not need the idea of equality; we can simply treat each case as the relevant substantive criteria dictate. We do not need to insist on treating the blind and the sighted "equally"; if we simply determine the appropriate criteria for voting eligibility and for drivers' licenses and apply these criteria consistently, then without ever intoning the word we will ipso facto be treating these groups as equality requires. Conversely, if we do *not* know what the relevant substantive criteria are, the idea of equality is no help, because we have no way of determining whether particular instances are relevantly like or unlike. "So there it is," Westen concluded:

> Equality is entirely "circular." It tells us to treat like people alike; but when we ask who "like people" are, we are told they are "people who should be treated alike." Equality is an empty vessel with no substantive moral content of its own. Without moral standards, equality remains meaningless, a formula that can have nothing to say about how we should act. With such standards, equality becomes superfluous, a formula that can do nothing but repeat what we already know.[73]

Westen's conclusion may have overreached in some respects, as his critics argued.[74] But a mildly more modest conclusion seems sound, and also tremendously important: in any genuine controversy, the notion of "equality" cannot carry us far toward any particular resolution. If there is a sincere disagreement about, say, whether same-sex marriage should be legalized, then insisting on "equality" is merely a distraction (albeit a polemically potent one, as we have recently observed). More generally, when we observe an advocate placing a great deal of weight on "equality," we have cause to suspect that something sneaky is going on.

Westen's article has been widely discussed, and most legal scholars will purport to acknowledge the central point. Moreover, advocates typically understand that they must say *something* about the substantive criteria or values they are invoking. Yet it remains common to observe even the most prominent and sophisticated theorists and advocates today featuring appeals to equality as their central discursive strategy on a whole range of issues, from same-sex marriage to religious freedom to free speech to just about any major issue you can name. And whenever we observe this strategy in action, we have reason to suspect that the real operative values are being smuggled in—or at least heavily subsidized—under the auspices of the venerable family of "equality."

Or if "equality" happens to be indisposed, the close family relations of "neutrality" or "reciprocity" can often be employed to do the same work. Consider Jürgen Habermas's claim that a "universal" ground for religious toleration (as opposed to more local and prudential grounds) can be found in the idea of reciprocity. Citing Pierre Bayle's classic argument, Habermas argues that reciprocity precludes Christians from forbidding Muslim proselytizing in Christian Europe while at the same time objecting to the suppression of Christian evangelization in Japan.[75] To those of us for whom a constitutional commitment to religious toleration has become close to axiomatic, this argument is likely to pass without objection. *Of course* religious toleration is a good thing—who today worth paying attention to doubts this? So a denial of toleration would be a clear violation of reciprocity. Wouldn't it? And wouldn't it seem merely churlish, and maybe a bit medieval, to quibble with Habermas's argument?

So then did the people in premodern Europe who resisted religious toleration—the Thomas Mores, the John Calvins—somehow fail to grasp or accept the idea of "reciprocity"? Not at all. Or at least they need not have opposed the idea. Rather, they might cheerfully acknowledge the legitimate demands of "reciprocity," and they might further concede that, *if* Christianity, Islam, and, say, Shintoism are relevantly similar, then if Christians expect to be permitted to evangelize in territories dominated by Islam or Shinto, they likewise ought to allow representatives of those religions to proselytize in Christendom. But that premise—namely, that these religions are relevantly similar—is precisely what the premodern believers

31

emphatically denied. In *their* view, one of the religions leads to salvation, while the others lead to damnation: that is hardly equivalence. And what could be more perverse than to insist that reciprocity requires truth to be treated in the same way as falsehood? It is as if a student were to argue, on grounds of reciprocity, that if the school gives credit for true answers on a test it must give equal credit for false answers.

To be sure, even the most devout adherents to the different religions might acknowledge that the religions are similar in the sense that their own followers believe them to be true. But is that similarity dispositive for the question of reciprocity? Well, it may be, if we assume, for instance, that belief, not actual truth (or salvific efficacy), is the relevant factor. And that assumption may seem natural enough—even obvious—to, say, a modern skeptic who supposes that none of the faiths is actually true in any strong sense anyway, or that in any event their truth is unknowable *to us*. Conversely, to a premodern true believer—to a Thomas More, once again, or a John Calvin—that assumption would likely seem as odd as would a claim by a failing student that since all humans (including teachers) are fallible, what should matter in determining grades is not whether the answers given on an exam are actually correct (about which we can never be absolutely confident anyway) but whether the student sincerely believed those answers.

We need not take sides in this particular disagreement here. The crucial point is simply that the division between partisans and opponents of religious toleration is not over the obligation of reciprocity—both sides may happily and wholeheartedly embrace that idea—but over whether reciprocity should be keyed to truth or instead to something like sincere belief. Piously insisting on "reciprocity" only serves to conceal that fundamental disagreement. Consequently, upon hearing the Habermasian argument (or similar arguments made by Rawls[76] or any number of other advocates), the opponent of religious toleration might say just what Dworkin says of public intellectuals today, and what Priel says of Dworkin: "You purport to be offering an argument, but in fact you aren't. You are simply begging the question, and your 'argument' is just a way of packaging the problem so as import—to smuggle in—the conclusion you were determined from the outset to reach."

The Necessity of Smuggling

A powerful and respectable family will naturally resist—and resent—any accusation of illicit behavior. By the same token, the numerous learned and respectable patrons of the autonomy and equality families might indignantly deny that those families are engaged in smuggling or illegitimate activity. Isn't it presumptuous of me, an obscure law professor, to be leveling such a charge anyway? What evidence can I produce to prove that honorable, venerable families of notions like liberty and equality are associated with a disreputable activity like smuggling?

It is a fair question, and I hasten to say that what I have done to this point is simply to lay out a story. You can observe the various conversations that make up public discourse and see for yourself whether the story fits. I do hope to raise your suspicions, but I understand that nothing I have said thus far and nothing I will say hereafter will amount to proof sufficient to sustain any universal indictment. Maybe a prosecutor with sufficient stature and intellectual clout—a Charles Taylor, an Alasdair MacIntyre[77]—could make a careful, comprehensive case strong enough to bring down the dominant secular families. But I very much doubt it—and in any case I am quite sure that I do not possess either the credentials or the intellectual wherewithal to attempt that task.

Indeed, I will offer a further concession: it is far from obvious that we should even want to crack down on smuggling at this point. Black markets are generally frowned upon, but an economy can be so dependent on a black market that shutting down that market will lead not to clean, honest commerce but rather to economic collapse. Or conditions can develop in which legitimate public authority has broken down, leaving people to depend on gangs or warlords for whatever order they enjoy. In a similar way, smuggling arguably allows modern discourse to function and to provide a measure of rationality and sense to our normative affairs. Conversely, ending such smuggling, even if that were possible, might, under current conditions, have the effect of paralyzing normative evaluation and leaving the public square vulnerable to openly cynical politics—or to brute force.

Even so, corruption is still less than ideal. So if in our current circumstances, we have little choice but to put up with smuggling (and, perhaps, to throw our support behind the benign smugglers rather than the malign or misguided ones), we ought at least to retain some awareness of what is going on. That is the objective of this book.

A Note about "Smuggling"

Before we pursue that objective, though, some clarification is called for. I have suggested that a good deal of modern discourse trades on "smuggling." But I have been less than precise about just what "smuggling" is. Is this just a provocative metaphor for flawed or inadequate reasoning? And hasn't discourse in all times and places been prone to flawed or inadequate reasoning? If so, isn't it a little misleading (even if true) to suggest that modern discourse exhibits and depends on smuggling, in the same way that it would be misleading (even if true) to say that most people in Alabama have two eyes and two ears but only one nose?

So it will be helpful to try to make the notion a bit more definite. "Smuggling" is a metaphor, obviously, not a technical term; but it is a metaphor that serves to depict one sort of discursive shortcoming. There are many ways in which discourse can be deficient—formal logical fallacies, simple errors of fact, and so forth—and most of them do not involve "smuggling." "Smuggling" is one kind of deficiency. But what kind?

Well, in the first place, smuggling implies that an argument is tacitly importing something that is left hidden or unacknowledged— some undisclosed assumption or premise. But relying on an unacknowledged premise or belief is not in itself enough to constitute smuggling, because *all* discourse does that, and could hardly do otherwise. Suppose you suggest that we should walk over to the deli for lunch because it's close and the food is tasty and not too expensive. Your suggestion assumes a staggering number of things: that saving time is good, that tasty food is prima facie to be preferred over tasteless food, that saving money is desirable, . . . that the deli still exists, that our legs still function, that the world is real, and so forth. But that sort of assuming is a virtue, not a shortcoming, because you have reason to be confident that these propositions are not controversial. It would be merely tedious for you to try to state *all* of your implicit assumptions, even if it were possible. In declining to say out loud what is assumed and doesn't need to be said, you are being sensible; you are not "smuggling."

The term "smuggling" seems to fit only if what you assume but do not explicitly disclose is somehow "illicit." But illicit in what sense?

Here, I believe, there are various possibilities. An undisclosed premise might be illicit because if it were made explicit it would be controversial: you would have to defend the premise, and you don't want to do that. Or your premise might be illicit because you yourself do not believe it: you like your conclusion, maybe, but you don't actually believe what would be necessary to support this particular argument for that conclusion. Perhaps, if you were to make your unstated premise explicit, you could be convicted of inconsistency, because you have contradicted that premise on other occasions.

Or your premise might be illicit because the conventions of the discourse you are engaging in purport to exclude it. You are involved with some matter—a hiring decision, perhaps, or a criminal trial—that isn't supposed to turn on race, but you manage obliquely to insinuate race into the discussion. So you tacitly do what you would not be allowed to do forthrightly.

An idea or belief or premise might be "illicit" in any of these senses. And if someone nonetheless makes an argument that implicitly depends on such illicit material and in that way manages to sneak this material into the conversation without open acknowledgment, it seems fair to describe this practice as "smuggling."

The term can be used, I think, without implying that a person who smuggles is necessarily in "bad faith" or even conscious of what she is committing (just as a tourist might innocently "smuggle" into the country contraband that had been surreptitiously stowed in his luggage by some stranger). On the contrary, smuggling might in many cases be unintentional or unconscious. As I will use the term, at least, someone who makes an argument that depends on an illicit and undisclosed premise is smuggling even if she is not consciously aware that she is relying on and thus importing that premise.

Once again, smuggling is only one kind of discursive shortcoming; there are any number of flaws or errors in discourse that do not involve "smuggling." Thus, an argument can be guilty of *logical fallacies* without smuggling. Conversely, it can smuggle without being guilty of any logical fallacy. If I say, "I know that Fido is a cow because cows have four legs and Fido has four legs," I have committed a conspicuous fallacy, but I have not smuggled. In a similar way, *mistakes of fact* are not equivalent to smuggling. Indeed, outright lying is not the same as smuggling: lying need not involve relying on illicit, undisclosed premises or propositions.

To return to the doubt posed a moment ago: it is surely true that discourse and argumentation at all times and in all places have often exhibited shortcomings. But it might be that particular kinds of discursive shortcomings thrive in particular kinds of situations. For reasons I have already suggested, I suspect that smuggling thrives in our contemporary situation. In saying this, however, I do not mean to contend that modern public discourse is necessarily worse—more futile or degraded or prone to error—than public discourse was two centuries or ten centuries or two millennia ago. In some respects modern public discourse may deserve higher marks than public discourse of many past times did; indeed, I suspect that this is so. So I am not making here (as some readers have supposed) any overall evaluative comparison of "secular" as opposed to "religious" discourse. "Religious" discourse—and of course there are many different kinds and forms of discourse that might be called "religious"—faces challenges and is prone to errors of its own. My suggestion is simply that the sort of discursive failing that can be described as "smuggling" is especially characteristic of our times, and of conversations carried on within the secular cage.

Which is not so surprising, since conversations in the secular cage could not proceed very far *without* smuggling. That at least is my claim.

The Plan of the Book

But how to support this claim? As I have already indicated, I doubt that anyone possesses the intellectual stature to succeed with any full-scale exposure and demonstration of illicit activities carried on under the auspices of the families of liberty and equality—but in any case I certainly do not. Still, just as a prosecutor or journalist who is unable to demonstrate wrongdoing by an entire family or syndicate may nonetheless try to pick off or expose the occasional hit man or boss, I can more realistically try to show smuggling on the part of particular modern thinkers or movements. That is what this book seeks to do.

Thus, the different chapters of the book deal with specific important thinkers or issues. Chapter 2 considers the much-discussed controversy over "assisted suicide." Chapter 3 discusses John Stuart Mill and Joel Feinberg and the enormously powerful "harm principle," perhaps the most influential modern notion for attempting to give practical content to the commitment to liberty. Chapter 4 turns to the vexed issue of religious freedom and the "wall of separation between church and state." Martha Nussbaum and the so-called capabilities approach, described by Nussbaum as "the most important theoretical development in human rights during the past two decades,"[78] are the subjects of Chapter 5.

My intention is that these chapters (2 through 5) can be read in isolation, and in any order, depending on which of the thinkers or subjects a reader may be most interested in. Although the particular subjects vary from chapter to chapter, a common theme runs through them, and my hope is that reading them in combination will provide support for a more general or cumulative criticism. That criticism, once again, is that the secular vocabulary within which public discourse is constrained to operate today is insufficient to convey our full set of normative convictions and commitments. We manage to debate normative matters anyway—but only by smuggling in notions that are officially inadmissible, and hence that cannot be openly acknowledged or adverted to. The pervasiveness of smuggling allows our conversations to be less pointless or ineffectual than they might be. But the fact that we must smuggle in, and hence cannot fully own up to, our real commitments—often cannot articulate them even to ourselves—ensures that our discourse will often be barren, unsatisfying, and shallow in the ways that critics like Jacoby and Dworkin say it is.

The chapters I have mentioned are all critical in nature: they attempt to put on exhibit the futility of our conversations in the secular cage. So then are we consigned simply to a perpetual practice of smuggling, and hence to conversations that will inevitably seem shallow, futile, often disingenuous?

I don't know. I have already said that under current circumstances, smuggling might be the best we can do. And I confess that given the entrenched secularism of the academy and the diversity of belief in the public at large, it is not easy to visualize just what a more satisfactory public discourse would look like. In criticizing thinkers like Rawls, I do not mean to deny that they have been struggling with very real problems—problems to which I do not purport to have a satisfying solution.

Nonetheless, the book concludes with two chapters that reflect on that question. Chapter 6 looks at a portentous issue—the potential of science to support human atrocities—and at a legal thinker, Joseph Vining, who in addressing that issue attempts to break out of the cage. Vining is less well known than Rawls, Nussbaum, Dworkin, and other thinkers I will notice in this book—and for understandable reasons. He does not conform to current conventions and assumptions, or even to academically fashionable forms of nonconformity. I do not know whether Vining's particular effort will succeed. But he is an important thinker nonetheless, and well worth considering, because his effort at least nurtures the hope that there is an alternative to simply resigning ourselves to life "in the cage."

Chapter 7 discusses the obvious practical question provoked by this diagnosis: What should we do? How *should* we talk? I suggest that something as exquisitely amorphous as a public discourse cannot be scripted, prescribed, or predicted. But we can recognize the error, and the irony, of the common view that a meaningful public discourse must be confined to the secular domain, and that nonsecular contributions—in particular religious contributions—would necessarily operate as a "conversation-stopper." If the thesis developed in these chapters is correct, this common prescription gets things exactly wrong: it is the imposition (under the heading of "public reason" or similar notions) of artificial constraints on discourse, and in particular the insistence that only secular talk is suitable for public discourse, that stifle conversation. In addition, we can acknowledge the need for greater openness to the alternative modes of discourse that already flourish in more secluded neighborhoods.

It may still turn out that in a pluralistic society such as ours, the barren secular discourse that Jacoby and Dworkin and others find so unsatisfying is the best we can do. But we won't know until we try opening up the cage.

2

Living and Dying in the "Course of Nature"

As the number of Americans eligible for membership in the AARP has risen over recent decades, increasing attention has naturally been focused on "end of life" issues. One set of questions—questions sometimes put under the heading of a "right to die"—is especially fraught with agonizing issues and implications, both ethical and existential. Should a person who believes his life has run its course—a person suffering from terminal illness and unremitting pain, perhaps—be permitted to "pull the plug"? And if so, should that person have a legal right to the assistance of a physician in bringing the last chapter to its close?

The issue was fiercely debated in the 1990s—Jack "Doctor Death" Kevorkian was perhaps the most conspicuous agent and provocateur—and it was actively litigated in the courts as well. The decade began with a landmark case, *Cruzan v. Missouri Department of Health*,[1] in which the Supreme Court appeared to conclude that patients have a right to refuse life-sustaining treatment, at least if they clearly declare this choice. (I say "appeared to conclude" because the decision was not without its central ambiguities.) So a patient can have a respirator or a feeding tube removed, even though the foreseeable result will be death.

But what if the mere refusal of treatment is not sufficient to bring about death? Or what if foregoing treatment will culminate in death—but only through the long and tortuous process of starvation or dehydration? Because suicide today is not illegal, a patient is legally free to end his life more expeditiously by, for example, taking a lethal dose of morphine. But what if the patient doesn't have the morphine, or isn't sure how to administer it, and so wants or needs a doctor's help in carrying out this decision? If a patient has a constitutional right to refuse treatment needed to sustain life, and in that way has the power to choose to die, should he or she not also have the right, say, to have a doctor prescribe and administer some death-producing medication?

Most states say "no": they prohibit doctors from assisting patients in terminating their lives. But do these prohibitions violate some constitutional "right to die"? That was the conclusion reached in the mid-1990s by federal Courts of Appeals on both the West Coast and the East Coast.[2] In the cases of *Washington v. Glucksberg*[3] (considering a Washington prohibition) and *Vacco v. Quill*[4] (considering a New York prohibition), the U. S. Supreme Court in turn reversed these appellate court decisions. The upshot is that, for now at least, you and I do not enjoy any constitutional right to a doctor's assistance in ending our lives.

Still, the issue continues to generate active debate and critical scholarship,[5] as well as attempts to secure the claimed right by legislation or litigation. Oregon enacted a statute permitting physician-assisted suicide; in 2008, Washington voters by a wide margin approved a similar measure. In that same year, a judge in Montana discovered a right to physician-assisted suicide in that state's constitution.[6]

The Supreme Court's *Glucksberg* and *Quill* decisions produced an array of opinions by the justices that amounted to, in Ronald Dworkin's description, "the fullest and most candid debate [of the relevant constitutional issues] for many decades."[7] Naturally, both the Supreme Court and the lower courts treated the question as one of constitutional law: only on this assumption did the courts have any excuse for involving themselves in the controversy. But in fact, the text of the Constitution says nothing explicit about euthanasia, or a "right to die," or physician-assisted suicide. So the judges' discussions inevitably moved beyond constitutional text and technical legal doctrine to reflect on the moral and political and historical dimensions of the choice to terminate life. That reflection was joined not just by judges and lawyers but by a host of scholars and pundits, including a "Dream Team of liberal political philosophers"[8] (John Rawls, Ronald Dworkin, Thomas Nagel, Judith Jarvis Thomson, Thomas Scanlon, and Robert Nozick), who submitted a much trumpeted "Philosophers' Brief."[9] The Supreme Court opinions together with the sometimes lengthy majority and dissenting opinions at the lower court levels and the accompanying commentary thus provided a thorough airing of views about the delicate question of deliberately ending life.

And yet, there was (and is) something inconclusive—something disconcertingly incomplete—about the array of arguments that were offered. Reflecting on the debate surrounding *Glucksberg* and *Quill,* we may find ourselves suspecting that proponents of the various positions were holding something back. Not that they were being disingenuous: in some instances, at least, the advocates were plainly sincere and even passionate in their various causes. But their arguments leave us with the suspicion that something was left out, or was concealed—from us, and perhaps from the advocates and judges themselves. Unbeknownst to the participants in the debates, perhaps, some premise or value—something that in fact led them to their various conclusions but that was not openly acknowledged—was, must have been, somehow smuggled into the debates.

In this chapter we will look at the arguments in *Glucksberg* and *Quill* to see whether something has gone missing. And we will ask what that something might be.

Hiding the Ball? The Court's Concealed Casuistry

In constitutional jargon, the issue in *Glucksberg* and *Quill* presented questions of "substantive due process" (sounding in the "liberty" theme) and "equal protection" (sounding, obviously, in the "equality" theme). Fortunately, though, we need no course in constitutional law to understand the substance of the debate. It is enough for present purposes to say that in justifying its rejection of the claimed right, the Supreme Court basically faced two challenges.

Constitutional doctrine holds that a state must have a "rational basis" for placing restrictions on liberty, and also for distinguishing, for legal purposes, between classes of people. So in order to uphold the New York and Washington restrictions, the Supreme Court first needed to show that a state can have a legitimate reason for prohibiting a terminally ill patient from receiving assistance in ending his or her life. In addressing this challenge, the

Glucksberg majority opinion offered a list of interests served by such a prohibition: these included preserving life, preventing suicide, "protecting the integrity of the medical profession," "protecting vulnerable groups" against "the real risk of subtle coercion and undue influence in end-of-life situations," and avoiding the slippery slope that might lead "down the path to voluntary and perhaps even involuntary euthanasia."[10] Although the character and sufficiency of these interests are surely contestable,[11] one or more of them was sufficiently attractive to gain the votes of all of the justices in the cases, whether liberal or conservative.[12]

However, the Court also faced a second and more difficult challenge. Like most states, Washington and New York *permitted* doctors to assist patients in terminating treatment (by removing food and hydration tubes, for instance)—even when the predictable consequence would be death. But also like most states, Washington and New York *prohibited* doctors from assisting patients in committing suicide (by, for example, prescribing a lethal dose of morphine). From some perspectives, though, this combination of prohibitions and permissions seemed cruelly incongruous. That is because there was no meaningful difference, or so it might seem, between what was permitted and what was prohibited—namely, between assisting a patient to end life-sustaining treatment and assisting a patient to commit suicide. Consequently, unless the Court and the states were to admit that these laws made arbitrary and irrational distinctions (which, in slightly different ways, constitutional doctrine under both the due process clause and the equal protection clause forbids), they needed to explain why one method of bringing about a patient's voluntary death should be legally protected while a different, arguably more efficient and humane method was treated as a criminal offense.

"Killing" versus "Letting Die"?

A familiar response asserts that there is a crucial difference between administering a lethal drug, which is a way of *killing* the patient, and refusing treatment, which merely amounts to *letting the patient die*. Though widely embraced,[13] however, this distinction is also elusive. "[W]hen we try to become clear about that distinction," Judith Jarvis Thomson observes, "we find ourselves in a philosophical mess and tangle."[14]

A majority of the lower court judges found the proffered distinction unpersuasive. "To us," Judge Stephen Reinhardt wrote for the Ninth Circuit Court of Appeals, "what matters most is that the death of the patient is the intended result as surely in one case as in the other."[15] The Philosophers' Brief agreed. "[T]here is no morally pertinent difference," Dworkin and Rawls and company asserted,

> between a doctor's terminating treatment that keeps [the patient] alive, if that is what he wishes, and a doctor's helping him to end his own life by providing lethal pills he may take himself, when ready, if that is what he wishes—except that the latter may be quicker and more humane.... If it is permissible for a doctor deliberately to withdraw medical treatment in order to allow death to result from a natural process, then it is equally permissible for him to help his patient hasten his own death more actively, if that is the patient's express wish.[16]

In the face of these objections, the Supreme Court tried to defend the distinction between "killing" and "letting die" through the refusal of treatment. Indeed, the Court offered two different rationales in support of the distinction. But neither rationale holds up well under inspection.

The "Causation" Rationale

The first rationale suggests that when a patient refuses—or, perhaps with a doctor's help, removes—life-sustaining treatment (such as feeding or hydration tubes), this human action is not tantamount to "killing" because it does not *cause* the patient's death. Instead, some underlying "natural" cause—starvation, perhaps, or dehydration—causes the death: the patient's and physician's actions amount to nothing more than a refusal to intervene to check or thwart this natural process. Conversely, if a doctor assists a patient to inject a lethal drug, say, then the doctor's and patient's actions actually *cause* the death, and hence "kill" the patient. "[W]hen a patient refuses life sustaining medical treatment," the *Quill* majority maintained, "he dies from an underlying fatal disease or pathology; but if a patient ingests lethal medication prescribed by a physician, he is killed by that medication."[17]

But the argument from causation wilts under examination. Compare the two characteristic situations. In one situation, at the patient's request a doctor removes the intravenous tube by which a patient is supplied with food and water, thus allowing the patient to die. In the other situation, at a patient's request a doctor prescribes a lethal drug and helps the patient to inject the drug. In each case, the most *immediate* cause of death is in a sense biological and "natural"—the heart stops beating, the brain stops functioning—while in each case human decision and deliberate action figure conspicuously in the more extended causal sequence that leads to death. If we understand "causation" in the familiar "but for" sense (Would B have happened *but for* A?), then the patient's decision and the doctor's cooperative action (As) *are* "but for" causes of the death

(B) in both cases. "But for" those actions, the death would not have occurred when it did.

In many situations, moreover, it would seem artificial or even absurd to deny that removal of a feeding tube *is* a cause of death, and that the person who removed the tube thereby killed the patient. Suppose, for example, that a doctor develops a dislike for a patient—he disapproves of the patient's politics, maybe, or her uncouth sense of humor—and so without the patient's consent he sneaks into the patient's room and unplugs her respirator. Charged with murder, the doctor protests, "Why are you accusing *me*? I didn't kill her. Suffocation did." We would think the plea outrageous.

Judith Jarvis Thomson illustrates the problem:

> If somebody is attached to a life-support system in a hospital, and I wander in and for my own purposes pull the plug, surely I do kill my victim. If a deep-sea diver is attached by a pipe to a breathing apparatus on board ship, and I'm a passenger and cut the pipe, surely I do kill the diver. . . . It seems to me counter-intuitive in the extreme to deny these things.[18]

As these examples suggest, moreover, the difference between "killing" and "letting die" cannot be satisfactorily explained by reference to the legal distinction between "acts" and "omissions" anymore than it can be explained by familiar notions of causation. Often the elimination of life-sustaining treatment will involve a conscious decision and affirmative steps by patient or doctor. So the exercise of that acknowledged right will often involve "acts," not mere "omissions." Thomson's example of the malicious interloper who sneaks into a hospital room and deactivates a patient's life support demonstrates the point: we would surely say that the interloper "acted" to "cause" the patient's death—to kill him.

So it seems that if in the ordinary "refusal of treatment" situation we decline to call the removal of the tube a "cause" of the death, we must be expressing a conclusion based on something other than merely empirical or conventional observations about the causal sequence.

The "Intent" Rationale

The inadequacy of a purely causal account of the "killing/letting die" distinction might suggest that the real difference lies in the intentions that animate the patient's and doctor's actions. In the "refusal of treatment" situation, the argument goes, doctor and patient may foresee that the result of their choices and actions will be death, but they do not actually intend to produce death. Death is merely a predictable consequence, or side effect, of what is directly intended—that is, avoidance or elimination of undesired treatment. In the "assisted suicide" situation, by contrast, doctor and patient consciously intend to produce the patient's death.

The *Quill* majority endorsed this rationale as well:

[A] physician who withdraws . . . life sustaining medical treatment purposefully intends, or may so intend, only to respect his patient's wishes and "to cease doing useless and futile or degrading things to the patient when [the patient] no longer stands to benefit from them." . . . . The same is true when a doctor provides aggressive palliative care; in some cases, painkilling drugs may hasten a patient's death, but the physician's purpose and intent is, or may be, only to ease his patient's pain. A doctor who assists a suicide, however, "must, necessarily and indubitably, intend primarily that the patient be made dead." Similarly, a patient who commits suicide with a doctor's aid necessarily has the specific intent to end his or her own life.[19]

The intent rationale typically provokes discussions of what moral philosophers sometimes call the "doctrine of double effect."[20] Though the doctrine can become highly technical, the basic distinction animating the doctrine is between consequences of an act that are actually *intended*—that provide the person's object or reason for acting—and other consequences that are *foreseen* but not actually desired or intended. Proponents of the double-effect doctrine typically maintain that it is morally impermissible to act with the intent to produce an evil effect, either as an end in itself or as a means to some other end: good ends do not justify evil means. But it is sometimes permissible to act with the intent to produce a good end even though the act will have foreseeable harmful side effects. To adapt an example offered by Judge Andrew Kleinfeld, dissenting from the Ninth Circuit's decision striking down the Washington law,[21] it is morally permissible for the Allied forces to invade Normandy to liberate Europe from the Nazis, even though the generals know that thousands of soldiers inevitably will die in the assault. But suppose the Nazis made a credible offer to withdraw if the Allies would deliberately execute a comparable number of randomly selected soldiers: only a grossly immoral government could accept such an offer.

By this "double-effect" reasoning, death in itself is an evil, so it is impermissible to act with the intent of producing death, even as a means of relieving suffering. Conversely, it *is* permissible to refuse treatment, or to administer heavy doses of pain medication, even when these measures will foreseeably hasten the patient's death—so long, that is, as the intent or reason for acting is not to produce death but rather to avoid objectionable treatment or to eliminate pain.

The doctrine of double effect has been debated at length in academic literature. Critics doubt that the distinction between "intended" and merely "foreseen" effects can bear the moral weight that the doctrine places on it.[22] Proponents answer that we all intuitively resort to some such distinction in sorting out our moral judgments.[23]

Whatever the merits of the doctrine of double effect, though, the problem with the doctrine in the assisted suicide context is that it does not appear to vindicate the legal distinction in question—the distinction, that is, between assisting in committing suicide and assisting in the removal of life-sustaining treatment. The distinction that the doctrine of double effect makes crucial, in other words, is between acts intended to produce death and acts undertaken without this intention. But although acts classified as suicidal are by definition intended to bring about death, the converse proposition—namely, that refusals of life-sustaining treatment are not intended to produce death—does not follow. The most that can be inferred, as the Court's language in *Quill* coyly acknowledges, is that the refusal of treatment *might not* be intended to produce death. But it is equally possible that a decision to refuse or terminate treatment *is* intended to do just that.

In some cases, such as that of the believer who refuses treatment for religious reasons, it may be plausible to characterize death as a foreseeable but unintended consequence. But in the broad run of cases in which a patient has decided after reflection to terminate treatment necessary to sustain life, it seems possible and even likely that the patient acts with an intent to bring about death—not as an end in itself, perhaps, but as a means of relieving suffering. Indeed, most patients would likely have difficulty even grasping the central distinction. "Is your intention [in refusing life-sustaining treatment, or in taking lethal medication] to end your pain, or to bring about death?" asks the double-effect theorist. And the typical response would likely be "Well . . . , umm, . . . yes."

Under the "double-effect" doctrine, it seems, such cases are morally indistinguishable: the end or objective (elimination of suffering) and the means (death) are the same in both kinds of cases. Thus, the Supreme Court's attempt to explain the distinction between suicide and termination of life-sustaining treatment in terms of different intentions was unpersuasive.

The Intrinsic Normativity of "Nature's Course"?

The frailty of the Court's efforts to rationalize a distinction between "killing" and "letting die," a distinction (or perhaps a pseudo-distinction) reflected in the laws of Washington and New York and most other states, might tempt us to conclude that these laws were arbitrary and irrational, and hence unjustifiable, and hence unconstitutional. And this was precisely what the appellate courts had concluded.[24]

Still, it is—or should be—no casual matter to dismiss as irrational a distinction that has been so long and so widely embraced. Perhaps a second look is in order. Might there be more to the "killing"/"letting die" distinction than initially meets the eye?

We might begin by noticing a slightly different formulation that often pops up in this context: proponents of the traditional position suggest that administering a lethal drug is "killing" while refusing life-sustaining treatment is merely "letting nature take its course." In this vein, Chief Judge Thomas Griesa of the Southern District of New York observed in *Quill* that "it is hardly unreasonable or irrational for the State to recognize a difference between *allowing nature to take its course*, even in the most severe situations, and intentionally using an artificial death-producing device."[25] The locution implies that there is a normative dimension intrinsic to something like a "natural course of life" that can serve as a standard of evaluation: actions are distinguishable by whether they artificially interfere with that natural course or instead respect and defer to it.

This again is an elusive notion. But we may get some help from a surprising source—Ronald Dworkin. "We believe," Dworkin asserts, "that a successful human life has a certain *natural course*. It starts in mere biological development—conception, fetal development, and infancy—but it then extends into childhood, adolescence, and adult life. . . . It ends, after a *normal life span,* in a *natural death*."[26] These stages combine to form a "natural course of human life."[27] And the termination of life at any stage before "natural death" is regrettable (Dworkin's pronouncement here is quietly and perhaps inadvertently portentous) as "a kind of *cosmic shame*."[28]

This last phrase is trenchant because it transforms what might otherwise be taken as a purely descriptive, morally neutral statement—as a matter of empirical fact human lives often follow a pattern of conception, infancy, adolescence, and so forth—into a claim fraught with normative force and content. But that transformation might also provoke objections. Doesn't the view outlined by Dworkin commit the classic fallacy of deriving an "ought" from an "is"? Human lives often *do* in fact follow a typical course; therefore (Dworkin seems to say), human lives *should* follow that course. It is a "cosmic shame" if they do not. At least since Hume, we know that such inferences of moral "ought" norms from natural "is" facts reflect a fundamental error in reasoning. Don't we?

Indeed, the attempt to draw normative conclusions from biological facts may seem a particularly egregious form of this error. Isn't this much like the kind of pre-Kitty Hawk thinking that insisted that "If humans had been meant to fly, we'd have been given wings"? Isn't it the same type of thinking that leads some people to draw contestable inferences about the proper role of women—or the "natural" form of sexuality, or the impermissibility of some kinds of genetic research or technology—from brute biological facts?

Perhaps. Surely one plausible response to Dworkin's assertion of what "We believe" is that, whether or not his statement is accurate in a Gallup poll sense as a description of widely held opinions, those opinions are also transparently fallacious—and hence incapable of providing a normative justification for a law restricting patients' liberty in a matter as fundamental as the choice between life and death.

Before peremptorily dismissing the appeal to "nature's course" as a basis for normative judgments, however, we might pause to notice a curious and troubling fact: even the judges in *Glucksberg* and *Quill* who *favored* a right to assisted suicide, and who most emphatically insisted on patients' autonomy as the decisive criterion, quietly betrayed a lingering commitment to the same kind of "nature's course" logic. These judges tacitly agreed that there is a normatively significant difference between deaths—even self-chosen deaths—that are "natural" and others that are not.

Thus, while supporting a right to physician-assisted suicide, these judges carefully limited that right to "terminally ill" patients.

And their explanations for this limit were terse but suggestive. Judge Barbara Rothstein, the lower court judge in the Washington case, ruled that the state's prohibition on assisted suicide was unconstitutional. But she explained that the right to assistance in dying should be limited to the terminally ill. Why? Because, Judge Rothstein explained, "[o]bviously, the State has a strong legitimate interest in deterring suicide by young people and others with a significant *natural life span* ahead of them."[29] Judge Eugene Wright likewise voted to strike down the Washington prohibition because he believed that the state's interest in preserving life, though real, diminishes "as *natural death* approaches."[30] The Court of Appeals in the New York case expressed the same view.[31]

Judge Stephen Reinhardt, writing for the Ninth Circuit majority, declared the Washington prohibition an unconstitutional infringement on the liberty of terminally ill patients. But Reinhardt also emphasized that the state has a valid interest in discouraging suicide by those who are not terminally ill: that is because in these instances suicide would amount to the "senseless loss of a life *ended prematurely.*" Conversely, suicide in the case of a terminally ill person is not tragic or "senseless," Reinhardt opined, because "death does not come *too early.*"[32]

These pronouncements were in tension with these judges' heavy emphasis on individual autonomy as the decisive consideration and with their dismissal of the states' own "natural course" logic. Imagine a person who is in severe pain and is horribly disfigured and disabled—by an auto accident or war injury, perhaps—but who with proper care still has years to live. Suppose this person decides that her life is an unbearable burden, and so after ample reflection and consultation with friends or family she decides to end her life (and seeks a physician's help in doing so). If the crucial criterion is individual autonomy or freedom of choice, as these judges insisted, then such a person ought to have the same rights as one who is terminally ill. Yet even the judges who voted to strike down the New York and Washington prohibitions explicitly rejected this view. Although these judges *said* that individual autonomy was the decisive factor, it seems that they did not fully believe—perhaps did not fully grasp—the implications of that position.

Rather, the assumption running through these judicial explanations is discernible: human beings enjoy a "natural life span," and even a competent person's self-chosen death that occurs before the fulfillment of that natural span is normatively to be regretted. Such a death is "senseless"—perhaps even, to borrow Dworkin's phrase, a "cosmic shame"?—because it is "premature" or "too early"; and the state is accordingly entitled to discourage or prohibit such unnatural deaths.[33]

In the end, therefore, and contrary to initial appearances, it seems that the deeper disagreement in the cases was not so much over whether there is normative significance in "nature's course," but rather over the proper interpretation of "nature" in this context. And in this respect, the cases tracked the larger public debate. One familiar view suggests that so long as a person's body can continue functioning—without extraordinary "artificial" support, perhaps?— then nature has not yet signaled that this person's part is over. But others interpret terminal illness—combined with extreme suffering, perhaps?—as a person's cue to exit; someone who insists on clinging to life under those conditions is like an actor who won't get off the stage even though his role is finished. Clinging to life under these circumstances is a breach of "dignity." To shift the metaphor, people disagree about whether particular death-hastening actions— removing a food or hydration tube, injecting a lethal dose of morphine—are like "running out the clock," as the rules of the game permit, or more like running off the field before the game is over.

For the *Glucksberg-Quill* majority, it seems, any death intentionally brought about by the patient and doctor through lethal medication or injection is not "natural." Or at least a state is permitted to make that judgment. By contrast, for judges like Reinhardt, this kind of self-chosen death is proper so long as it occurs during the terminal stage of life. But a self-chosen death that occurs earlier in life is "premature" or "too early," and thus not a "natural death"; so even the much lauded value of individual autonomy does not entail a legal right to choose that sort of unnatural end.

It is hard to assess these competing views, however—or even confidently to articulate them—because none of the judges gave any explicit account of how "nature" could have the normative significance they subtly ascribed to it. The judges' moral intuitions can be cautiously extrapolated, but their overall normative frameworks remain mostly hidden—from us and, possibly, from the judges themselves. Thus, the *Quill* majority attempted to explicate its moral intuitions in the terms of causation and intent but, as we have seen, that vocabulary is inadequate fully to convey or support what is evidently a more subtle and elusive understanding of "nature's course." And the deeper normative assumptions of judges like Reinhardt, Wright, and Rothstein are even harder to fathom, since on the surface these judges stressed individual autonomy as the key moral criterion: but, as we have seen, it seems that these judges did not fully grasp or believe the position they purported to take.

But why should it be so difficult for seasoned judges to explain their fundamental normative premises, to us and perhaps to themselves as well? To think about that question, we need to step back and look at *Glucksberg* from a more long-term historical perspective.

The Separation of Normativity and "Nature": Emancipation or Collapse?

Moral reflection—about death, about countless other, more mundane matters—is something that as humans we necessarily engage in. How should I live? It is the quintessential Socratic question, and none of us can escape it. To be sure, we rarely pause to notice or articulate the larger intellectual frameworks within which our moral musings proceed. Even so, inadequacies in these larger frameworks may in turn manifest themselves in moral reasoning that is unsound or unsatisfying. And upon inspection, it appears that the shortcomings in *Glucksberg* are a manifestation of just this sort of moral malaise.

We might begin by observing that allusions to "letting nature take its course" in controversies like *Glucksberg* are vestiges of thinking on subjects like suicide and euthanasia that has occurred over the centuries, but that often has been more forthright about its assumptions with respect to the normative dimension of nature. Indeed, from classical until at least early modern times, the sort of thinking that we classify as "moral" typically proceeded unapologetically on the assumption that the cosmos itself—or "nature," or "human nature"—contain or reflect some sort of intrinsic normative order. Depending on whether it was traceable more to Jerusalem or to Athens, such an assumption might or might not have a theistic component. Leon Kass observes that the classical, teleological conception of nature appeared in a variety of versions:

Perhaps the two grandest and most influential alternatives are
these: The biblical view of a teleological and created world with its
various forms specially created after God's plan, and the Aristotelian view of a teleological but eternal nature with its various
forms kept in being, generation after generation, by the immanent
workings of eternal species *(eide)*.[34]

In this view, the function of moral reasoning is to determine
what actions, or what kind of life, conform to a normative order
inherent in nature itself. Thinking on issues like suicide often
reflected some such assumption. Thus, Michael Seidler explains
that "[t]o answer the general question of legitimation facing the
potential suicide, some Stoics turned occasionally to the idea of
divine calling which Socrates had already used as a justification . . . : it is wrong to leave life, to forsake our post in the world,
unless God calls us."[35] In a similar vein, John Locke maintained
that "men being all the workmanship of one omnipotent, and
infinitely wise maker, . . . they are his property, whose workmanship they are, made to last during his, not one another's pleasure." From this premise, Locke inferred, it followed that "[e]very
one . . . is *bound to preserve himself,* and not to quit his station
wilfully."[36]

A good deal of thinking about suicide, and about moral questions generally, still operates on some such assumption.[37] In much
public discourse, however, and especially in academic and legal
contexts, explicit appeals to a normative dimension in nature are
typically deemed inadmissible. Moral reasoning is supposed to
operate without reliance on religious or metaphysical premises.
In part, this modern approach may reflect the conclusion that
the older view of nature as harboring some indwelling "telos" is

ruled out by modern science. Nobel Prize–winning physicist Steven Weinberg's observation is typical: "The more the universe
seems comprehensible, the more it also seems pointless."[38] Bertrand Russell waxed rhapsodic on the theme of ultimate cosmic
meaninglessness:

> That man is the product of causes which had no prevision of the
> end they were achieving; that his origin, his growth, his hopes and
> fears, his loves and his beliefs, are but the outcome of accidental
> collocations of atoms; that no fire, no heroism, no intensity of
> thought and feeling, can preserve an individual life beyond the
> grave; that all the labors of the ages, all the devotion, all the
> inspiration, all the noonday brightness of human genius, are
> destined to extinction in the vast death of the solar system, and
> that the whole temple of man's achievement must inevitably be
> buried beneath the debris of a universe in ruins—all these things,
> if not quite beyond dispute, are yet so nearly certain that no
> philosophy which rejects them can hope to stand. Only within
> the scaffolding of these truths, only on the firm foundation of
> unyielding despair, can the soul's habitation henceforth be safely
> built.[39]

In some (especially academic) quarters, some such view is virtually axiomatic—at the core of "what we know now." It is, to borrow a metaphor from Wittgenstein, part of the "scaffolding" on
which contemporary thinking does its work.[40] Or, to change the
metaphor: respectable academic conversations today are carried
on, as I have put the point earlier, in the iron cage of secular
rationalism.

In political and especially legal contexts, the classical approach
may seem ruled out by a different kind of consideration as well. The

classical view of nature, even in its less overtly theistic versions (such as Aristotle's), strikes the modern eye as suspiciously religious. By contrast, public and especially legal discourse are supposed to be secular.[41] And it has become axiomatic in modern constitutional law that government can act only for "secular," not "religious" purposes.[42] Such thinking is apparent in Justice John Paul Stevens's rejection, in "right to die" and also abortion cases, of a state's asserted interest in protecting life on the ground that the interest is "theological."[43]

And what are the consequences of cutting off normative or moral reasoning from its classical foundation in nature? Opinions differ—antithetically.[44] One view, unsurprisingly common in academic contexts, is that moral reasoning is thereby liberated from influences and impediments that served mainly as obstructions to clear thinking. Just as science could develop more freely when unencumbered by older, animistic assumptions or superstitions, so moral theorizing can operate more rationally when released from religious or metaphysical shackles. In this vein, Martha Nussbaum (whose views we will look at more closely in Chapter 5) asserts that "if we really think of the hope of a transcendent ground as uninteresting or irrelevant to human ethics, as we should, then the news of its collapse will not change the way we think and act. It will just let us get on with the business of reasoning, in which we were already engaged."[45]

But the analogy to science might also elicit the opposite conclusion. How would science fare, we might wonder, if cut off from its connections to the natural world? And the answer, it seems, would be that science could not survive such a separation. The natural world is science's essential subject matter. Consequently, if appeals to the natural world were deemed inadmissible, science would no longer be possible: whatever might go on under the label of "science" would not in fact be *science*.

In a similar way, if moral reasoning is—or was—reasoning about how to live in accordance with the normative order intrinsic in nature, then if appeals to that order come to be forbidden (either because we no longer believe any such order exists, or because such appeals offend cultural or constitutional constraints against "religious" or "theological" reasons), moral reasoning will no longer be possible. Anything that goes on under that label will be something quite different—and probably, if it fails to recognize this revolutionary change, something profoundly confused.

This more critical assessment may be endorsed by thinkers of different stripes. One sort of thinker happily accepts the modern verdict that there is no normative order intrinsic in nature, and shares as well in the sort of optimism expressed by Nussbaum—but concludes that the only sensible kind of evaluative talk is consequentialist in nature. How can we achieve the most of the things that we in fact want—pleasure, happiness, satisfaction of human wants and needs? That is the kind of discussion worth having. To this sort of thinker, misty talk about "duties," "rights," and "obligations" that haunt us from some spooky deontological domain seems obscurantist and nonsensical, or almost literally incomprehensible[46]—unless, perhaps, such talk is understood as an obfuscating translation of more consequentialist considerations. In this vein, John Stuart Mill argued that Kantian morality must be understood in consequentialist terms, Kant's own protestations notwithstanding. "To give any meaning to Kant's [categorical imperative], the sense put upon it must be, that we ought to shape our conduct by a rule which all rational beings might adopt *with benefit to their collective interests*." "Otherwise he uses words without a meaning."[47]

Of a different view and temperament are thinkers who are not prepared to relinquish the belief in an intrinsically normative nature, or who acquiesce in the more modern view but with a profound sense of real and perhaps irreparable loss. The loss is suggested in Weber's lugubrious term—the "disenchantment" of the world. In this vein, Alasdair MacIntrye has famously argued that modern moral discourse consists of the now incoherent fragments of a kind of reasoning that made sense on older metaphysical assumptions.[48] His diagnosis elaborated on a view more succinctly expressed in a classic essay by Elizabeth Anscombe.[49] The Australian philosopher Raimond Gaita observes that "[t]he secular philosophical tradition speaks of inalienable rights, inalienable human dignity and of persons as ends in themselves. These are, I believe, ways of whistling in the dark, ways of trying to make secure to reason what reason cannot finally underwrite."[50]

John Rist contends that in fact there are only two coherent metaethical positions: a robust metaphysical moral realism and . . . nihilism. With an allusion to Thrasymachus, the nihilistic antihero of Plato's *Republic,* Rist concludes that "all other possibilities [are] good-natured muddles to be collapsed by the clear-headed into Thrasymacheanism."[51] Positions that purport to be neither objectivist nor nihilist (i.e., many of the positions commonly defended by contemporary philosophers) are maintained only through "deception and self-deception (including outright lying)"—which is one source of the "deceptions, equivocations, and outright lying and humbug in public debate."

Between these extremes there is of course a series of gradations in views. Thinkers like Richard Joyce and John Mackie suggest, for example, that normative considerations are in fact pragmatic or consequentialist in nature and that morality of the more deontological sort is a "myth" or "fiction." But it is a valuable fiction—a sort of internal policeman that helps enforce conformity with mutually beneficial rules that individuals might otherwise be tempted to break. Consequently, old-fashioned moral notions amount to a fiction that (contrary to the more straightforward, or perhaps cruder, consequentialist view) we should not be in a hurry to abandon. There are no "moral duties"—not really—but it is good for all of us if people believe there are.[52]

From any of these more critical perspectives, the sort of distinctively "moral" discourse practiced in academic and legal contexts is almost predestined to produce an unedifying spectacle. Unmoored from its subject matter, necessarily trading on suppressed premises and commitments, such discourse is inherently deceptive and deficient. And its deficiencies routinely manifest themselves, the critic may remark, in the performances of moral reasoning that we regularly observe—performances that in addition to being unpersuasive are also distinctly peculiar.

Suppose you try reading a representative sample of contemporary applied moral theorizing of the academic variety on just about any issue you might choose—euthanasia, abortion, human rights. You will find that such theorizing typically attempts to reflect and impose some sort of order on—and to draw inferences from—the "moral" intuitions people have about various problems. Often the intuition-generating scenarios are fictional and fanciful:[53] thus, we encounter meditations about violinists biologically hooked up to sleeping strangers,[54] or seemingly endless variations on the hypothetical case of the trolley car that will kill several people unless you deliberately divert it onto a different track where it will kill only one person.[55] Such reasoning can be impressive in its intricacy; its foremost practitioners are veritable virtuosos. But their performances rarely persuade anyone not already well disposed to the reasoner's conclusion.

More importantly, there is no apparent reason why anyone *should* be persuaded. After all, what credentials can these intuitions claim?[56] Whether intuitions are reliable is, of course, always a question, but in this case the problem goes deeper: it is not at all clear exactly what the intuitions are even intuitions *about.* Suppose I do have a "moral" intuition (whatever that is[57]) that, say, polygamous relationships are "wrong" (whatever that means). So what? I may also harbor an obsessive fear of traveling on airplanes, or an abiding premonition that something horrible will happen if I leave the house on Friday the thirteenth, or a sense of profound disgust when I look down at my plate and see that the peas have gotten mixed with the potatoes. Unless these feelings, intimations, or intuitions are grounded in something rational and objectively real, the proper response in each case, it seems, would be therapeutic in nature; it would be a response calculated to help me and anyone else subject to such debilitating feelings and intuitions to "Get over it!"

Conversely, insofar as contemporary deontological thinkers forego the therapeutic response and instead treat such intuitions with utmost respect, it is hard to resist the suspicion that they are acting on lingering assumptions—their own, possibly, or perhaps those of the people whose intuitions provide them with their material—about some sort of intrinsic normative order. Moral intuitions might be our way of apprehending this order. Or at least if some such assumption is not in the background, so that the "intuitions" are nothing more than attitudes or mental states of the intuiters, then once again the question arises: Why should anyone care about these intuitions?

This is not the place, of course, and I am not the person, to try to resolve metaethical debates between those who believe that moral reasoning can get along just fine, thank you, without any metaphysical or theological support and those who believe that such reasoning is an exercise in futility and self-delusion. But we can perhaps say this much: *if* the critical diagnosis of our situation is correct, then we would expect moral arguments on controversial subjects to leave us with the suspicion that the considerations that in fact propel the various advocates to their preferred conclusions are not being candidly presented, but instead have been smuggled in without full acknowledgment. We would expect, in other words, to see performances such as those in . . . *Glucksberg* and *Quill*. And not just in the majority opinions, but in the concurring and lower court opinions as well.

The Malaise of Modern Moral Discourse

Glucksberg would not be unique, of course, as a manifestation of the moral malaise. We would expect to see similar embarrassments elsewhere—in lots of places, in fact—including in other judicial decisions and doctrines. And we do. Thus, in his classic critical treatment of modern moral reasoning, Alasdair MacIntyre picked the then recent affirmative action case of *Bakke v. Regents* as an example. The various opinions in *Bakke* revealed, MacIntyre thought, how an issue such as affirmative action exceeds the resources of modern moral discourse to resolve;[58] and certainly nothing in the Supreme Court's affirmative action jurisprudence since *Bakke* has shown this judgment to be mistaken.[59]

Though they are hardly unique, however, the assisted suicide cases stand as a distinctively powerful manifestation of our condition. In part this may be because, as is often observed, life-and-death decisions can pose moral questions in a particularly wrenching form: get it wrong, and someone who should be living—some human being, some person—will be dead. There is an awful, sobering finality about being dead. And perhaps for that reason, the question of terminating life forced judges on all sides of the issue, at some point, to fall back on assumptions about an intrinsic normative order implicit in the "natural course of life"—assumptions that the judges could neither openly avow nor entirely conceal. In this way, the earnest inefficacy of *Glucksberg* and *Quill* paid powerful if oblique witness to the predicament of modern moral reasoning.

And yet . . . in life as in law, moral and political-moral questions arise—they will not patiently wait for the development of some satisfactory theory—and so answers must be given. A court cannot simply decline to decide a case with the excuse that "This is a really a tough one. We're honestly not sure what to say." Instead, the court must give an answer of some sort, somehow. In the same way, society, and the state, and each of us as individuals, will often have to give some answer to the questions that are thrust upon us, however ill equipped we are to address those questions. Moreover, in some contexts (and court cases are again an especially vivid instance), we are expected to support our answers or our decisions with *reasons*. "I decided the way I did because . . . well, I just sort of felt like it" is not good enough.

So then if we must decide and we must give reasons but the moral discourse available to us does not provide adequate reasons, what are we supposed to do? What *can* we do?

I have already suggested one answer: we can smuggle. But to smuggle effectively, we need discursive equipment—a trusty vehicle, perhaps—suitable for sneaking values or premises that are officially inadmissible into the cage, and into our accounts. For the various judges in *Glucksberg* and *Quill,* the elusive notions of "autonomy," "causation," and "intention" served as such vehicles.

In the next chapter, we will look at another piece of equipment—one that on many issues and for many advocates over the last century or so has been the vehicle of choice.

3

Trafficking in Harm

Among the various instruments in the toolbox of modern liberal thought, surely one of the most popular—and most powerful—has been what is often called "the harm principle." Presented by John Stuart Mill as *"one very simple principle* . . . entitled to govern absolutely the dealings of society with the individual in the way of compulsion and control . . . ,"* the principle holds that "the sole end for which mankind are warranted, individually or collectively, in interfering with the liberty of action of any of their number, is . . . *to prevent harm to others.*"[1]

Mill's principle is invoked frequently, and with potent effect, in debates on a range of issues from prohibitions on obscenity to regulations of marijuana to the hot-button controversy of the moment: same-sex marriage. Courts have occasionally declared the harm principle to be part of our fundamental law.[2] Students often suppose the same thing: Andrew Koppelman, a law professor at Northwestern, notes that "each year at least one of my students recites the [harm] principle as if it were part of the Constitution, and everyone else in the room nods with approval."[3] The students assume too easily: in fact, the harm principle is nowhere articulated in the constitutional text, nor has the Supreme Court ever conferred constitutional status on Mill's principle—not officially and explicitly, at least. Nonetheless, observers sometimes discern the principle's not-so- subtle influence in the Court's decisions.[4]

The harm principle's sway within the academy is, if anything, even more potent. Bernard Harcourt observes that

> over the course of the 1960s, '70s, and '80s, Mill's famous sentence began to dominate the legal philosophic debate over the enforcement of morality. Harm became the critical principle used to police the line between law and morality within Anglo-American philosophy of law. Most prominent theorists who participated in the debate either relied on the harm principle or made favorable reference to the argument.[5]

Perhaps the most impressive defense and elaboration of the harm principle occurred in a four-volume work by the legal philosopher Joel Feinberg that has become an oft-cited jurisprudential classic.[6] Like others in the liberal tradition, Feinberg was not quite a "harm principle" absolutist: he accepted a hint from Mill in allowing for limited restrictions on liberty to prevent serious "offense" to others.[7] In the main, though, Feinberg's opus amounted to a massive sympathetic exposition of the harm principle, and it generated lavish praise, even from scholars who disagreed with Feinberg on important points.[8]

Unlike some other darlings of legal and political philosophy, however (such as the Rawlsian notions of "public reason" or the "original position"), the harm principle is not merely or even mainly an academic phenomenon. On the contrary, much of its power derives from its resonance with views and adages that pervade popular political discourse. Although terminology may vary, you are as likely to hear the harm principle invoked (albeit without attribution) in a popular discussion of obscenity or drug policy or abortion as in an academic discussion.

Because of its widespread appeal and its apparent significance for a range of current and highly contested issues, the harm principle deserves continuing and close scrutiny. Is the principle as strong and sound as it often seems to be? Should it play a significant or even decisive role in resolving the issues of the day?

A few hardy souls have argued that it should not. Thus, a half century ago, in what evolved into a celebrated debate with the Oxford legal philosopher H. L. A. Hart, the English judge Lord Patrick Devlin argued that the harm principle is misconceived and that society *should* sometimes prohibit immoral conduct even when the conduct is not discernibly harmful.[9] The debate was a reprise of an exchange a century earlier between Mill, the harm principle's renowned author, and James Fitzjames Stephen.[10] The position taken by Devlin and Stephen suggests that the harm principle is substantial but contested—that it has definite content that is accepted by some and rejected by (at least a few) others.

In this chapter I will offer a different, and in one sense a dimmer, assessment. My argument will be that the harm principle is not so much misguided as empty. It is a hollow vessel, alluring and even irresistible but (or because) without any intrinsic content, into which adept advocates can pour whatever substantive views and values they happen to favor. The principle is attractive and useful—useful, that is, for smuggling purposes—precisely because at its core it means pretty much whatever you want it to mean.

The Irresistibility of the Harm Principle

As articulated by Mill, the harm principle holds (a) that the only justification (with perhaps a few small and grudgingly granted qualifications) for coercively restricting liberty is to prevent harm and (b) that the harm that may justify such restrictions must be harm to others. So government should not restrict liberty to prevent people from harming *themselves*. This latter component—the antipaternalism component—has been defended by Mill, Feinberg, and others; but it has been questioned or rejected by others in the liberal tradition (notably H. L. A. Hart[11]), and it has seemingly been less influential than the core principle itself in debates about legal issues. For present purposes, therefore, we will focus on the basic harm principle, bracketing the antipaternalism corollary.

Thus qualified, the harm principle seems practically irresistible. Its allure arises from two features. First, the principle is (or at least it presents itself as) a "very simple principle," as Mill observed. Simplicity is powerfully attractive to judges, legislators, and debaters of all sorts. Second, the principle's animating precept—that government should restrict freedom only to prevent harm—resonates with pervasive intuitions and popular notions that make the precept seem almost self-evidently correct.

Start with the feature of simplicity. Appearances can be deceiving (as this one will turn out to be), but at least on its face the harm principle seems to live up to this part of Mill's advertising. If your actions cause harm, government has the authority to restrict those actions. If they don't, it doesn't. Looks pretty straightforward, doesn't it? Thus, Bernard Harcourt remarks that "the harm principle offered a bright-line rule. A rule that was simple to apply. A rule that was simply applied."[12]

To be sure, this bright-line rule purports to tell us only what activities government *may* regulate, not what activities it *should* regulate. If an activity is not harmful, government must leave it alone. Conversely, if the activity causes harm, government may regulate it. Even so, regulation may or may not be prudent or expedient, and Mill's "very simple principle" does not purport to resolve such issues of prudence. To put the point differently, the harm principle purports only to delineate government's coercive "jurisdiction,"[13] so to speak; it does not tell government how to act within the scope of such jurisdiction. Still, if the principle could persuasively chart the scope of legitimate coercive jurisdiction, that would be no small contribution.

In addition to its simplicity, the basic precept animating Mill's proposal seems almost self-evidently true. It resonates with intuitions most of us have, with adages that are standard fare in everyday exchanges, and with familiar wisdom about the role of and justification for government.

The basic intuition is often expressed as a "none of your business" appeal: what doesn't injure or affect you is "none of your business." Freedom in itself is a good thing—who doubts this?—so as long as a person is exercising her freedom in ways that cause no harm, why is it anybody else's "business" (including government's) to tell her she can't? The intuition is powerful and widespread, and though the phrasing may seem inelegant, in fact the eminent thinkers who have addressed the issue have often resorted precisely to that "none of your business" language to convey the point.[14]

The "no harm" precept also resonates with an adage that all of us must have heard a thousand times, beginning in grade school or before: we could call this the "somebody else's nose" adage. "Everyone must understand," as a West Virginia court put it, "that his right to swing his arm ends at the other chap's nose."[15] The inculcation of this principle often starts early. Thus, the teacher tells a third grader on the playground to stop doing something that is bothering or threatening other students. The obstreperous student whines: "Why can't I? It's a free country, isn't it?" And the teacher patiently explains that freedom is not absolute. "You have the right to swing your arm, Johnny, but only up to the point where it runs into somebody else's nose: at that point your freedom ends." The harm principle and the "somebody else's nose" adage seem nicely congenial, if not virtually identical.

In slightly more dignified terms, government is often conceived in the Anglo-American liberal political tradition as the product of a social contract that extricated us from a figurative "state of nature" or "pre-political state" in which we imaginatively lived (or would live) before (or without) the institution of government. The state of nature had its attractions—there was no official authority to boss us around—but it also had its drawbacks. In particular, there were no officials and no police to prevent other people from doing whatever they wanted to do *to us:* hence, life could be "solitary, nasty, brutish, and short."[16]

So we formed a government, the familiar story says, in order to remedy this deficiency, preserving as much of our erstwhile liberty as possible while providing a mechanism to prevent people from injuring each other. From this picture it seems to follow that government may step in to prevent some citizens from harming others: that is why we formed government in the first place, isn't it? Conversely, if someone wants to do something that does *not* injure or affect others, then it seems that government's commission—its reason for being—is not implicated; so the earlier rule of freedom should remain in force.

For those (like Mill) who are averse to fairy tales about states of nature and social contracts,[17] the same idea can be expressed in less mythical terms. We might simply say that the purpose of government is to protect and promote human welfare, or perhaps "human flourishing." After all, this is why we pay taxes and submit to government, isn't it? Freedom to choose and to act is surely part of human flourishing. And it seems to follow almost inexorably (bracketing again the issue of paternalism) that if a person wants to do some action that will bring her pleasure or satisfaction or benefit, and if this action will cause no harm to anyone else, then government will diminish rather than enhance human welfare by prohibiting the person from engaging in this harmless conduct.

In short, the precept that animates the harm principle seems virtually irresistible. Resonating powerfully with familiar intuitions and adages and political theories, the basic idea seems almost self-evidently sound. H. L. A. Hart nicely made just this sort of appeal to the apparently self-evident quality of the harm principle:

> [A] very great difference is apparent between inducing persons through fear of punishment to abstain from actions which are harmful to others, and inducing them to abstain from actions which deviate from accepted morality but harm no one.... [W]here there is no harm to be prevented and no potential victim to be protected, ... it is *difficult to understand the assertion that conformity ... is a value worth pursuing,* notwithstanding the sacrifice of freedom which it involves.[18]

It is difficult to understand indeed! The harm principle is powerful—*too* powerful, perhaps. The lack of justification for restricting conduct that some people want to engage in and that harms no one seems so obvious that it provokes a suspicion: Does anyone really disagree? And if everyone in fact accepts this elementary idea, what exactly is going on when one party of advocates picks up the principle and uses it to club another party?

The Central Dilemma

The question prompts us to consider a prior and pressing question that we have thus far tacitly deferred: What *is* "harm" anyway? As it turns out, this question confronts us with a dilemma. I will preview the dilemma here and then try to elaborate on it in the remainder of the chapter.

What is "harm"? Well, one alternative would be to understand harm in a subjective sense. We might, in other words, defer largely to individuals' own evaluations—much in the way economists defer to consumers' choices about what has value for them. So if people sincerely believe and report that they are "harmed" by some occurrence, they are. In the alternative, we might instead try to use the term in a more technical and normatively "objective" sense. Individuals' sincere reports that they have been "harmed" would not be conclusive: instead, we would examine claims of injury reflectively, perhaps with the aid of some theory of human interests and rights, in order to decide whether the reported injuries should count as cognizable harms or not.

Both possibilities—the subjective approach, and the technical and objective approach—are open to us. And the resulting dilemma is this: the features that make the harm principle so irresistible— its simplicity, and its resonant or truistic quality—attach to and grow out of the subjective understanding of harm. But this understanding would also render the harm principle wholly unsuitable for achieving its central purpose of limiting government and protecting liberty. Conversely, we can make the principle more useful for liberal purposes by defining harm in a more crafted or technical sense; but in doing so we sacrifice the principle's intuitive appeal.

So, how have Mill, Feinberg, and company resolved this dilemma? The answer is less than edifying. To be blunt, they have equivocated. They have tried to have it both ways. Millian liberals have acknowledged that subjective understandings of harm would subvert the liberal purposes of the harm principle, and so they have proceeded to refine the concept in various ways—to make it more technical and normative. But having made the desired refinements, they have nonetheless proceeded to trade rhetorically—tacitly, perhaps, but prodigiously—on the subjective sense of the term to carry themselves and their readers to their desired conclusions

Harm as Subjective

Consider the first alternative. In deciding what counts as harm, we might defer to subjective evaluations: if people sincerely report that they have been harmed by some occurrence, they have been. This approach seems nicely compatible with what Joel Feinberg sometimes calls "the spirit of the harm principle":[19] after all, a proposal designed to make room for individual choices and beliefs seemingly ought to respect individuals' judgments about what does and does not cause them "harm."

The Utilitarian Conception

One way of implementing this subjective approach would use a utilitarian framework to register harm. And indeed, Mill himself prescribed, or appeared to prescribe, a utilitarian conception of harm.[20] Utilitarianism, to be sure, has no single or canonical formulation; rather it has become a broad umbrella for a family of ethical theories, of which Mill's own version may be somewhat idiosyncratic. For our purposes, it is enough that by drawing upon the remarks at the beginning of Mill's discussion in *Utilitarianism* together with the writings of his predecessor Jeremy Bentham, we can extract two slightly different versions, either of which might supply a subjective conception of harm that seems congruent with everyday understandings.

The most familiar version, endorsed by Bentham and recited by Mill, understands utilitarianism as a position favoring the maximization of happiness, which in turn is understood in terms of pleasure and the absence of pain. Bentham had declared that the correct moral principle "approves or disapproves of every action whatsoever, according to the tendency which it appears to have to augment or diminish the happiness of the party whose interest is in question," and Bentham had understood "happiness" in terms of those "sovereign masters, *pain* and *pleasure*."[21] Mill at least appeared to concur:

> Utility, or the Greatest Happiness Principle, holds that actions are right in proportion as they tend to promote happiness, wrong as they tend to produce the reverse of happiness. By happiness is intended pleasure, and the absence of pain; by unhappiness, pain, and the privation of pleasure.[22]

On these premises, it would seem, "harm" might naturally be understood as *pain*—or, more accurately, as pain or the deprivation of pleasure. So my conduct harms you if it causes you pain or if it deprives you of some pleasure you would otherwise have experienced. This conception of harm is subject-based in the sense that if you report (sincerely) that you experience pain because of some action or state of affairs, then you have suffered harm.

A slightly different version of utilitarianism would focus not directly on pleasure/pain as the central desideratum but on the satisfaction or frustration of *preferences*. A page after asserting that pleasure and pain are the basis of right and wrong, Mill casually shifted to the vocabulary of preference.[23] The shift was calculated, it seems. Mill wanted to justify the satisfaction of "higher pleasures" over what he viewed as lower, vulgar ones: contrary to Bentham's well-known dictum, he did not concede that pushpin is more valuable than poetry just because people get enthused about pushpin (whatever that was: substitute, if you like, poker or professional wrestling) but are bored to tears by poetry. "It is better to be a human being dissatisfied than a pig satisfied," Mill famously insisted—"better to be Socrates dissatisfied than a fool satisfied."[24] Mill's nobler (or elitist) predilections are difficult to square with a hedonic utilitarianism emphasizing mere "pleasure" as the ultimate good. But focusing on "preferences" seemed more promising: that is because Mill thought that "competent judges"[25] would in fact prefer "higher" pleasures over more debased ones, and would prefer to be a morose Socrates rather than a cheerful pig.

There is much to comment on—or to be amused by?—in Mill's mix of down-to-earth utilitarian and democratic commitments with what easily might be viewed as intellectual and cultural snobbery, but let this pass. What matters for present purposes is that if we opt for a utilitarianism oriented to preferences rather than to pleasure and pain, we would understand "harm" not in terms of inflicting pain but rather in terms of frustrating preferences. I harm you, on this view, if I act in a way that prevents you from obtaining something you would prefer to have, or that brings about a state of affairs different from what you regard as the preferable state of affairs. Again, this conception of harm is subject-based: if you report (sincerely) that your preferences have been frustrated, then you have suffered harm.

Whichever of these alternatives we choose, the utilitarian versions of "harm" preserve that principle's attractive features of simplicity and of conveying an idea that seems commonsensical and almost self-evidently true. Suppose we opt for the "pleasure/pain" version. Then the harm principle will mean that it is illegitimate for government to restrict my conduct except to prevent me from inflicting pain on others[26] or depriving them of pleasure. That idea seems simple enough, at least as an abstract matter, and it also seems intuitively attractive. If I really desire to do something (perhaps because it brings me pleasure), and the thing I want to do will not cause anyone else pain or deprive anyone of pleasure, then what justification could a utilitarian government have for stopping me? No doubt some caveats and refinements might be needed, but the powerful appeal of the basic idea is apparent.

Or suppose we adopt the "preference" version. Now the harm principle means that government can restrict my freedom only to prevent me from acting in ways that frustrate other people's preferences— that impose on them states of affairs that they do not prefer. Again, the basic idea seems both straightforward and attractive.

In this vein, the philosopher Richard Arneson argues that "a plausible liberal doctrine should incorporate a utilitarian value theory."[27] And Arneson explains the rationale for this utilitarian approach: "[I]n deciding on state policy, why should we care about anything except what will help make people's lives go best *according to their own personal values?*"[28]

Paralyzing the Harm Principle

These two familiar and commonsensical versions of utilitarianism both supply conceptions of "harm" that preserve the harm principle's simplicity and truistic quality. Unfortunately, these conceptions also render the principle incapable of protecting liberty—which of course was the whole reason for proposing the principle in the first place. That is because any sort of conduct to which some people object *will* inflict pain of various sorts, and will interfere with the satisfaction of some people's preferences, and hence it will be within the realm of conduct that government may permissibly decide whether or not to regulate.

Take a common example—one that seems to present the sort of issue liberal theorists have wanted the harm principle to address.[29] Suppose I live in a community in which prudish Victorian types are numerous and wield considerable political influence. The community as a whole thus tends to favor rigorous restrictions on materials that residents regard as pornographic. As it happens, I am a solid citizen with a family and a steady job, but one who happens on occasion to enjoy watching hard-core, XXX films in my living room. I watch these films alone, or sometimes with a few adult friends—academic colleagues, maybe—who have been fully advised about the nature of the materials and have freely chosen to partake. After particularly grueling and inane faculty meetings, perhaps, these ribald festivities help us to loosen up and recover our sanity. But although these viewings are as private as my friends and I can possibly make them (we keep the volume down and make sure to close the curtains), they transgress the community's antipornography ordinance. So my nosy neighbors (as I regard them) somehow learn of what I am doing, and complain, and the local authorities move to enforce the ordinance against me.

Naturally, I resent this invasion of my freedom. As long as I watch these films strictly in private, and as long as no one except fully informed and consenting adults participates, what business is it of the community (I ask indignantly) to tell me I can't do this? I invoke Mill: the community has no right to restrict my freedom, I protest, so long as I am not *harming* anyone.

The city council patiently explains, though, that at least according to the utilitarian conceptions of harm, I *am* harming other people, in a variety of ways. How? I ask, and the council obliges by explaining two obvious ways in which I am causing harm. These forms of harm will not elicit my sympathy, of course, and on a prudential balance they may not warrant restricting my liberty. Liberals—and others—have typically treated them with derision. But whether or not they deserve this treatment, the crucial point is that they *are* real and perfectly genuine forms of harm *according to the utilitarian conceptions*.

First, and most obviously, the knowledge that I am watching XXX films in my home causes emotional or psychic distress to my prudish neighbors, who view my practice with abhorrence. Millian liberals will surely respond, of course, that this is not the kind of harm they had in mind. We can concede the point, and we can further concede that government would be ill-advised to restrict freedom merely to avoid psychic distress to officious neighbors. But the immediate point is simply that some citizens *do* feel emotional distress because of what I am doing. Indeed, it may be obvious that they are deeply unhappy about my movie-watching predilections and practices. Nor can I deny that emotional distress *is* a kind of suffering, or pain. After all, in other contexts (in tort law, for example) we readily acknowledge that the prevention of emotional or psychic distress is a perfectly legitimate state interest.[30] Or, if we want to make the point in terms of the "frustrated preferences" conception of harm, then it is plain that a state of affairs in which citizens like myself watch XXX films in our homes frustrates the preferences of citizens who would prefer to exclude such materials and practices from the community.

Change the facts, and this sort of harm might even elicit the sympathies of liberal-minded citizens. Suppose, for example, that the question is not whether to regulate pornography, but instead whether to permit gladiatorial contests between consenting combatants who fight to the death before consenting, paying spectators. Richard Arneson suggests that "we should think of citizens who would be appalled at the thought of living in a community that tolerates Roman-style gladiatorial spectacles as *harmed by the bare knowledge that such events are occurring.*" And he observes more generally that "emotional reactions to what one's neighbors and fellow citizens are doing can be powerful and can be virtually unavoidable for persons who have not detached themselves from all personal concern for the quality of life in their community."[31]

So my movie-watching practices harm my Victorian neighbors by causing them emotional pain. But the city council goes on to explain that by watching XXX movies in my home I am also causing harm in another way that is more indirect but arguably even more substantial. I insist, once again, that my conduct is purely private, affecting no others against their will (except insofar as they are being intrusive busy-bodies). But the defenders of the antipornography restriction point out that I am being, or at least am pretending to be, sociologically naïve: I can maintain my position only by narrowly confining my field of view in an artificial and implausible way.

More specifically, what my consenting adult friends and I do in private will surely have some influence over the kind of people we are. Our movie-watching habits will affect how we talk, how we spend our time, what activities we choose to engage in and support: while we are watching adult films behind closed curtains we are not attending the high school musical or the baseball game. Our activities will influence what we find interesting, and valuable, and humorous. In this way, our conduct will immediately influence and help to form *us*. And because we interact with the community—as teachers and lawyers and business people and consumers—it will affect others in the community as well.

In addition, even if for now I limit the audience for my XXX films to a few adult friends, it would be unrealistic to suppose that other people—our children, for example—will not be in some measure influenced in their own attitudes about what sorts of films are available, and acceptable, and interesting. Perhaps as they get older my own children and those of my friends will be permitted to participate in some of our activities. You on the other hand would prefer that your children steer clear of such materials, but realistically, it will be much more difficult for you to inculcate these values if many of your children's associates and friends are participating.

Indeed, you might even be afraid that in a certain kind of community *you yourself* will come to develop a liking for such materials, and that this would be a regrettable moral or cultural decline. Arneson describes this sort of concern as "self-paternalism," and he argues that "self-paternalism is in principle a legitimate reason for instituting criminal prohibitions."[32]

I might argue, of course, that if you prefer this level of cultural innocence you always have what we might call "the Amish option": you can opt out of normal society. But you would point out that for many people this is not in fact a viable option (remember *Mosquito Coast?*); and in any case, it would be a massive imposition on your life and your preferences to put you to that choice. Why should you and your friends (who are by hypothesis a sizable majority in our town) be the ones who are forced to take that drastic course? Why not tell me that if I really care so much about my XXX movies I always have "the Babylon option"? Why shouldn't I move to some less squeamish community—New York, maybe, or San Francisco, or Denmark? I would immediately recognize the exorbitant cost—the harm—that this forced choice imposes on me: but if left unregulated, the movie-watching and related habits of people like me will impose similar harmful costs on you.

Over time, in short, what we do in private will almost certainly have a gradual and subtle, but very real, influence on the sort of community all of us experience. And even citizens with no independent desire to be officious or to interfere in the lives of others will often have a strong personal interest in the kind of community in which they (and their children) live. Robert George thus compares public morality to a kind of "community's 'moral ecology'—an ecology as vital to the community's well-being, and, as such, as integral to the public interest, as the physical ecology which is protected by environmental laws."[33] Consequently, conduct that is likely over time to make a community incongruent with the values of many of its residents, or even just less to their liking, causes these residents pain and frustrates their preferences. Such conduct undeniably harms them, at least in the familiar utilitarian senses.

If harm is understood in utilitarian terms, in short, then my conduct (or *any* conduct that members of the community might in fact want to restrict) *does* cause harm, and the harm principle accordingly renders public regulation of that conduct legitimate (though not necessarily prudent or expedient[34]). This is an obvious point, actually, and thoughtful proponents of Millian positions—Ronald Dworkin, for instance—sometimes acknowledge it.[35] I have nonetheless lingered on the point because I think a clear appreciation of the problem helps us to perceive the "confession and avoidance" strategies to which Millians have typically resorted, and which we must now examine.

Getting Technical

Understandably, Mill and his followers have been reluctant to concede that the harm principle is useless—or, even worse, illiberal. Instead, in a quick stipulation, they typically acknowledge the sorts of difficulties just discussed but treat them as a warrant *not* for abandoning the harm principle, but rather for rejecting subjective conceptions of harm. They then proceed to define "harm" in narrower, more technical terms. The notion of "harm" must be refined, Feinberg explains, because otherwise the principle "might be taken to invite state interference without limit, for virtually every kind of human conduct can affect the interests of others to *some* degree, and thus would properly be the state's business."[36]

So it turns out that not every inflicted pain or frustrated preference will qualify as a "harm." Instead, the determination of harm comes to turn on a more theoretical reflection.

The Narrowing of "Harm"—Mill

Consider what Mill himself does with the concept of "harm." Almost immediately after announcing the harm principle, Mill asserts that he "regard[s] utility as the ultimate appeal on all ethical questions," and this assertion might lead us to think that he understands "harm" in something like the straightforward, utilitarian senses just discussed. But before even finishing his sentence, he already begins to back away from the position. "Utility" is the ultimate criterion, *but*—Mill hastens to add—"it must be utility in the largest sense, grounded in the *permanent interests of man as a progressive being*."[37] Evidently, the frustration of less "permanent" interests, or of interests associated with less "progressive" conceptions of humanity, will not count as harm.

These suggestions are obscure, but as the essay proceeds, Mill gives at least glimpses of his "progressive" view of what a good life and a good society would be. And his conception of what should be regarded as "harm" is intimately tied to those views.

Thus, in a chapter on freedom of expression, Mill emphasizes the value of lively, independent thought.[38] It may be, as Mill concedes (nay, insists), that only a few select souls are actually capable of this sort of lofty reflection. Those of us who are not among that elite company might be tempted to conclude that lively thought (which, alas, is beyond our attainment) is not so important *for us* after all. But this is not Mill's conclusion. He argues, rather, that humanity achieves its highest status and receives its general benefactors in a few "[p]ersons of genius"—the "highly instructed One or Few."[39] "I insist thus emphatically," Mill gushes, "on *the importance of genius, and the necessity of allowing it to unfold itself freely both in thought and practice*."[40]

Other Millian commitments emerge as the essay proceeds. Mill places great value on "Individuality"; his use of the upper case conveys the emphasis. He praises whatever causes "human beings [to] become a noble and beautiful object of contemplation."[41] He finds a rich diversity in ways of life highly appealing.[42] "Originality" is much to be prized.[43] More generally, Mill yearns for strength and intensity (at least in the intellectual realm) over moderation and calm—for "great energies," "vigorous reason," "strong feelings controlled by a conscientious will."[44]

For Mill, these values determine the meaning of "harm." Contrary to what his avowed pleasure-pain utilitarianism might lead one to expect, "mere displeasure" turns out not to count as a harm at all.[45] But conduct or restrictions that impair lively thought or originality or individuality or nobility or beauty *are* harms.

Later in his essay Mill introduces, almost as an afterthought, a further drastic limitation on what can count as "harm." The conduct that society can expect of us, Mill remarks in what is offered as a sort of summary of the preceding discussion, consists "in not injuring the interests of one another . . ."—now the crucial qualification—"or rather *certain interests,* which, either by express legal provision or by tacit understanding, *ought to be considered as rights.*"[46] Injury to others' interests will not count as cognizable "harm," it seems, unless those interests are of the type to be regarded as "rights." Consequently, a person's conduct may be "*hurtful* to others without going the length of violating any of their constituted rights": such hurtful (but not "harmful," in Mill's increasingly rarified sense) conduct may be "punished by opinion, though not by law."[47]

This limitation of "harm" to injuries inflicted on interests protected as "rights" seems at once sensible, even inevitable, and also hugely problematic. Let's be reasonable, Mill and his followers might implore: it's perfectly obvious that not *all* injuries to *all* interests can justify legal restrictions. Suppose my business (in which I surely have an "interest") suffers because you start a competing and more efficient business and thereby drive me into bankruptcy.

Should I be able to say that you "harmed" me, and hence that your business should (or at least *could*) be prohibited?[48] Of course not!

Even so, by limiting harms to injuries to "rights," Mill drastically undermines the ostensible simplicity of the harm principle. He also severs "harm" from what it would mean in ordinary understanding, in which in many contexts it would seem a kind of double-talk to distinguish "harming" from "hurting." And, as we will see, he arguably renders the whole concept of "harm" question-begging and circular.

The Narrowing of "Harm"—Feinberg

In attempting to salvage the harm principle for liberal purposes, Joel Feinberg remodels the concept of "harm" in ways that directly parallel Mill's qualifications. More forthrightly than Mill, Feinberg disavows standard or Benthamite utilitarianism, noting (as Mill could not bring himself to do) that within a utilitarian framework the distinction between "harms" and "moral evil" would disappear.[49] Feinberg also explicitly acknowledges that "harm" as he uses the term will not correspond closely to ordinary usage, and that there will accordingly be "clear examples of harm as the term is used in ordinary language" that will not count as harms within his own theoretical framework.[50] More specifically, Feinberg defends two limitations that operate to disqualify numerous injuries that people might ordinarily think of as "harm."

First, Feinberg says that "harm" consists of a "thwarting, setting back, or defeating of an interest." An "interest," in turn, is something in which a person has a "stake."[51] These terms are opaque, but Feinberg attempts to clarify them; in doing so he emphasizes distinctions between "harms" on the one hand and the "[u]nhappy but not necessarily harmful experiences" that he describes as mere "hurts" and "offenses" on the other.[52] Feinberg offers a lengthy and macabre list of nonharmful "hurts," explaining that these are not "harms" because "[t]here is no interest in not being hurt as such, though certainly we all want to escape being hurt, and the absence of pain is something on which we all place a considerable value."[53]

Feinberg's list of these nonharmful hurts is worthy of perusal. He divides the hurts into two categories—physical and mental.

> Physical pains include pangs, twinges, aches, stabs, stitches, cricks, and throbs, as caused by cuts, bruises, sores, infections, muscle spasms, over-dilated or contracted arteries, gas pressures, and the like. Roughly analogous to these are various forms of mental suffering (they "hurt" too): "wounded" feelings, bitterness, keen disappointment, remorse, depression, grief, "heartache," despair. Nonpainful forms of physical unpleasantness include nausea (which can be even more miserable a condition than pain, but does not, strictly speaking, *hurt*), itches, dizziness, tension, hyperactivity, fatigue, sleeplessness, chills, weakness, stiffness, extremes of heat and cold, and other discomforts.[54]

None of these unwelcome phenomena will count as "harms" that can justify restricting anyone's liberty.

But Feinberg places a second and severe limitation on what can count as a "harm." Like Mill, he makes harm dependent not only on a theoretically limited set of interests but also on preexisting "rights." Thus, he argues that a setback even to what is admittedly an "interest" cannot count as a harm unless it is wrongfully inflicted— which is to say that it is inflicted in violation of a right. "To say that A has harmed B in this sense is to say much the same thing as that A has wronged B, or treated him unjustly. One person *wrongs* another when his indefensible (unjustifiable and inexcusable) conduct violates the other's right."[55]

So it turns out that only a carefully delimited subset of the universe of injury qualifies as "harm" in Feinberg's scheme. The limitations are so restrictive that Feinberg is pushed to acknowledge various other kinds of "harmless" misfortunes—or of what Feinberg himself calls "evils." We have already noted two such harmless evils—"hurts" and "offenses." But in the final volume of his project Feinberg goes on to offer an elaborate taxonomy of "evils."[56] On the most general level he distinguishes between what he somewhat curiously calls "theological evils" (such as natural disasters and "killer diseases") and "legislative evils," which are the result of human action.[57] He further subdivides the latter category into "grievance evils"—"harms" belong in this subcategory—and "nongrievance evils."

Among the latter are "free floating" evils, which are so named because they "'float free' of [human] interests, needs, and desires."[58] The nature of these free-floating misfortunes is mysterious. Why should we call something an "evil" if it has no detrimental impact on human concerns? Of course, utilitarians and others might plausibly consider injury to nonhuman but sentient beings—dogs, cats, dolphins—to be evils, but this is not mainly what Feinberg has in mind. Instead, his (arguably circular) explanation is that although these misfortunes neither "harm" nor hurt or offend anyone, they are nonetheless "evils" in the sense that they are "rather seriously to be regretted" because "the universe would be a better place without [the evil]."[59] Feinberg gives examples of what he regards as free-floating evils: these include violation of moral taboos, false belief, extinction of a species, and "the wanton, capricious squashing of a beetle (frog, worm, spider, wild flower) in the wild."[60]

Unlike Mill (who himself occasionally vacillates), Feinberg does not finally contend that the harm principle is the only possible justification for restrictions on liberty.[61] He allows for coercion to prevent some types of offensive conduct.[62] More generally, he concedes that "[s]ince evils are by definition something to be regretted and prevented when possible, it seems to follow that the prevention of an evil, *any* evil, is always a *reason* of some relevance, however slight, in support of a criminal prohibition." The concession might seem to have the effect of casually giving away the liberal store. But Feinberg attempts to minimize this relaxation of the harm principle by arguing that evils other than "harm" (and to a limited extent "offense") have little weight and hence will rarely justify curtailing liberty.[63]

Harm to Discourse

In sum, both Mill and Feinberg (the author and the most careful expositor, respectively, of the harm principle) self-consciously depart from conventional or generic usages and from subjective senses of "harm." On first impression, it is hard to fault liberal theorists for departing from conventional usage and making the notion of "harm" into a term of art. Doesn't careful consideration of an issue often require us to try to achieve more precision in our basic terms than those terms would have in ordinary conversation?

Nonetheless, refinements of the notion of "harm" introduce serious mischief into political and legal discourse. We can notice some of these problems, beginning with the less grave and proceeding to the more serious.

Loss of Simplicity

Most obviously, the numerous refinements and qualifications introduced by proponents of the harm principle deprive the principle of the simplicity that Mill claimed for it. Cosmetically, the principle is still simple—government can restrict liberty only to prevent "harm"—but since "harm" itself is not now a simple fact but rather the conclusion of a controversial and complex normative reflection, the simplicity is illusory. It is as if someone were to say that there is one "very simple principle" that can readily be applied to resolve all conflicts between a state and its citizens: "Let justice be done." Okay, but. . . .

It may be, of course, that such matters are simply not amenable to simple propositions and nice generalizations. Nonetheless, as we have seen, its apparent simplicity is one of the harm principle's major attractions. By depriving the principle of this attractive feature, liberal refinements make it much less useful than it at first appears.

Equivocation

A second and closely related drawback of the Millians' technical conceptions of "harm" is that these conceptions, though attempting to make the concept of "harm" more precise, risk promoting confusion in discussions of the issues to which the harm principle is addressed. Without great care, discussants are likely to use the term "harm" sometimes in the complex and technical senses elaborated by thinkers like Mill and Feinberg and at other times in the more generic senses of the term.

It might seem that this is a risk that could be avoided by paying careful attention to how the term is being used. Perhaps—but such attentiveness is more easily preached than practiced. In everyday conversations, it would be remarkable if equivocation and the ensuing confusion could be avoided. And as we will see, this risk is often realized in academic discussions as well, even in the written work of careful theorists like Feinberg.

Circularity

Liberals and others use the harm principle to argue for their favored positions on questions of individual freedom, often in the context of specific controversies over obscenity, regulation of sexual conduct, abortion, or similar issues. But, reversing directions, they also use their favored positions on issues of individual liberty to argue for understanding "harm" in particular ways—and for excluding from the category of "harm" injuries that are in fact harmful in any ordinary sense not skewed to reach (or avoid) particular favored (or disfavored) conclusions. So it seems that premises and conclusions are constantly switching places. A *conclusion* ("no regulation of . . .") is said to be justified because it follows from the *premise* (the harm principle). But a contested interpretation of the *premise* (subjective injuries *x*, *y*, and *z* should not be counted as "harms") is justified because it is necessary to support the preferred *conclusion*.

Thus, we have already noted that although injuries in the utilitarian senses are in fact harms in any ordinary or subjective sense of the term—I *do* "harm" you by inflicting pain on you, or by frustrating your preferences—proponents of the harm principle peremptorily dismiss these senses of the term. They do so simply and unapologetically because, so construed, the harm principle would permit limitations of freedom that liberals oppose. A narrow, technical conception of harm is imperative, Feinberg contends, because "otherwise we shall find ourselves defending the legitimacy of state interferences with liberty that, preanalytically, we would find dubious or wrong."[64]

We have also noticed that both Mill and Feinberg are willing to count as "harms" only injuries to interests protected by "rights." But what "rights" we have against governmental interference with our liberty was precisely the question—or at least one way of stating the question—that the harm principle was supposed to help us answer in the first place. So it seems that we cannot know whether something counts as a "harm" unless we know what "rights" we have, but we cannot know what "rights" we have unless we know what will count as "harm."

Feinberg notices, and briefly addresses, this apparent circularity.[65] He acknowledges that the circularity would be vitiating if the rights invoked to determine which interests can be the subject of "harm" were *legal rights*. But Feinberg argues that the circularity can be avoided by specifying that the rights used to classify interests are *"moral rights merely."*[66] Whether an activity can properly be prohibited depends, in this view, on whether the interests it injures are protected by a *moral* right.

This suggestion might seem to demote the harm principle into a minor corollary of some larger theory or doctrine of "moral rights": only by first ascertaining what moral rights we have can we then determine what interests are protected by such rights, and hence what injuries count as "harms." But Feinberg eschews any such approach. Instead, he tries to explicate the notion of "moral rights" by asserting that *"any* indefensible invasion of another's interest (excepting of course the sick and wicked ones) is a wrong," and hence an infringement of a "moral right."[67]

Far from resolving the circularity, however, this response merely complicates the problem with additional normative questions. Which among the interests people think they have are genuine and valid, as opposed to "sick and wicked"? Traditional moralists, after all, have typically claimed that ostensible interests in viewing pornography or engaging in homosexual conduct are sick, wicked, or disordered. And how do we know which invasions of interests are "indefensible"? It had seemed that these were exactly the sorts of questions that the harm principle was supposed to help us answer. But it turns out that we cannot even use the principle unless we already know the answers to these questions.

In sum, it seems that in many ostensible applications of the harm principle, the conclusion is justifying the premise, not vice versa. An injury cannot be deemed a "harm" because saying it is one would justify restrictions that we know, somehow—"preanalytically," as Feinberg says—to be improper.

Indeed, Feinberg is sometimes endearingly candid as he trims and tailors the harm principle to fit conclusions favored in advance. In the final volume of his series, he considers a situation much like our earlier example of the Victorian community in which a few friends and I want to watch pornographic movies at home. In Feinberg's comparable example, "a community of like-minded puritan fundamentalists" discover—and want to restrict—a member who "has been secretly reading romantic novels in the privacy of his quarters, occasionally drinking a can or two of beer, and listening (at low volume of course) to popular music on his tiny radio."[68] Feinberg confesses that when he wrote his first volume, *Harm to Others,* it had not occurred to him that moralistic citizens might seek to justify a restriction by asserting—quite plausibly, as he now admits—that they *are* harmed by their neighbors' practice because "their paramount interest in living in a community of a certain sort has definitely been set back."[69] (I myself find this confession revealing and, frankly, startling.) "If that had occurred to me in time," he forthrightly acknowledges, "I no doubt would have tried to control the damage to my liberalism by adding another 'mediating maxim for the application of the harm principle,' one which would place constraints on the way appeals to harm prevention can be made in those quite common circumstances in which interests are opposed."[70]

Having now noticed the difficulty, Feinberg goes on to propose just such a further refinement—one favoring "personal" interests over "external" ones.[71] Whether this distinction could succeed in salvaging Feinberg's position need not concern us here (though we might in passing note that other liberal theorists have been pushed to propose virtually the same distinction, for similar reasons, and that the distinction has been powerfully criticized, including by other liberal theorists).[72] Nor is there anything necessarily unseemly about revising one's premises upon further reflection, and indeed Feinberg's candor in the matter is impressive. The pertinent point for now is simply that when "harm" is severed from its conventional and more straightforward meanings, the relation between ostensible premise and ostensible conclusion is placed in doubt. It is hard to know whether the premise is carrying the conclusion or the conclusion is carrying the premise.

Free (or Heavily Subsidized) Riding

But this is still not the most serious objection provoked by the exquisitely crafted definitions of harm to which Mill and his followers have been forced to resort. The greatest problem is that the possibilities of confusion and equivocation and circularity created by different meanings of "harm" permit liberal thinkers to "free ride" on the irresistible appeal of the harm principle in its more ordinary or generic senses.

Such "free riding" is possible because, as we have seen, in its ordinary sense the harm principle states what seems to be almost a self-evident normative truth—one that resonates both with familiar intuitions and popular adages and with more developed theories of legitimate government. If I want to do something, and if what I want to do doesn't harm anyone, what justification could the government have to stop me? Once "harm" has been redefined in a more technical and much narrower sense, however, proponents of the harm principle forfeit their claim to rely on these familiar intuitions. If what I am doing "hurts" and "offends" others, and if it causes them pain and frustrates their preferences, then perhaps as a prudential matter I should still be allowed to do it; but I can hardly claim in good faith that the reason I should be allowed to do it is that my conduct doesn't "affect" them.

By rights, then, proponents of the harm principle ought to forego any reliance on the "doesn't affect anyone" appeal (and on the related intuitions). But the multiple meanings of "harm" would make it difficult to exclude such an appeal, even if liberal thinkers wanted to earn their own way. And in any case, it seems they are *not* inclined to be so scrupulous. On the contrary, a close reading of their arguments suggests that they pervasively, even flagrantly, exploit the equivocation involved in "harm" to piggyback their arguments and conclusions onto the more conventional or straightforward senses of "harm" that they elsewhere disavow.

Mill as Free Rider

Thus, in the same paragraph in which he introduces the harm principle, Mill gives it a powerful rhetorical boost by asserting that an individual's freedom should be respected in that part of his conduct "which *merely concerns himself*."[73] This language is repeated, over and over again, throughout the essay.[74] Almost as numbingly frequent is an appeal framed in "not affecting" language. A person should not be "restrained in things not affecting [others'] good."[75] He should be free in "conduct which affects only himself."[76] Society has no coercive jurisdiction over a man in "conduct which does not affect the interests of others in their relation to him."[77] Or the protection of the principle may be said to cover the individual's "judgment and purposes in what *only regards himself*."[78]

The effect of these recurring appeals is to create a depiction of the sort of regulation that Mill is resisting (and that an overbearing society is ostensibly eager to impose) as almost wholly gratuitous—an officious effort to interfere in and curtail conduct that simply does not "concern," "affect," or "regard" anyone other than the actor. Little wonder that such gratuitous interference would provoke Mill's opposition: who other than the most insensitive meddler would *not* be indignant at such gratuitous interference?

Even a moderately careful reading of Mill's essay shows, of course, that *this* indignation is unwarranted, because the crucial terms— "concern," "affect," "regard"—are actually being used in narrow and highly artificial senses. As Mill quietly acknowledges, the same conduct that in his special usage does not "affect" or "concern" other people may very well be "hurtful" to them, and may have a powerful detrimental impact on "interests" that (alas for them) do not rise to the level of "rights." Viewed in this light, Mill's position seems much more fragile. Is it so obvious that individuals have an "absolute" right to do things that are "hurtful" to others so long as they do not "harm" others, in Mill's special and convoluted sense? How much of the rhetorical appeal of Mill's position is traceable to free or at least subsidized riding—to artful equivocations involving terms such as "harm," "concern," and "affect"?

Feinberg as Free Rider

As noted, Joel Feinberg is more deliberate in his analysis and his use of terms. Nonetheless, Feinberg fully exploits the rhetorical possibilities of equivocating about the meaning of "harm."

For instance, we have earlier noted that people who value a particular kind of community or culture might plausibly argue that they do in fact suffer "harm" from actions that undermine that community or culture. (Whether such harm is sufficient as a prudential matter to justify restrictions on the liberty of others is, once again, a different and more complicated question.) Although at times Feinberg appears to concede the point, in his more elaborate taxonomy this sort of injury is typically classified as an "evil" but not a "harm." And in arguing passionately that no one's liberty should be restricted to prevent this kind of evil, Feinberg makes tacit but powerful use of the more generic sense of "harm."

So he protests that restrictions aimed at protecting community character, by limiting the freedom of some individuals, would inflict "palpable harms" merely to avoid "states of affairs that *harm no one*."[79] Such an exchange—of "palpable harms" for the cessation of harmless conduct—seems manifestly unreasonable, to be sure. But then, of course, it is only in Feinberg's highly artificial sense of "harm" that the loss of a valued culture or community "harm[s] no one": in any less gerrymandered sense of the term such a loss might be viewed as a very serious harm indeed.

It is likewise wrong, Feinberg insists, "[i]f I am forbidden on pain of criminal punishment and public humiliation from acting as I prefer in ways that *harm no one.*"[80] Same response. And again: "The free-floating evils . . . *do not hurt anybody;* they cause no injury, offense, or distress. . . . To prevent them with the iron fist of legal coercion would be to impose suffering and injury *for the sake of no one's good at* all."[81] And yet again: "[I]t is *no reason whatever* to restrict *A*'s behavior simply because *B* disapproves of it, in the absence of harm or offense."[82] The same response applies: these protests may seem powerful and persuasive, but their power is dependent on the more subjective and generic senses of harm. Conversely, if we keep constantly in view that Feinberg is using "harm" in a "special narrow sense,"[83] as he puts it, and that in fact the behavior he wants to immunize *does* cause harm in any ordinary or practical sense of the term, his pleas lose much of their force.

Imagine an extreme case in which someone—call him Mr. Boorish—wants to engage in some course of conduct that does not interfere with the sorts of interests in which, by Feinberg's analysis, citizens have a "stake" and a "right," but which pervasively inflicts the sorts of "evils" that in Feinberg's catalogue rise only to the level of nonharmful "hurts." Boorish wants to engage in activities, in other words, that cause his fellow citizens to suffer "pangs, twinges, aches, stabs, stitches, cricks, and throbs, . . . cuts, bruises, sores, infections, muscle spasms, over-dilated or contracted arteries, gas pressures, and the like." In addition to these physical hurts, Boorish's activities will cause his neighbors to feel "nausea . . . , itches, dizziness, tension, hyperactivity, fatigue, sleeplessness, chills, weakness, stiffness, extremes of heat and cold," and also "bitterness, keen disappointment, remorse, depression, grief, 'heartache,' [and] despair."[84] Boorish's activities will cause all of these "hurts"—but nothing worse. Nothing that rises to the level of actual "harm."

The community acts to curb Boorish's hurtful activities, but (flourishing his copy of Feinberg) Boorish protests that under the harm principle, the community has no coercive jurisdiction to restrict his conduct. That is because, technically speaking, none of the "hurts" or "evils" he is inflicting on his neighbors qualifies as "harm." It is an outrage, Boorish declares with righteous indignation, that "[I should be forbidden] on pain of criminal punishment and public humiliation from acting as I prefer in ways that *harm no one*."[85] How appealing is the harm principle now?

Thus, Feinberg's appeals depend on a rather egregious sort of equivocation. Indeed, it might be argued that Feinberg quietly depends on equivocation as the major source of support for his position generally. In a perceptive and in some respects admiring review of Feinberg's opus, Gerald Dworkin attempts to clarify just what the harm principle as advocated by Feinberg entails. Having done so, Dworkin asks, "What is the argument for it?" The response is sobering: "In truth, I cannot find a clear argument in Feinberg." So Dworkin comments wryly that "[a]s Bertrand Russell observed with respect to logical matters, postulation has all 'the advantages of theft over honest toil.' "[86]

Perhaps it seemed that no justification was needed. Perhaps Feinberg imagined himself, as theorists sometimes self-consciously do, to be engaged in a conversation with people who already share his basic assumptions and commitments,[87] so that only refinements, not full-scale defenses, were needed.[88] Or perhaps the efficacy of the principle just seemed self-evident. Thus, after presenting a number of potentially controversial refinements in and applications of the harm principle, Feinberg comments sanguinely that "[a]s it has been formulated here, the harm-to-others principle is virtually beyond controversy."[89]

His almost childlike confidence on this point seems astonishing. It may be true, as discussed earlier, that the core idea contained in the commonsensical statement of harm principle *is* a virtual truism. Unfortunately, the truism and Feinberg, though sharing the term "harm," are not talking about the same thing. Not even close. But unfortunately, Feinberg (and Mill, and other deployers of the harm principle) often seem to forget that inconvenient fact.

The Hollowness, and the Indispensability, of the Harm Principle

The harm principle holds that government should restrict liberty only to prevent "harm." But "harm," as we have seen, turns out to be a receptive vessel into which advocates can pour virtually any content they like, or that they can persuade others to swallow.

Once we recognize the hollowness of the notion of "harm," it becomes apparent that there is no reason why anyone needs to object to the harm principle. As a matter of rhetorical strategy, to be sure, an advocate—a Lord Devlin, or a James Stephen—may choose to raise objections. Perceiving how others are using the principle, or what content others have fastened onto it, a critic may opt to acquiesce in that usage and then criticize or reject the principle itself. But there is an alternative, and anyone is free to choose it: simply embrace the principle and count as "harms" injuries to the sorts of values or interests for which protection would be prescribed by your own commitments, or theory of government, or conception of the good life.

If, instead of Mill's "progressive" view, for example, you hold the sort of "perfectionist" view that teaches that moral character is essential to the good life and that government has a role in "making men moral,"[90] then you will naturally and logically want to recognize "moral harm."[91] Different visions or political theories will produce different inventories of harms. But there is no reason why anyone needs to quarrel with *the harm principle* itself.

It would seem to follow that responsible and meaningful debates would neither contend over the harm principle nor expect it to do any real work in resolving contentious issues. Instead, they would engage with the larger theories or visions or commitments from which particular understandings of "harm" are derived.[92] "As we discourse on public affairs," John Courtney Murray observed, "we inevitably have to move upward, as it were, into realms of some theoretical generality—into metaphysics, ethics, theology."[93] Our discussion in this chapter supports Murray's observation. If conversations about "harm" are to be anything more than obfuscating and question-begging, they need to carry us to consider our deeper commitments and their bases in such things as "metaphysics, ethics, theology."

And there is the rub. Because it is precisely those sorts of matters that the cage of modern secular discourse operates to keep out of the conversation.

So, how can we argue about the desirability or justice of restrictions on abortion, or marriage, or drug use, *without* somehow drawing upon our larger visions of the good life, and upon the religious or philosophical assumptions that give rise to and inform those visions? It is a large question. But the short answer, it seems, is that we cannot. And thus we see the deeper reason why the harm principle has been so ubiquitous in modern political-moral discourse in the secular cage.

The cage purports and attempts to keep out the resources we need to articulate and ground and defend our views on the issues we must address. The exclusion leaves us little choice but to resort to smuggling operations: we must somehow smuggle into the cage, and the conversation, the resources we need to carry on the discussions we need to have. Not surprisingly, modern political-moral discourse has developed a number of devices for carrying out those smuggling operations. The harm principle is hardly the only such device, but for many it has been the instrument of choice.

In the end, the harm principle may be analytically useless. It may operate as a sort of license for a whole enterprise of deceptive, circular, question-begging, discursive practices. For smuggling. In our current circumstances, though, in which the cage of secular rationality makes smuggling all but inevitable, that same quality—namely, the principle's proficiency in facilitating intellectual smuggling—also makes it invaluable, even indispensable. And so, despite (or rather because of) its hollowness, we can expect the harm principle to do a brisk discursive business for a long time to come.

4

Disoriented Discourse:
The Secular Subversion of
Religious Freedom

How secure is religious freedom in the United States?

Looking backward at history, or looking around the world today, we may find cause to congratulate ourselves. In sixteenth-century Europe, hundreds of devout believers—Catholic, Protestant, Anabaptist—were burned at the stake for their religious beliefs.[1] In the mid-seventeenth century, Mary Dyer was led to the scaffold and hanged for insisting on professing her Quaker beliefs within the confines of Puritan Massachusetts. Today, in stark contrast, Quakers and more unorthodox or exotic believers of various sorts travel freely in Massachusetts—even live and worship there—without the slightest apprehension of being stoned, hanged, or burned (or even noticed). Unlike people of minority faiths in various countries today, Americans of all sorts openly confess our diverse faiths, or lack thereof, or hostility thereto, without fear of legal repercussions. We join, leave, switch, or stay away from churches. For the most part we do not worry about being excluded from government jobs, or from the best universities, for not belonging to some approved religion.

As they say in Lake Wobegone, "it could be worse." Much worse.

Even so, expressions of concern are common. One frequently articulated worry comes from people who associate religious freedom with a "wall of separation between church and state," and who perceive that in recent years the legendary wall, once officially described as "high and impregnable,"[2] has been crumbling.[3] Legal scholar Stephen Gey worries about indications that "the new majority on the Supreme Court is about to embark on a wholesale reinterpretation" which "would abandon any pretense of church/state separation."[4] More apocalyptic writers foretell an imminent "theocracy."[5]

Another cause for concern in some quarters is the Supreme Court's perceived lack of commitment to protecting the free exercise of religion. From about the mid-twentieth century until almost the end of the century, the Court at least *said*—actual practice notoriously fell short of professed principles—that in the absence of a "compelling" reason, government could not require a person to act against his or her religious convictions.[6] And the Court seemed inclined to construe "religion" expansively.[7] At least on paper, these pronouncements expressed a strong commitment to the free exercise of religion. In 1990, however, the Court abruptly changed course, ruling that government was free to burden the consciences of its citizens so long as it acted under religiously "neutral" laws and did not discriminate against religious practices *because* they were religious.[8] The Free Exercise Clause of the Constitution is now interpreted to forbid the "persecution" or "targeting" of religion—nothing more. In this newer regime, special constitutional protection for conscience is said to be a "luxury" that we can no longer afford.[9]

Disoriented Discourse

Even in the period when the judicial commitment to church–state separation and free exercise was at its peak, however, a different and more intellectual kind of concern was often voiced, and this concern has if anything become more urgent in recent years.

The concern is most often put in terms of *incoherence:* the courts' doctrines and decisions are said to exhibit no intelligible or coherent pattern. Steven Gey observes that "[o]ne of the few things constitutional scholars of every stripe seem to agree about is the proposition that the Court's Establishment Clause jurisprudence is an incoherent mess."[10] But this incoherence is not merely a product of judicial ineptitude. It reflects a deeper difficulty—a difficulty in *justification.* Both the constitutional text and the American political tradition appear to prescribe that "religion" is a matter requiring special legal treatment of some sort. But *why?* Justices have occasionally tried to suggest rationales for giving religion a special place at the constitutional table, and theorists have devoted even greater thought and energy to the task.[11] But the rationales that have been put forth often seem, upon inspection, contrived and unconvincing. And if you are unsure about *why* you are doing something, it should come as no surprise that you are also confused about *how* to do it, and dumbfounded when it comes to explaining and justifying *what* you have done.

It seems, in short, that although we have inherited a strong sense that religious freedom is a precious constitutional possession, we have a devil of a time *talking about* religious freedom—talking about it coherently and intelligently, that is. As long as the commitment to religious freedom appeared strong, this embarrassment may have seemed largely academic. We somehow seemed to do the right thing; who cares if we could not articulately explain what we were doing, or why? But as the practical commitment itself has deteriorated (or so many suppose), it is natural that not only theorists but also pundits and even citizens generally begin to worry, and to ask what has gone wrong and who is to blame.

And it seems that lately, the most common answer to that last question (albeit one that I will argue is shortsighted) has been . . . the so-called religious right.

Pernicious Religious Conservatism, or Subversive Secularism?

Recent antitheocracy books and articles differ in their details, but in broad outline they tell a common story, which goes roughly like this: The nation's founders devised a Constitution that created a "wall of separation between church and state." And at least during the mid-twentieth century and for some decades later, the Supreme Court was committed to maintaining that wall. Problems have arisen, though, basically because from approximately the Reagan years on, an increasingly influential movement of religious conservatives, working through and upon the Republican Party and Republican appointees to the federal bench, have conspired to tear down the wall.[12]

It is hardly surprising that this assessment has become commonplace. For one thing, the assessment contains a large measure of at least local truth. In recent decades, conservative evangelists like Pat Robertson as well as conservative politicians, writers, and scholars *have* often been outspokenly critical of the "wall" and the principle of separation, at least as the courts have construed that principle.[13] Then-Justice William Rehnquist wrote perhaps the most vigorous criticism of the "wall" metaphor by a Supreme Court justice—a sort of belated dissent to the seminal separationist decision in *Everson v. Board of Education*[14] that inaugurated modern judicial involvement with religion. Since then, Rehnquist's conservative colleagues, Justices Antonin Scalia and Clarence Thomas, have been as energetic as anyone on the Court in resisting or undoing separationist doctrines and decisions.[15]

So there are good or at least understandable reasons for ascribing the decline of the wall of separation to conservatives, especially religious conservatives. Even so, that ascription is, to be candid, near-sighted, simplistic, and fundamentally misleading. Complacently offered or accepted, it does a serious disservice to our understanding of the long-term causal influences that have combined to corrode separationist commitments and to bedevil the discourse of religious freedom. Indeed, from a more detached perspective, the diagnosis ascribing the decay of these commitments and this discourse to religious believers and their political representatives is almost exactly wrong. It would be more accurate, ultimately, to attribute our current malaise to secular influences than to religion.

This claim may seem paradoxical, to be sure. It has long been supposed, by both critics and proponents of the notions, that "separation of church and state" and "secularism" (or at least *governmental* secularism) go hand in glove:[16] How then can secularism be responsible for the erosion of separation? In this chapter, I will nonetheless try to explain and support that claim.

The commitment to church–state separation, I will suggest, has a long, distinguished (albeit tumultuous and sometimes sordid or even violent) history—one that antedates Thomas Jefferson and the American constitutional experiment by many centuries. And this commitment is indeed closely tied to what we might call the *classical* notion of the "secular." But the concept of the "secular" has undergone a radical transformation:[17] the modern conception—the conception expressed, for example, in Weber's imagery of the secular "cage"—is not only different from but is in some respects antithetical to the classical conception in which the commitment to church-state separation had its origins and its secure foothold. Far from providing a suitable foundation for any "wall of separation between church and state," modern secularism relentlessly chips away at that foundation.

Thus, proponents of separation and of secularism in its *modern* sense have inadvertently been promoting mutually antagonistic positions. And it is hardly surprising that at least one of those incompatible positions—in this case, the separationist position—might begin to totter (along with the associated commitment to freedom of conscience). Nor is it surprising that the discourse of religious freedom would come to seem profoundly befuddled.

Foundations: Separation and the Classical "Secular"

It is a rarely challenged commonplace, in constitutional discourse and academic theory generally, that the U. S. Constitution establishes a "secular" government.[18] But what does this idea mean, and how does the notion of the "secular" relate to the principle of separation of church and state? The questions turn out to be more complicated than we typically suppose, and they push us to consider how the dominant meaning of the "secular" has changed over the centuries and how that change in meanings affects commitments to separation of church and state.

The "Secular," Classical Style

Charles Taylor observes that "'[s]ecular' itself is a Christian term, that is, a word that finds its original meaning in a Christian context."[19] More specifically, the concept is rooted in the view, evident in the New Testament, that life and reality are divided into two realms or orders of reality that, though related in important ways, nonetheless have independent value and integrity. Different terms have been used to denote these realms—"earth" and "heaven," the "temporal" and the "spiritual," "this world" in contrast to another world.[20] In this vein, Jesus is believed by his followers to be in some sense a king, but his kingdom, as he himself declared, is "not of this world."[21]

In its more eschatological moods, Christian scripture anticipates that the division between the realms will ultimately be healed. As the words made familiar by Handel's "Hallelujah Chorus" declare, "the kingdom of this world" will become "the kingdom of our Lord."[22] But in the meantime (which is the very long time, from our mortal perspective anyway, in which we live as beings in human history), each realm makes its separate and valid claims on us. So we must "render unto Caesar the things which be Caesar's, and unto God the things which be God's."[23]

This two-realm teaching of the New Testament has persisted through Christian history. Thus, Augustine famously developed, at great length and with sophistication, the metaphor of the *two cities*—the City of God and the City of Man.[24] Medieval thinkers devoted much effort to explicating the biblical metaphor of the *"two swords."*[25] Luther and Calvin emphasized the doctrine of the *two kingdoms*.[26] Christians generally contrast "time"—the here and now of mundane history—with a more ethereal "eternity."[27]

Within this two-realm worldview, the term "secular" has denoted one of the two realms—the realm of "this world." The "secular," Taylor explains, described "profane time, the time of ordinary historical succession which the human race lives through between the Fall and the Parousia [or second coming of Christ]."[28] Thus, the "secular" existed as one component within a more encompassing reality that we could describe (with misgivings) as "religious." The secular domain, Nomi Stolzenberg notes, was "a specialized area of God's domain."[29]

> "The secular" was, in fact, originally a religious concept, a
> product of traditional religious epistemological frameworks. The
> concept of the secular always served the function of distinguish-
> ing religious from nonreligious domains. But nonreligious
> domains did not, in the premodern view, exist outside the religious
> epistemological framework. On the contrary, the framework of
> meaning was all-encompassing, overarching, comprehending
> within it every domain of human (and nonhuman) action and
> cognition, both the spiritual and the temporal, the holy and the
> unholy, the ecclesiastical and the secular, the sacred and the
> profane.[30]

Stolzenberg's observation is borne out by the familiar plea from the "Lord's Prayer" or "Our Father," regularly recited by Christians over the centuries: "Thy will be done on earth as it is in heaven."[31] Two realms are here distinguished—"earth" and "heaven"—but both are (or ought to be) governed by God's will. Her observation is borne out as well by the familiar classification of priests into the "regular" and "secular" clergies. A "secular" priest is plainly not one who is "not religious"; rather, he is a priest who instead of retreating into a monastery serves in a parish—in "the world."[32]

In sum, the classical view recognized two realms, related but independent, each with its own valid claims.[33] As with other such pairs—teacher and student, parent and child—the realms are at the same time separate but also related, and the relations between them are real and important: indeed, each term gets its meaning in part from its relation to the correlative term in the dichotomy. Thus, both the spiritual and the secular, as we have seen, are ultimately part of a single reality and are to be governed by a unified, overarching truth.[34] And we human beings are simultaneously subjects of both realms.

The Classical, Jurisdictional Problem: God and Caesar

The two-realm worldview, though a familiar part of our own heritage, seems to be distinctive to Western civilization. Or at least the view that each realm has its principal institutional representative— the state representing the secular realm and the church the spiritual—seems distinctive. Bernard Lewis explains, for example, that "[c]lassical Islam recognized a distinction between things of this world and things of the next, between pious and worldly considerations."[35] But "[t]he dichotomy of *regnum* and *sacerdotium,* so crucial in the history of Western Christendom, had no equivalent in Islam."

> In pagan Rome, Caesar was God. For Christians, there is a choice between God and Caesar, and endless generations of Christians have been ensnared in that choice. In Islam there was no such painful choice. In the universal Islamic policy as conceived by Muslims, there is no Caesar but only God, who is the sole sovereign and the sole source of law.[36]

The two-realm worldview has powerfully influenced Western history and culture,[37] including conceptions of the state, law, and individual rights. The eminent medieval historian Brian Tierney notes, for example, that "[n]atural rights theories seem to be a distinctively Western invention" and that "[m]edieval society was saturated with a concern for rights."[38] The two-realm worldview did not exactly generate this commitment to rights, Tierney suggests, but it provided an intellectual climate in which such thinking could flourish. "Since neither the spiritual nor temporal power could wholly dominate the other, medieval government never congealed into a rigid theocratic absolutism in which rights theories could never have taken root."[39]

The two-realm view also gives rise to a distinctive challenge—one that manifests itself on both the personal and political levels. The basic problem is this: because the realms are at once independent and yet significantly interrelated, and because both make their valid claims on us, we must somehow find a way to honor both kinds of claims. We must give both Caesar and God their due. But what exactly *is* Caesar's, and what is God's? It would not be an exaggeration to say that addressing this challenge, or negotiating the complex demands of the temporal and the spiritual, has been *the* central ethical and existential problem for Christians from the religion's inception.

This ethical problem passes into the realm of politics because each of these realms—the spiritual and the temporal—is subject to its own set of institutional authorities. In the medieval understanding, the spiritual realm was subject to the church. The temporal or secular realm was subject to God, ultimately, but more immediately to kings and princes.[40] Consider the characteristic explanation of a prominent twelfth-century thinker, Hugh of St. Victor:

> There are two lives, one earthly, the other heavenly, one corpo-
> real, the other spiritual. . . . Each has its own good by which it is
> invigorated and nourished. . . . Therefore, in each . . . life, powers
> were established. . . . The one power is therefore called secular,
> the other spiritual. . . . The earthly power has as its head the
> king. The spiritual power has as its head the supreme pontiff.
> All things that are earthly and made for the earthly life belong
> to the power of the king. All things that are spiritual and
> attributed to the spiritual life belong to the power of the
> supreme pontiff.[41]

In this framework, the problem of church and state was basically a matter of sorting out how God had allocated authority as
between the church and the secular rulers. What is the proper
jurisdiction of the state? Of the church?[42] And how should these
institutions deal with and relate to each other? This problem of
delineating jurisdictions is simply the manifestation, in the political domain, of the central Christian problem of dealing with the
independent, sometimes competing and sometimes overlapping
claims of the spiritual and the temporal.

As we will see, the problem of church and state itself is no longer
typically conceived of in this way, but we can appreciate the jurisdictional perspective with the help of other contemporary analogies. Thus, international and constitutional law routinely address
issues posed by conflicting jurisdictions of independent or partly
independent entities: different nations, different states, the states
and the national government, state and federal courts. In the classical view, church and state were themselves independent jurisdictions, and immense effort was devoted to trying to sort out the
jurisdictional lines.

Then and now, jurisdictional battles are fought on different levels. They can be fought on an *intellectual* plane, as participants deploy whatever intellectual resources and authorities are available to delineate the respective jurisdictions of the different institutions. In the classical context, these intellectual resources were found in the overarching truths believed to govern both the temporal and spiritual realms. So arguments about the proper domains were commonly framed in theological terms, or in the form of interpretations of biblical passages or other religious authorities thought to be repositories of truth.[43] Advocates might appeal to a sort of natural theology in which, for example, relations between pope and king were understood based on a supposed parallel to the relation between the sun and the moon.[44]

To be sure, advocates could also appeal to more pragmatic or political or philosophical considerations (especially after the revival of jurisprudence in the twelfth century and of Aristotle in the thirteenth century).[45] But the arguments were carried on to a significant extent in theological terms. Indeed, though the extracts we typically read today may not disclose the fact, even a later theorist of the secular state such as Hobbes—recently lauded as the seminal rejecter of "political theology" and advocate of the "Great Separation"[46]—devoted more pages in his classic *Leviathan* to supporting his views on government through painstaking scriptural exegesis and theological exposition than through the more secular social contract reasoning we focus on today.[47]

Jurisdictional disputes could, and can, also become "battles" in a more literal sense. Just as modern jurisdictional struggles sometimes generate not just political or legal analysis but also violence and bloodshed—the Civil War would be the horrific example in American history—so the classical jurisdictional debates stimulated outpourings of learning and polemic but also more fleshy and sometimes fatal thrusts and parries. In the eleventh century, Pope Gregory VII excommunicates the emperor Henry IV for interfering in the church's prerogative to appoint bishops, then forgives an apparently penitent Henry—only to be driven out of Rome by Henry's vengeful armies.[48] A century later, Archbishop Thomas Becket feuds with King Henry II over conflicts between the royal and ecclesiastical jurisdictions, flees Henry's wrath to spend years in exile on the Continent, but eventually returns only to be murdered by Henry's nobles in Canterbury Cathedral.[49] Later, the "man for all seasons," Thomas More, born about a block away from Thomas Becket's birthplace, is sent to the scaffold by his former friend Henry VIII (rulers named Henry seem to have been especially prone to jurisdictional quarrels) for refusing to recognize the king's supremacy over the church.[50]

The Response: Separation of Church and State, and (Later) Freedom of Conscience

Although princes, popes, and scholars often disagreed, sometimes bitterly or violently, over the proper division of jurisdictions, they virtually all agreed on one thing: the jurisdictions of church and state were different, and separate. "There were through the mediaeval centuries great overlap and great conflict between Church and state," Charles Taylor explains, "but in all versions, and on all sides, it was axiomatic that there had to be a separation of spheres."[51]

This is of course an oversimplification. Then as now, church and state did not inhabit separate universes; if they had, separation of church and state would simply have been a physical fact, not a problem or a principle requiring intellectual and political effort to achieve and maintain. In addition, bishops and priests often served both temporal and spiritual functions. William Placher observes that

> [i]n theory, everyone agreed that the church and the empire or kingdoms had separate tasks, both given by God. But in practice, when the church owned vast stretches of land and provided many governmental officials, it was hard to know where to draw the line between the two. Gregory [VII] saw lay investiture as illegitimate interference in the church, but to Henry [IV] it seemed necessary to have some right to choose his own leading landowners and officials.[52]

Because church and state existed alongside each other, the jurisdictional challenge was to delineate both the ways in which church and state should be separate and the ways in which they were related—the ways in which they might defer to but also cooperate with each other in exercising their respective jurisdictions. Nonetheless, separation was an essential part of the overall project. Indeed, the metaphor of the wall of separation is usually attributed to Roger Williams, who was working very much in the religious, two-realm worldview in which the "secular" state was contained in a more encompassing "religious" reality and was subject to the overarching religious truths.[53]

Not surprisingly, different thinkers, different political and ecclesiastical actors, and different eras developed this basic commitment to separation of church and state in different ways. Thinkers of the High Middle Ages gave much thought to how church and state should be separate, but their conclusions differed drastically among themselves, with some thinkers giving more and others less scope to the church's jurisdiction vis-à-vis the state's.[54] Medieval conclusions differed as well from those of the Massachusetts Puritans, who much later also reflected carefully on the issue, and who established a polity based on a strict separation of church and state as *they* conceived it[55] (but *not*, of course, as their colleague and then adversary Roger Williams conceived it, or as Jefferson and Madison would later conceive it.)

We need not attempt any survey of the dizzying variety in conceptions of separation that have been proposed or embraced over the centuries.[56] However, one historical development—namely, the rise of an intense concern with the protection of conscience commonly associated with the Protestant Reformation—deserves attention because it bears heavily on modern American jurisprudence.

From Freedom of the Church to Freedom of Conscience

Conscience is hardly a distinctively Protestant idea. On the contrary, the sanctity of conscience was recognized in medieval Catholic teaching and canon law,[57] and there has perhaps been no more eloquent and devoted champion of conscience than the fiercely Catholic lawyer, and Lord Chancellor, Sir (and Saint) Thomas More, who, as noted a moment ago, chose to go to the scaffold rather than betray his conscience.[58] ("A man may lose his head and have no harm," he explained.[59]) Nonetheless, the Protestant Reformation altered the significance of conscience in a way that profoundly affected, and to some extent redirected, historical commitments to the separation of church and state.

The alteration can be understood as the product of two changes associated with the Protestant Reformation. First, the fragmentation of Christendom resulting from the Reformation, combined with the tendency of both Protestants and Catholics to resort to invoking the aid and protection of secular princes in the ensuing struggles, had the effect of bringing churches under state control. Such arrangements came to be described as "Erastian." Jose Casanova observes that following the Reformation, "[t]he churches attempted to reproduce the model of Christendom at the national level, but all the territorial national churches, Anglican as well as Lutheran, Catholic as well as Orthodox, fell under caesaropapist control of the absolutist state."[60]

Second, in Protestant thinking the conception of the church itself changed. In simple and somewhat overstated terms,[61] the change was this: whereas Catholic teaching had emphasized the indispensable role of the church as an intermediary between God and humans, Protestants sought to cut out (or at least downsize) the middle man, so to speak, and to encourage a more direct relation between the individual and God. In the "priesthood of all believers," anyone could read the Bible for himself or herself and could commune with God directly without the intercession of priests, saints, or sacraments.[62] In this spirit, Luther passionately and defiantly set his own understanding of scripture against the decrees and practices of the church—"Here I stand; I can do no other"[63]— and thereby, as his biographer observes, "liberated the Christian conscience...."[64] Two-and-a-half centuries later, Thomas Paine, a radical protestant in temperament and outlook if not in substantive doctrine, put the idea in characteristically pithy form: "My own mind is my own church."[65]

This change can be overstated. For Protestants the church remained important as a community of believers and as a vehicle through which the word of God is preached. Moreover, the sacraments of baptism and communion were typically retained. But the spiritual center of gravity had shifted, as the position and functions formerly controlled by the church came to be transferred to the individual and his or her conscience: God spoke to people most compellingly, it came to be thought, not through the church but through the individual conscience.[66]

As a consequence of these developments, the medieval commitment to separation of church and state, and hence to keeping the *church* independent of secular jurisdiction, was partially rerouted into a commitment to keeping the *conscience* free from secular control. "The old claim that the church ought not to be controlled by secular rulers," Brian Tierney explains, "was now taken to mean that the civil magistrate had no right to interfere with any person's choice of religion."[67] Thus, the medieval slogan proclaiming *libertas ecclesiae*—"freedom of the church"[68]—begat the more modern theme of "freedom of conscience."[69] (Like many a parent and child, the two themes—freedom of the church and its offspring, freedom of conscience—would thenceforth be sometimes mutually supportive and sometimes in conflict: modern devotees of "conscience," forgetful of their origins, are as likely to see in "the church" a threat as a nurturing progenitor.)

Both the generative connection and the jurisdictional cast are manifest in the declaration of the eighteenth-century Connecticut legislator and Yale rector Elisha Williams: "[I]f CHRIST be the *Lord* of *Conscience*, the sole King in his own Kingdom; then it will follow, that *all such* as in any Manner or Degree *assume* the Power of directing and governing the Consciences of Men, are justly chargeable with *invading* his rightful Dominion; He alone having the Right they claim."[70] This theme grew to be powerfully influential in Protestant societies and became a central component of the American version of religious freedom.[71]

America as Legatee

By the time Jefferson and Madison took their places on the historical stage, therefore, the tradition of honoring—and sometimes fighting or even dying for—separation of church and state and freedom of conscience was already centuries old. Jefferson and Madison and their fellow citizens in turn accepted that inheritance and developed it in their own distinctive ways.

The American founders' commitment to religious freedom is often viewed as a decisive break from the past.[72] And in view of the more Erastian intermission that immediately preceded the American founding, this supposition is understandable. Nonetheless, the strand of continuity in the founding was as important as the fact of discontinuity.[73] Jefferson and his contemporaries were in reality the heirs to a tradition that was already centuries old, and they still had at least one foot firmly planted in the classical worldview.[74]

Thus, unlike most modern commentators and justices, Madison justified religious disestablishment in openly theological terms.[75] For his part, Jefferson officially argued for disestablishment and freedom of conscience on the overtly theological premise that "Almighty God hath created the mind free," and that governmental coercion in matters of religion represented "a departure from the plan of the Holy Author of our religion, who being Lord both of body and mind, yet chose not to propagate it by coercions on either, as was in his Almighty power to do."[76] And of course, Jefferson deployed the "wall of separation" metaphor in a letter to a group—New England Baptists—who were heirs of Roger Williams, and who had struggled for a version of separation of church and state on unapologetically religious grounds.[77]

In addition, founding era separationist commitments retained the jurisdictional aspect of classical thinking, and of the Protestant adaptation of this thinking to the domain of individual conscience.[78] The Protestant emphasis on a relation—an *unmediated* relation—between God and the individual was central to the argument in the famous *Memorial and Remonstrance* that James Madison wrote in support of religious freedom in Virginia.[79] "It is the duty of every man," Madison contended, "to render to the Creator such homage, and such only, as he believes to be acceptable to him." And on this assumption "[t]he Religion then of every man must be left to the conviction and conscience of every man." Madison was thereby led to conjoin church-state separation and free exercise of religion, and to conceive of both in strikingly *jurisdictional* terms. "Before any man can be considered as a member of Civil Society," Madison reasoned, "he must be considered as a subject of the Governor of the Universe." Consequently, duties to God are "precedent both in order of time and degree of obligation, to the claims of Civil Society," and entrance into society can only occur "with a saving of the allegiance to the Universal Sovereign." From these premises Madison drew his jurisdictional conclusion: "[I]n matters of Religion, no man's right is abridged by the institution of Civil Society, and . . . *Religion is wholly exempt from its cognizance.*"[80]

But if Americans were heirs to a centuries-old separationist tradition, can we at least say that the American constitutional system came to favor a *greater* or *more complete* separation than pre-Jeffersonian thinkers did? Alas, no—not in such categorical terms, anyway. In reality, compared to the classical models, the separation established in the American constitutional system was indeed more complete or pronounced in some respects, but it was discernibly *less* rigorous in others.

In the medieval world popes backed up their dictates to secular rulers not only through instruction and criticism but also by wielding the potent weapons of excommunication, and also of interdict (i.e., cessation of sacraments and church services within a ruler's jurisdiction[81]) and the threat of deposition. And the princes at least sometimes felt obliged to comply. Gregory VII deposed the emperor Henry IV, "releas[ing] all Christian men from the allegiance which they have sworn or may swear to him, and ... forbid[ding] anyone to serve him as king," and in order to regain the support of his subjects, Henry was compelled to stand for three days in the snow outside the castle at Canossa, ragged and barefoot, in order to obtain the pope's forgiveness.[82] Pope Innocent III imposed an interdict on England's hapless King John (of Magna Carta notoriety), and John was eventually forced to submit by actually turning England over to the pope and receiving it back as a fief in return for swearing an oath of vassalage and agreeing to pay an annual tribute to Rome.[83] Nothing of the sort would happen today: in this respect, modern separation does indeed seem more complete.

In addition, in premodern and early modern times it was common to suppose that church officials could determine what heresy consisted of and who was guilty of it; and it then became the task of the state actually to punish heretics.[84] At least in this country today, the prevailing assumption is that the state has no business bothering with heresy at all.[85] In this respect as well, the distance separating church and state is considerably larger today than it once was.

Conversely, some older conceptions separated church and state by forbidding clergy to hold public office;[86] that severe sort of separation has been repudiated in American jurisprudence.[87] And the medieval notion that ecclesiastical courts have exclusive jurisdiction over some persons, crimes, and claims that are beyond the cognizance of the civil courts[88]—the notion for which Thomas Becket became a martyr[89]—reflects a commitment to an extreme kind of jurisdictional separation that would be almost inconceivable in modern jurisprudence. Likewise, medieval thought and practice embraced an extreme version of separation with its notion of "the right of sanctuary," under which a criminal taking refuge in a church could claim to be beyond the reach of secular authorities. Robert Rodes observes that "[i]n some cases, [churches] became ultimately not a refuge but a center from which [the felon] could sally forth for further depredations or a hostel in which he could live in comfort on his ill-gotten gains."[90] Again, the practice brings to mind modern jurisdictional analogies—bandits fleeing across the Rio Grande into Mexico, white-collar criminals secreting away stolen funds in a Cayman Islands bank—that underscore the degree of separation reflected in the notion of "sanctuary." But that notion—that form of radical separation—has been peremptorily rejected when raised in tamer modern versions.[91]

In the end, then, we can confidently say that a commitment to separation of church and state has a very ancient and distinguished pedigree, and that conceptions of how church and state should be kept separate have differed significantly from time to time and from thinker to thinker. But it is hard to represent those complex differences on any one-dimensional metric of *more* or *less*. Americans have, to be sure, developed the separationist tradition in our own distinctive ways. But we have also witnessed and even presided over changes that threaten to bring the tradition to an end.

Subversion: Separation, Conscience, and the Modern "Secular"

"[T]he concept of the secular has itself, ironically, been secularized and modernized," Nomi Stolzenberg explains, "which makes it hard to grasp the original meaning of the secular."[92] The process by which this development has occurred has of course been complex. But, simplifying, we can discern the broad outlines of what has happened.

The Transformation of the "Secular"

As a starting point, we might recall the daunting challenge that the classical two-realm view poses on both the personal and political levels. God and Caesar. The spiritual and the temporal. Dual authorities, both imposing their valid claims on us. At times the claims emanating from these realms appear to conflict. How then are we to negotiate them? Given the difficulty of this challenge, it should not be surprising that many have tried to deflect it by simply ignoring or rejecting one of the realms, or by reducing the two realms to one.[93]

One way to achieve this simplification would be to renounce, to the extent possible, the temporal realm—to deny that this world, with its demands and desires, lays any valid claims on us. Many Christian sages (or eccentrics) over the centuries have advocated or practiced this course to some extent: St. Simon Stylites sitting atop his pillar for thirty-seven years in an attempt to escape the world is an extreme and exotic example.[94] But rejection of the world has not in fact been the dominant Christian response. On the contrary, Christian orthodoxy has characteristically cautioned against—

indeed, has condemned as heretical—an excessive negation of the claims of this world.

Thus, in response to early "gnostics" who disparaged the physical world, orthodox Christianity emphasized that the world itself was made by a benevolent God for humans, and that even in its fallen condition the world is still fundamentally good.[95] Mortal life, beginning with birth and ending in death, may be infinitesimally short (from the perspective of eternity anyway), but it is precious nonetheless; the world visible to the eye and audible to the ear is full of horror and discord—but also of joy and beauty. It is a gift of God to be cherished, not despised.

That conclusion might point in the direction of a different, opposite (and, to most of us, more congenial) reductionist path to simplification, though one that orthodox Christianity also disapproves. We might regard the secular realm—"this world" and this life—as the *only* reality, or at least as the only reality we can be confident of or need to concern ourselves with. And if the first way was that of monastic withdrawal, it would be natural to describe the opposite approach, which makes this "secular" world our exclusive concern, as "secularist." But now the term comes to have a different meaning than it had in its original or classical context. "Secular," rather than denoting one realm within an encompassing and ultimately "religious" reality, now describes a comprehensive view of life and the world[96]—a view in which the "spiritual" or the "holy" or "supernatural" are denied, subordinated, or at least reduced to this-worldly terms.

"Modern secularism," Nomi Stolzenberg observes, is "reductive." It "eliminates the tension between [the sacred and the profane] by simply preserving one and discarding the other."[97] In this way, we arrive at the core modern meaning of the "secular," in which the term means, basically, "not religious"[98]—so that secularism describes a sort of worldview that is fundamentally naturalistic rather than religious. Owen Chadwick describes the common usage in which "'secularization' is supposed to mean, a growing tendency in mankind to do without religion, or to try to do without religion. . . ."[99]

It is in this modern sense—of the "secular" as the encompassing framework that is "not religious"—that scholars and lawyers typically expect the state to be "secular." A "secular" government, in other words, is one that acts purely for this-worldly purposes and is "not religious" in its assumptions, motivations, and deliberations.[100] Once again, this statement is too simplistic to capture the messier reality in which we actually live; we will notice some complications shortly. Nonetheless, it is on approximately this assumption—that the state is supposed to be secular in the sense of "not religious"— that contemporary jurists and scholars typically debate problems of church and state.[101]

Problem and Nonproblem: From Jurisdiction to Justice

In the classical, two-realm worldview, as we have seen, the problem of church and state was one of delineating jurisdictions. But suppose now (simplifying the much messier historical developments that have in fact occurred) that we discard the classical worldview, with its conception of the secular as "a specialized area of God's domain,"[102] and embrace instead a more modern view and conception. Now the "secular" describes an encompassing worldview or framework, and the state is supposed to be "secular" in the sense of "not religious." What will happen to the classical problem of church and state?

Well, in the first place, it seems that the problem of jurisdiction will disappear. We might still at times describe issues using jurisdictional language in an attenuated or metaphorical sense.[103] But the bottom line is that actual legal and political jurisdiction—sovereignty—will now belong to the state, period. The state may defer to the church for various reasons and in various ways, but the church will ultimately enjoy as much freedom or immunity, and *only* as much, as the state sees fit to allow it. And when disagreements arise, it is the state that will decide them. Churches, of course, may sometimes be severely critical of governmental decisions or policies. But that a church might assert its own sovereignty to reject a secular legal decision, backing its refusal with threats of excommunication, interdict, and deposition, and that the government might feel obliged to back down in deference to the church: such a scenario will now seem almost inconceivable.[104]

In short, in the modern secular state the problem of jurisdiction effectively disappears. Instead, we now have a problem of justice, broadly conceived.[105] If the state is or aspires to be liberal and just, that is, it will be committed to respecting citizens' rights, to treating them as equals, and to promoting the public interest. The church will be one unit or association among many that are within the state's legal and political jurisdiction, and that the state will seek to treat as liberal justice requires.

In addressing the demands of justice, moreover, and thus in determining the proper treatment of churches, the modern liberal state will be expected to act on grounds that are "secular"—secular, once again, in the sense of "not religious." Thus, the sorts of theological or biblical arguments that once dominated discussion of the proper relations between church and state will now seem suspect or inadmissible.

In sum, though we might talk about something like "the problem of church and state" in both the classical and modern settings, such language is apt to mislead. In reality, we are talking about two distinctly different problems: a problem of *jurisdiction* has given way to a problem of *justice*—one that will be addressed and resolved within the state's secular jurisdiction and in secular terms. That fundamental (though perhaps unnoticed) transformation has crucial implications for the issues of "separation of church and state" and freedom of conscience.

The Wall as Relic?

One such implication is that the legitimacy of the classical "wall of separation" between church and state is called into question. The venerable construction may come to seem reminiscent of Hadrian's Wall, built in the second century to protect Roman civilization against the Picts and now running in time-worn, weather-beaten fragments across northern England: it is a hoary holdover from earlier times and earlier needs—charming and quaint, perhaps, but functionally obsolete with respect to the world we live in now.

This is not a proposition, to be sure, that will or should be accepted casually. Doubt will be fed in part by the fact that in reality the world is not thoroughly secular in the sense of being "not religious." But it will be helpful to begin by abstracting from the more cluttered reality we inhabit and trying to consider the pure case.

In performing this thought experiment, we must suppose that although government is now entirely secular, society as a whole is not. If society itself were wholly secular in the modern sense of being not religious, religion would presumably simply wither away (as so many thinkers over the last century or so have predicted or perhaps hoped it would), and the question of church–state separation would recede along with it. We must suppose that the government, although secular, is also tolerant; otherwise it might view religion in the way aggressively secular governments have sometimes done—that is, as a sort of reactionary and irrational element that should simply be suppressed to the extent possible.[106] Thus, we must imagine a situation in which some citizens are religious while the government itself is wholly secular, but also liberal and tolerant. In this situation, what stance would government take—as a matter of secular logic—toward the idea of separation of church and state?

In such a society, government would of course be little influenced by the church as a *religious* organization, or as a repository of religious truth; government's secularity would immunize it against that sort of influence. Threats from the church of excommunication or interdict would be impotent, even laughable. Nor would government have any apparent incentive to establish a religion as the official religion for the society. So church and state would be, as a matter of fact, separate from each other.

At the same time, there would be very little reason to embrace any notion of separation of church and state as a distinctive and constitutive commitment. Instead, religious citizens and religious groups or organizations would simply be one class among many that the government would need to deal with. And government would presumably deal with them in basically the same ways it deals with other citizens and other comparable (by secular criteria) groups—no better and no worse.

Thus, to the extent that government regulates, say, voluntary associations of various sorts to protect and serve the public interest (to prevent tortious conduct, for example, or race and sex discrimination), government would presumably impose similar regulation on religious organizations. If government taxes other comparable associations, it would likewise tax religious associations (and vice versa).[107] Similarly, property disputes within churches would be resolved in the courts by applying the same "neutral principles" used when such disputes arise within nonreligious organizations.[108]

To be sure, doctrines of privacy or freedom of association might provide some limited immunity from regulation for religious organizations in the same way that such doctrines partially insulate other sorts of private or charitable organizations.[109] But there would be no special claim to immunity arising simply from the fact that an organization is religious. By the same token, insofar as the state is viewed as having authority to dispense benefits—financial subsidies, for instance—to citizens and groups that it deems meritorious (or that have the political clout to extract such benefits), there would be no special reason to prohibit religious citizens and groups from receiving such benefits.[110]

A church, in short, would be much like General Motors[111]—or, perhaps more precisely, like the Rotary Club, or maybe the Red Cross. These organizations are all independent of government, and in that sense "separate" from it, but no special constitutional barrier prevents government from regulating, or subsidizing, or working in cooperation with them. The same would be true of churches: there would be no place for any distinctive constitutional commitment to "separation of church and state."[112] More particularly, the claim that anchored the commitment to separation of church and state in the classical context— namely, that the church is beyond the jurisdiction of the state because it is the representative of a different realm of reality that transcends the secular and hence the state—would now become noncognizable, even nonsensical.[113] On modern secular assumptions, there *is* no realm of reality—no realm cognizable by the state, at least—that transcends the secular.[114]

Similarly, insofar as a commitment to the free exercise of religion or the sanctity of conscience was derived from the more jurisdictional claims made for the church (conscience having partially occupied the place formerly held by the church), that commitment would likewise be undermined. There would be no plausible justification for religion-specific "free exercise exemptions"—that is, for exempting citizens from some laws just because the laws happen to burden their religious practice. On the contrary, such special treatment would seem a departure from the liberal requirement that all citizens be treated equally.[115]

To this point, we have been talking hypothetically: we have been asking what our legal world *would* look like if the secular worldview were wholeheartedly embraced, for purposes of governance at least, and if the implications of that view were consistently implemented. In fact, though, our actual legal world has come to look increasingly like the hypothetical world we have been contemplating (as my footnotes will suggest if you take the trouble to turn to them). As noted at the outset of this chapter, constitutional decisions in recent years seem to have relaxed or retreated from the earlier commitment to church–state separation. And they have moved away as well from earlier professions of affirmative protection for free exercise of religion. So our legal world is looking more like the hypothetical, secular world. And, as we will see, prominent theorists would push us even farther in that direction.

Still, the actual legal world is at least much messier than the hypothetical one we have been sketching. Why?

The Deterioration of Discourse

The preceding discussion has suggested that *if* government operated in purely secular fashion (in the modern sense), there would be little or no justification for any special constitutional commitment to "separation of church and state" or the free exercise of religion—or indeed for treating "religion" as a special legal category at all. In our actual world, however, that "if" condition is only imperfectly realized, for various reasons.

In the first place, it is true that a secular, nonreligious worldview has come to dominate some sectors of our society, including academia and law. But most American citizens, presumably including some academics and judges, remain religious,[116] and so inevitably religious beliefs and more classical notions of the secular continue to infiltrate and influence academic and public discourse. Frederick Gedicks observes:

> It is as if public religious discourse were driven into the mountains by public secularism, which then decided that it was not worth the trouble to complete the messy task of total eradication. As a result, religious discourse now makes periodic, guerilla-like forays into the public domain of secular neutrality.[117]

In addition, neither government nor the academy in fact operates in the coolly detached and rationalistic manner contemplated in the preceding discussion, in which basic assumptions are soberly and dispassionately articulated and then specific practical conclusions are worked out in some merely logical and disembodied fashion. Human thinking and practice rarely work in that way. Instead, as William James explained, typically "we keep unaltered as much of our old knowledge, as many of our old prejudices and beliefs, as we can. We patch and tinker more than we renew."[118] If James's observation holds for philosophical and academic endeavors, it is even more true in politics and law, where expectations and constituencies typically develop around, and thus serve to solidify and maintain, entrenched doctrines and principles.

Not surprisingly, thinking about religious freedom and church-state separation has unfolded in this more lurching and haphazard fashion. In this context, we are the heirs of centuries of thought and action—some of it heroic or violent, resulting in sacrifice and even martyrdom—in which separation of church and state, freedom of religion, and the sanctity of conscience have been struggled for. These notions are by now central to our intellectual universe and our national self-understanding,[119] and they are not about to be lightly cast aside just because a theoretical reflection on the implications of modern secular assumptions does not readily yield satisfying justifications for them. Ancient commitments and assumptions can be eroded, but the erosion is likely to occur gradually, as the implications of more contemporary assumptions are worked out and assimilated, sometimes peacefully, sometimes through litigation or political conflict.[120]

This erosion has occurred in part through the efforts of justices and theorists to articulate reasons for maintaining a wall of separation between church and state (and more generally for treating religion as a special legal category)—and through their inability to discharge that task with anything like manifest success. The modern project of justifying the special constitutional treatment of religion began somewhat belatedly. Thus, when the modern Supreme Court entered the field in *Everson,* the Court purported simply to enforce the historical decision made in the founding period; it did not pretend to offer any explicit contemporary justification for the wall of separation.[121] And indeed, as late as the 1980s, and even more recently, scholars noticed that surprisingly little attention had been given to providing convincing justifications for treating religion as a special constitutional category.[122] Writing in 2002, Noah Feldman observed that "the Establishment clause has generated comparatively little academic writing about why (as opposed to how) church and state should be kept distinct."[123]

In fact, a few legal scholars *had* addressed that issue,[124] however, and the project of justifying the special treatment of religion has accelerated in recent years.[125] But the results have been less than satisfying.[126] The project is by now extensive, and no detailed review or assessment is possible here. But for survey purposes it may be helpful to divide the project into three stages: rationalization, revision, and renunciation. The division is artificial, because the stages blur into each other, and in fact arguments of all classes are made in all periods. Even so, the schema may serve to impose some order on an unruly phenomenon.

Rationalization

In the first stage, judges and theorists forego appeals to classical or religious arguments but nonetheless attempt to support traditional commitments—to separation of church and state, to free exercise of religion or freedom of conscience—on secular, nonreligious grounds. In this vein, for over half a century judges and theorists have advanced secular rationales—albeit often casually or in ad hoc and haphazard fashion—to explain the distinctive treatment given to religion in American constitutional law.[127] Usually such rationales are not wholly lacking in plausibility. But they tend to be overbroad and underinclusive, and they often leave one with the sense that the advocate embraces a doubtful premise because of the instinctively favored conclusion it leads to, not vice versa.

For example, one of the most familiar rationales for attempting to separate religious arguments and symbols from the public sphere is that religion is dangerously divisive. Among current jurists, Justice Stephen Breyer in particular has stressed this rationale.[128] And Breyer plainly has a point: religion *can* be divisive. But then other interests, subjects, and perspectives besides religion can also be divisive. Religion, conversely, is not always divisive, and can in fact be a source of unity, especially in times of national crisis or tragedy: it is hardly surprising that solemn public displays of religion figured prominently in the American response to September 11.[129] Moreover, efforts to exclude religion from the public sphere can provoke as much contention and conflict as religion itself would: think of the furor provoked by the Ninth Circuit's attempt to excise the words "under God" from the Pledge of Allegiance.[130] In the end, it is hard to resist the suspicion that the divisiveness rationale, though not wholly lacking in plausibility, is embraced by proponents like Breyer to support conclusions or policy preferences arrived at in other ways or on other grounds.[131]

In a similar way, theorists have tried to develop secular rationales for a special constitutional commitment to free exercise of religion, or freedom of conscience, but these efforts have not been notably successful. One scholar, John Garvey, after surveying the inadequacies of familiar rationales, tentatively suggested in the 1980s that perhaps free exercise of religion is specially protected because religion is like insanity: both are immune to rational influences and considerations.[132] A decade later, Garvey renounced this rationale and candidly concluded that the special constitutional protection for religious exercise probably cannot be justified on secular grounds, so that the only plausible justification is a religious rationale.[133]

It would be rash to conclude, of course, that the project of providing secular rationales for commitments to separation of church and state, or freedom of conscience, is predestined to fail. Thus, theorists continue to develop and debate such rationales, as they should.[134] And yet a persistent question looms over these efforts: would we—would anyone—really find these rationales compelling if we were not already predisposed to embrace separation of church and state or freedom of conscience?

Revision

As secular rationalizations of traditional commitments come to seem less than satisfying, judges and theorists may almost imperceptibly and perhaps unconsciously shift to a different strategy: rather than trying to *justify* a commitment, they may quietly *revise* it to fit more current conceptions and rationales. The result of this sort of revision may be that the commitment is effectively converted into something different—something more cognizable and acceptable in contemporary terms—but the conversion is largely concealed because the new commitment still goes under the traditional title.

Perhaps the most ingenious such revision with respect to the venerable commitment to church–state separation has been offered by the prominent scholar and litigator, Douglas Laycock.[135] Laycock's basic commitments, forcefully and articulately expounded in a series of scholarly articles,[136] are to religious voluntarism and governmental neutrality toward religion. In this vein, while acknowledging that "separation" has been and continues to be an authoritative principle, Laycock proposes that the Constitution should be interpreted to require "separation," yes—but separation *not* (as virtually everyone had supposed) of *church and state,* exactly, but rather of *governmental influence* from *religious choice.*[137] Governmental "neutrality" toward religion, Laycock argues, is the best way to achieve that sort of "separation."

On this interpretation, the common assumption that "separation" means that government should not give aid to religion turns out to be mistaken. In some contexts, on the contrary, government may or even must affirmatively support or subsidize religious causes and institutions, so that they will not be disadvantaged relative to nonreligious causes and institutions that government also supports or subsidizes.[138]

Laycock's interpretation preserves the *word* "separation." But this sort of separation is a distinctly different sort of animal from the classical or traditional American versions of separation of *church and state.* Laycock has recently conceded as much—his effort to merge separation into neutrality "maybe...was a bridge too far"[139]—and he now advocates the outright abandonment of the vocabulary of "separation."[140]

Laycock's suggestion is only one noteworthy instance of a much broader movement that would baptize and convert classical commitments to both church–state separation and freedom of conscience into the more contemporary orthodoxy of equality, nondiscrimination, or "neutrality." Indeed, the Supreme Court itself has largely translated its doctrines under both the establishment and free exercise clauses into this more fashionable idiom.[141] Thus, the "no aid" corollary of nonestablishment, which at least in the American tradition has been closely associated with "separation of church and state,"[142] has evolved (or, depending on one's perspective, degenerated) into the requirement that the state be "neutral" or "evenhanded" in dealing with religion, neither favoring nor disfavoring it relative to "non-religion."[143] Similarly, free exercise doctrine, which once ostensibly offered some protection for religious exercise even against unintended state-imposed burdens,[144] has now been reinterpreted to mean only that government must act under generally applicable, religion-neutral laws, not persecuting or discriminating against religion.[145]

In these ways, classical commitments to separation of church and state and freedom of conscience, though preserved in name, have been refashioned in the enormously influential language of equality and neutrality. The basic commitments themselves have been substantially transformed in the process, because "separation" and "neutrality" have divergent and inconsistent implications. Frederick Gedicks explains that "[s]eparation requires that the government sometimes treat religion worse, and sometimes better, than comparable secular activities." By contrast, "government satisfies neutrality when it treats religious beliefs and practices no better, but also no worse, than comparable secular activities."[146] A full embrace of "neutrality" would thus amount to a repudiation of traditional "separation."[147]

One small but troublesome manifestation of the discrepancy is the so-called ministerial exception to employment discrimination laws.[148] The problem is this: both state and federal antidiscrimination laws typically prohibit employers from discriminating on the basis of sex, but some churches hold as a matter of doctrine that women cannot serve as priests or clergy members. So, aren't these churches in stark, officially proclaimed violation of the laws? And if so, do they have any constitutional immunity?

In a classical "separationist" framework, the answer to these questions would seem to be quite clear. Drawing jurisdictional lines can be difficult in many cases, as we have seen, but it seems that this particular issue would not lie near the border. A sovereign clearly oversteps its jurisdiction if it attempts to dictate to another sovereign who can and cannot be employed in important offices within that other sovereign's own jurisdiction. Thus, under a classical, jurisdictional notion of "separation of church and state," the state could no more dictate to the church that it must employ women as priests than the United States could order England to revise its qualifications for membership in the House of Lords. And indeed, some such conclusion was plausibly (if contestably) explained under free exercise doctrine as it was understood until 1990.[149]

Under current doctrine, by contrast, this conclusion seems anomalous. As noted, the Supreme Court currently holds that so long as laws burdening religion are "neutral" toward religion and generally applicable, no exemptions from such laws are constitutionally required.[150] Antidiscrimination legislation is applicable to employers generally; it does not discriminate against churches or single them out for special burdens. Why, then, should churches be entitled to a constitutional exemption permitting them to discriminate against women in the clergy? Richard Garnett notes the obvious question: "If ... it would be illegal for Wal-Mart to fire a store-manager because of her gender, then why should a religiously affiliated university be permitted to fire a chaplain because of hers?"[151]

Some scholars would indeed draw this conclusion: sex discrimination by churches *should* be forbidden.[152] Most courts, however, continue to shield churches in this respect.[153] But under current constitutional doctrine, explanations for *why* churches enjoy this immunity seem strained.[154] The "ministerial exception" looks like an aberration[155]—a holdover from a more classical framework that has now been officially abandoned. The anomalous quality of the exception is testimony to the transformation that has in fact occurred as old commitments have been (incompletely) recast in more modern molds.

Equality and neutrality, however, do not provide the exclusive vocabulary into which classical commitments can be converted. Revisers may instead turn to the language of "personal autonomy":[156] this seems an especially apt idiom for presenting the classical commitment to freedom of conscience. But, once again, the traditional commitment is radically transformed in the revision. Thus, Marie Failinger remarks that freedom of conscience "began as an argument that government must ensure a free response by the individual called distinctively by the Divine within" but by now "has come to mean very little beyond the notion of personal existential decision-making."[157] In a similar vein, Ronald Beiner suggests that a book on the subject by David Richards alters—and demeans—the concept of conscience.

> The spuriousness of this recurrent appeal to the sacredness of conscience is very clearly displayed in the discussion of pornography. How can this possibly be a matter of *conscience?* What is at issue here, surely, is the sacredness of consumer preferences.

And Beiner goes on to scoff that "[b]y [Richards's] contorted reasoning, the decision to snort cocaine constitutes an act of conscience."[158]

Renunciation

As it becomes apparent that current constitutional commitments, though passing themselves off under the same names as more classical commitments, are substantially different in substance, an obvious question arises: wouldn't it be better just to drop the facade? Why not just admit that we no longer can give persuasive reasons for the older commitments—and then bid those commitments adieu? Might not this candid renunciation be a promising first step toward reducing the confusion that notoriously prevails in religion clause jurisprudence?

Courts, to be sure, may be understandably reluctant to announce that they are repudiating principles long thought to be contained in the Constitution. Scholars, by contrast, have more freedom to acknowledge and embrace changes that seem indicated. And recently, some scholars have openly advocated the renunciation of classical commitments to religious freedom and the separation of church and state.

Thus, in a provocative article called "Who Needs Freedom of Religion?" philosopher and law professor James Nickel offers a list of nine "basic liberties" that deserve legal protection; these include such liberties as "freedom of belief, thought, and inquiry," "freedom of association," and "freedom to follow an ethic, plan of life, lifestyle, or traditional way of living."[159] "Freedom of religion" does not appear on the list; however, Nickel argues that whatever is valuable about the traditional commitment to freedom of religion will be protected by the other "basic liberties." It is better to dissolve religious freedom into other liberties, Nickel contends, among other reasons because this approach "can gain widespread acceptance in a religiously and ethnically diverse society that includes many nonreligious individuals."

> Religious liberty is more secure when nonreligious people see it,
> not as a special concession to the orthodox, but rather as simply an
> application of liberties and rights that all enjoy.[160]

Nickel's position is not hostile to religion—nor, for that matter, favorable to it. His argument amounts to a plausibly presented claim that under modern assumptions and commitments, there simply is no adequate reason to treat religion as a special category for purposes of legal protection.

Though Nickel does not specifically call for renunciation of the principle of separation of church and state, his logic surely points in that direction. Martha Nussbaum's recent treatment moves farther along the road to rejection of separationism. Nussbaum does not call for outright repudiation of separation, but she subordinates it to other themes—especially "equality"[161]—and she repeatedly criticizes appeals to any more vigorous or independent idea of separation. Such appeals are in her view productive mostly of confusion.[162] "[T]he principle of separation of church and state as an end in itself," Nussbaum argues, "has muddied the waters, clouding analysis based upon the equality principle."[163]

A more vigorous criticism of separation is provided in a recent book by Christopher Eisgruber, Provost of Princeton University, and Lawrence Sager, Dean of the University of Texas Law School. Explaining that both establishment clause and free exercise doctrine have been powerfully influenced by an ideal of "separation," Eisgruber and Sager comment on "how odd and puzzling the idea of separation is."[164] For one thing, the idea has wreaked conceptual havoc. "[M]etaphors and slogans about 'walls' and 'separation' can never provide a sensible conceptual apparatus for the analysis of religious liberty,"[165] they contend. "The result has been a crazy quilt of special privileges and restrictions that seem ad hoc at best and incoherent at worst."[166]

In addition to causing confusion, church–state separationism is, in the view of Eisgruber and Sager, simply unjustifiable—and unjust.[167]

The separation-inspired approach to Establishment Clause questions is the mirror image of the separation-inspired approach to the Free Exercise Clause questions about special exemptions for religiously motivated conduct. They form an odd couple. Both insist that religion is an anomaly, requiring exotic constitutional treatment different from anything else. Yet in free exercise cases, the idea of special immunities demands that religious believers be given an extraordinary benefit enjoyed by no one else; in Establishment Clause cases, the idea of separation insists that religion and religion alone be starved of public benefits available to everyone else. . . . The result is a curious position that requires government both to grant religion special privileges and to impose upon it special restrictions.[168]

From a classical perspective, of course, what Eisgruber and Sager view with puzzled disdain as a "strange, two-faced constitutional response"[169] and an "injustice"[170] in fact seems utterly unremarkable. If church and state are viewed as independent jurisdictions, then it is no more odd—no more anomalous or unjust—that governmental noninterference will sometimes relieve churches and their disciples of both the benefits and the burdens of the state's law than that citizens of Mexico are neither subsidized nor restricted under many laws and programs of the United States. Conversely, once the two-realm, jurisdictional perspective is discarded or forgotten, the point made by Eisgruber and Sager seems apt: there is no longer any good excuse for what now looks like a sort of schizophrenic, constitutional love–hate complex extending to religion both special immunities and special disabilities.

In place of separation, Eisgruber and Sager propose a principle of "Equal Liberty." The core idea is that "minority religious practices, needs, and interests must be as well and as favorably accommodated by government as are more familiar and mainstream interests."[171] Most of their book is devoted to elaborating on this idea and applying it to a range of familiar issues involving religion or churches.

Eisgruber and Sager have gone as far as anyone down the road away from the two-realm origins of religious freedom. Even so, critics have wondered whether Eisgruber and Sager fully grasp and embrace their secular assumptions. At times they seem influenced by a lingering commitment to classical separation, or at least to its residue.[172] For example, they defend the exception to employment discrimination laws allowing churches to discriminate against women in the selection of clergy as an application of "associational freedom."[173] But since other comparable associations (comparable on secular criteria, at least—private schools, for instance) usually do not enjoy any such immunity from antidiscrimination legislation, this rationalization seems frail.[174] In the end, it is hard to resist the suspicion that some of Eisgruber's and Sager's particular conclusions reflect a residual—and "separationist"— sense that religion and government simply are not supposed to go together.[175]

Despite this residue of separationism, however, Eisgruber's and Sager's book at least attempts to renounce the "wall" metaphor, the separation principle and its corollaries, and the derivative commitment to special protection or immunity for the free exercise of religion. In that respect, the book may be the starkest recent manifestation of the conclusion this chapter has argued for—namely, that the wall of separation lacks any secure foundation in modern secularism.

Dark Secular Discourse

If the modern discourse of religious freedom seems profoundly confused, that confusion ultimately traces back to the fact that it is hard to give good justifications either for a wall of separation between church and state or for the historically derivative commitment to freedom of conscience from within the cage of modern secular discourse. One remedy, advocated both by a few religionists and by a few secularists (like Eisgruber and Sager), would be simply to give up the game—to abandon the wall of separation.

But that prescription is likely to go unfilled, in the short run at least, because Americans generally remain deeply committed to church-state separation, even as they disagree about its meaning and its justifications. Gerard Bradley remarks that "'[s]eparation of church and state' is right up there with Mom, apple pie, and baseball in the American iconography."[176] As one vivid if amusing manifestation, Bradley quotes the first President Bush's recollection:

> Was I scared floating around in a little yellow raft off the coast of an enemy-held island, setting a world record for paddling? Of course I was. What sustains you in times like that? Well, you go back to fundamental values. I thought about Mother and Dad and the strength I got from them—and God and faith and the separation of Church and State.[177]

What has deteriorated, it seems, is not so much our commitment to church-state separation and freedom of conscience as our ability to justify and expound those commitments in public discourse. Nomi Stolzenberg observes the "modern cultural deformity that finds expression in frightening levels of mutual incomprehension between 'the religious' and 'the secular' that we see today."[178] It is that incomprehension that afflicts our modern conversations about religious freedom. And so long as the incomprehension persists, the celebrated incoherence of our church–state jurisprudence seems destined to flourish as well.

5

The Heavenly City of the Secular Philosophers

In April of 1931, as Herbert Hoover was vainly struggling to contain the Great Depression, Adolph Hitler was plotting his way into power, and Joseph Stalin was implementing a five-year plan that would soon produce a devastating famine in the Ukraine, the eminent historian Carl Becker delivered the prestigious Storrs Lectures in the more genteel environs of the Yale Law School. In an impressive display of erudition and gently cynical wit, Becker inspected an intellectual problem that he seemed to view as a sort of delicious performative irony acted out by the partisans of the eighteenth-century Enlightenment.

His lectures, published under the title of *The Heavenly City of the Eighteenth Century Philosophers,* became a minor classic that continues to warrant attention, because in fact Becker's analysis illuminates more than he intended. Without quite realizing it, Becker had stumbled onto a fundamental conundrum that continues to afflict much modern thought. Indeed, it is just possible that Becker's discussion revealed more about his own plight, and that of his secular successors, than about his historical subjects.

The Enlightenment of Self-Deception

Becker's focus was on the so-called philosophes—the progressive thinkers of the period of Voltaire, Diderot, Hume, Franklin, and Jefferson. It was in these thinkers that Becker detected the problem that became the subject of his book—and of this chapter.

Morality without Religion

The eighteenth-century progressive thinkers, Becker reported, saw themselves as "engaged in a life-or-death struggle with Christian philosophy and the infamous things that support it—superstition, intolerance, tyranny."[1] Though they attacked traditional Christianity, however, the philosophes were far from being ethical nihilists. On the contrary, they were in fact the conspicuous champions of justice and morality.

In part, their patronage of morality reflected a self-serving concern about their own public image.[2] Thus, David Hume declared himself "much more ambitious 'to be esteemed a man of virtue than a writer of taste.'"[3] But the philosophes' devotion to morality went beyond reputational concerns. At its core, Becker observed, the Enlightenment program was one of social reform[4]—its proponents hatched innumerable projects ranging from the mundane (upgrading of roads in winter) to the grandiose (universal peace)[5]— and social reform presupposed normative standards by which the society they strove for could be judged superior to the society they wanted to supercede. Having repudiated traditional Christianity, therefore, the philosophes were determined "to replace the old morality by a new and more solidly based one."[6]

And how was this task to be accomplished? The moral vocabulary of the eighteenth century, Becker noted, pervasively invoked "nature" and "natural law" as the definitive ethical standard.[7] There was nothing new about these ideas, of course—or at least about these words; appeals to "natural law" were perfectly familiar to classical, medieval, and early modern thinkers. But the philosophes understood "nature" in a radically different way than their predecessors had.

In earlier centuries, Becker argued, "nature" was the doorway to a theological or philosophical system. In the eighteenth century, by contrast, "nature" became secular and assumed a scientific, empirical cast; the term referred to observable facts, not to a priori concepts or categories.[8] (This was Becker's interpretation, at least, though of course other scholars would give—and have given— different interpretations.[9]) Investigating nature, consequently, became "a matter of handling test tubes instead of dialectics."[10]

In short, "nature" now referred to solid empirical realities—not to metaphysical fantasies (as the Enlightened thinkers took the older notions to be). Unfortunately, this more scientific view created a serious problem when the devotees of Enlightenment looked to nature as a source of ethical standards. Once deprived of its normative dimension, how could "nature" or "natural law" serve as sources of evaluative criteria or judgments? How could one squeeze moral values, or judgments about justice, or interpretations of the "meaning" of it all, out of brute empirical facts? The philosophes were committed to using "reason," yes, but reason does not manufacture moral criteria ex nihilo. It needs something to work with, and nature as they understood it (or as Becker supposed they understood it), was stingy in supplying that need.

Thus, the most acute philosopher of the period, David Hume, demonstrated that "[r]eason is incompetent to answer any fundamental question about God, or morality, or the meaning of life."[11] And the period's leading philosophical poet, Alexander Pope, expressed what seemed the natural conclusion in poetic (if slippery, and contestable) terms: "One truth is clear, *Whatever is, is right.*"[12]

Pope's dictum can be taken to indicate a sort of morally blank universe: whatever is simply *is*, and no independent normative Archimedean point or standard is available by which what *is* can be judged "right" or "wrong." Becker thought that this was what Pope's pronouncement meant, at any rate,[13] and he also thought that Pope was right. Or at least he believed that the amoralist proposition expressed the conclusion that a dispassionate exercise of reason would have drawn from the Enlightenment thinkers' scientific view of nature.

The problem, Becker explained, was that this amoralist position was also flatly unacceptable to the partisans of Enlightenment. In the first place, the notion expressed in Pope's line seemed a conceptual or semantic travesty. "To assert that all that is, is right, was to beat all meaning out of the word 'right.'"[14] The amoralist position also seemed to fly in the face of Enlightened good sense: how could it be that the Bastille, or the practice of torture, or the "superstition, intolerance, and tyranny" associated with traditional Christianity, were right?[15] Perhaps most distressingly, the amoralist position threatened to thwart the philosophes' reformist aspirations. "A society so obviously wrong could never be set right unless some distinction could be drawn between the custom that was naturally good and the custom that was naturally bad."[16]

In short, Pope's dictum seemed to imply a sort of incipient moral nihilism that was categorically unacceptable to the philosophes. So . . . what to do?

One possibility would have been to return to the Christian world-view of revealed religion, or perhaps to the telos-infused worldview of classical Athens, as a basis for moral judgments. But this was a course that the philosophes were constitutionally unable to take—or at least to admit to taking. Kant's Critical morality might (or might not) eventually offer an escape from the predicament—Becker ventured no judgment on that point, nor need we—but in the cultural milieu of Becker's study the Kantian philosophy was not yet on offer.

So instead, Becker argued, the philosophes opted for a "strategic retreat" from reason and its impertinent implications.[17] If reason led to the amoralist conclusion, then reason would just have to be, for the moment and for certain practical purposes, suspended.

Naturally, though, the philosophes did not and could not have put the point in quite these stark terms—not even (or perhaps especially not) to themselves. "Reason," after all, was their banner and their battle cry; conversely, transgression against the authority of reason was the principal sin of which they accused their traditionalist and Christian foes. So instead of openly acknowledging the shortcomings of reason, the partisans of Enlightenment adopted a more complicated strategy—one that (we can see in retrospect) could never actually satisfy the unflinching requirements of reason, but that could at least serve to conceal the philosophes' embarrassment behind a rationalist veil.

More specifically, they resolved to derive values from "human experience" and "human nature"[18] by means of historical research—the eighteenth-century equivalent of modern social science—conducted in a reflective and scientific spirit. The point of this philosophical history would not be simply to record facts, as in their estimation past historians had done, but rather to discern what is essential in human nature—to separate out the "really human" (to borrow a phrase that we will see much more of shortly) from the accidental or contingent manifestations of corrupted culture. Becker explained:

[T]he task of the philosopher-historian, theoretically speaking, was to note the ideas, customs, and institutions of all peoples at all times and in all places, to put them side by side, and to cancel out as it were those that appeared to be merely local or temporary: what remained would be those that were common to humanity. From these common aspects of human experience it would then be possible, if at all, to discover, as Hume put it, the "constant and universal principles of human nature" and on these principles to base a reconstructed society.[19]

From a distance it is easy enough to appreciate the shortcoming in this strategy. How is the theorist to know which "ideas, customs, and institutions" should be classified as essential and universal, and hence good, as opposed to those that are merely lamentable corruptions? In all times and places that the historian or anthropologist might study, she will likely discern features that we would applaud—but also features that we would regard as unfortunate or unjust or downright evil: there will be altruism, charity, and humane sympathies, yes, but also self-interest, cruelty, and exploitation. The philosophes "wished to get rid of the bad ideas and customs inherited from the past; quite as obviously they wished to hold fast to the good ones, if good ones there were";[20] but mere empirical observation would be incapable of making this sort of discrimination.

Enlightened Delusions

Undaunted (or perhaps oblivious), the Enlightenment thinkers forged ahead to reach righteous judgments on the basis of their social science project. Or at least they purported to. So, how did they manage to do this?

Very simply, Becker explained: they cheated. (Or, we might say, smuggled.) While purporting to derive ethical guidance *from* human experience, in fact they systematically imported their own preconceived values and imposed these values *onto* human experience. So they studied history, but "they were unwilling or unable to learn anything from history which could not, by some ingenious trick played on the dead, be reconciled with their faith."[21] And they pretended to ground their principles of ethics and justice in their empirical research and reflections, but in fact "the principles they are bound to find are the very ones they start out with."[22]

In this way, Becker suggested, the Enlightenment thinkers were in fact following in the steps of the medieval thinkers they regarded with such disdain, thereby producing an updated, secular version of the Heavenly City. To be sure, the substantive contents of the medieval and Enlightenment moralities were discernibly different. At least as Becker described them, the philosophes' moral and political views were, if not identical, at least strikingly similar to modern liberal notions (as we will see shortly). But the basic method was the same: the partisans of Enlightenment "were engaged in that nefarious medieval enterprise of reconciling the facts of human experience with truths already, in some fashion, revealed to them."[23]

Becker revels in the irony. The partisans of Enlightenment—of holding the world up to the critical examination of "reason"—were blissfully oblivious, it seems, to the workings of their own minds. "[A]t every turn [they] betray their debt to medieval thought without being aware of it."[24] Their very sophistication makes them seem almost comic—"at once too credulous and too skeptical."[25]

Still, in the end Becker is indulgent—and for a curious and, unbeknownst to him, portentous reason. "[T]hey are deceiving us, these philosopher-historians," he declares. "But we can easily forgive them for that, since they are, even more effectively, deceiving themselves."[26] So the Enlightened ones should be forgiven because, notwithstanding all of their castigating of foes for superstition and ignorance, and despite all of their paeans to truth and reason, they knew not what they were doing. Their grand moral and political aspirations were grounded in presuppositions of which they were unconscious, and which indeed they took pride in having repudiated. The Enlightenment—that "bright springtime of the modern world"[27]—was constituted at its core by a practice of pervasive deception and self-deception.

The "Old Insoluble Question"

It is a commonplace that in their presentations of the past, historians often reveal as much about themselves and their own times as they tell us about their ostensible subjects of study. Could this be true of Becker, himself a quintessential "philosopher-historian"? Becker's book obviously partakes of the wit and urbane cynicism that, he said, we most admire in Enlightenment thinkers.[28] Did it also reflect the insouciance he ascribed to them? And if it did, as I suspect, was the shortcoming peculiarly Becker's? Or did it reflect a deep conundrum of a secular age?

There is, we might notice, a troubling tension in Becker's treatment of the Enlightenment. Becker criticized the philosophes—albeit in a gentle, genial spirit—for the intellectual blunder he believed they committed and acted out with so much childlike energy and enthusiasm. And for the most part he treated that blunder as a historical curiosity—a local error that by now we could not be so naïve as to duplicate. Beneficiaries of decades of additional experience and sophisticated thought, we today would never be so innocent as to commit this sort of elementary mistake. Would we?

Yet Becker himself never actually proposed any solution to the philosophical predicament in which the philosophes found themselves. Given their views of nature, how *could* the thinkers of the Enlightenment have grounded or supported their moral values or commitments? Was there any alternative to the intellectual cheating that Becker depicted with such relish? What other response could the philosophes have made to what he called "the old insoluble question of the foundations of morality and the good life"?[29]

With respect to these more enduring questions, Becker kept mum. His silence raises a disturbing question about the nature of the blunder that the philosophes are said to have committed. Did their error lie in embracing a false solution to the problem of morality when a better solution was available? Or, rather, was their mistake to continue to adhere to normative commitments at all when the new, scientific worldview had rendered ideas like justice and morality anachronistic?

The light-hearted tone of Becker's treatment might seem to support the former interpretation. Nothing so portentous as the "death of morality" would seem to be at stake. But Becker's levity may mislead in this respect—mislead both us and himself. Indeed, his description of the moral problem as "insoluble" coupled with his apparent inability to point to any better answer to the philosophes' problem lends weight to this interpretation. "If it does not bore us too much," he remarked at one point, "we ask a perfunctory question, What is morality? and pause not for an answer."[30] The proper response to the "old insoluble question," it seems, is that we should just stop worrying about that question.

Should we then simply regard philosophical questions about the nature of morality as nonsensical—relegate them to the "angels on the head of a pin" category? Maybe. But it hardly takes the perception of a great historian to realize that humans have not adopted this nonchalant attitude, and we are not about to do so any time soon. The twentieth century was surely as charged with moral passions of one kind or another (some noble, and some deadly[31]) as the eighteenth century was, and such passions naturally provoke thinking about just what sort of thing "morality" might be. So if we cannot leave the philosophes' question alone, and if the new naturalistic worldview supports no satisfactory answer to that question (or at least none that Becker could point to), how could he be confident that the Enlightenment error he dissected so gleefully would not be repeated in his own time—or in ours?

Indeed, the conditions that spawned the mistake are, if anything, more stark now than they were two or three centuries ago. Other historians might doubt that the eighteenth-century thinkers actually embraced the disenchanted secularism that Becker ascribed to them.[32] But Becker, along with many of his contemporaries—and successors—surely *did* embrace it (or at least they tried to, and they thought they did). Thus, Becker intoned that it is now "quite impossible for us to regard man as the child of God for whom the earth was created as a temporary habitation. Rather must we regard him as little more than a chance deposit on the surface of the world, carelessly thrown up between two ice ages by the same forces that rust iron and ripen corn."[33] And any escape from the challenge through return to a more faith-filled or metaphysically thick world-view is by now almost inconceivable, he declared. So the older types of moral arguments inherited from classical and medieval times are no longer viable: "the world pattern into which they were so dexterously woven is no longer capable of eliciting from us either an emotional or an aesthetic response."[34]

At the same time, the notion that morality and justice are dead anachronisms—that "whatever is, is right"—is just as categorically unacceptable today as it was to the Enlightenment. Indeed, the moral commitments that Becker discerned in the eighteenth century are not so different from the commitments that mainstream political and legal thinkers would be espousing at the end of the twentieth. "The essential articles of the religion of the Enlightenment," he explained,

> may be stated thus: (1) man is not natively depraved; (2) the end of life is life itself, the good life on earth instead of the beatific life after death; (3) man is capable, guided solely by the light of reason and experience, of perfecting the good life on earth; and (4) the first and essential conditions of the good life on earth is the freeing of men's minds from the bonds of ignorance and superstition, and of their bodies from the arbitrary oppression of the constituted social authorities.[35]

Leave out the first two items (which today would seem so obvious, to progressive sensibilities anyway, that they would hardly need to be said), tone down the third item a bit, and Becker's list might almost be mistaken by a reader today, going on four-score years later, for prediction, not historical description. Indeed, the fourth and final element—"freeing...men's minds from the bonds of ignorance and superstition, and...their bodies from the arbitrary oppression of the constituted social authorities"—has been *the* project—*the* cherished, central, defining aspiration—of a mass of modern theorizing, polemicizing, and politicking on political-moral topics.

The relevant conditions and imperatives, in short, have not changed drastically, except perhaps by becoming even more firmly entrenched. So why would we *not* expect to find modern progressive thinkers practicing the same kind of elegant intellectual cheating, and the same cheerful and good-hearted self-deception, that Becker discerned in the eighteenth-century progressives?

Reenacting the Enlightenment?

It would not be difficult to paint some prominent thinkers of the past century into the picture that Becker sketched of the philosophes. Take John Dewey, that darling of the first half of the twentieth century and then again of many in the second half. With his earnest insistence on deriving values not from metaphysics or religion but from science and human "experience,"[36] Dewey would mix nicely in the company of Becker's philosophes.[37]

In a different way, John Rawls's famous devices of the "original position" and the "veil of ignorance" reflect an effort, quite reminiscent of the philosophes', to strip away the accidental and the distortingly contingent from humanity and thereby to call forth the pure, unencumbered human being—who can then consent to principles of legitimate government. As critics have often pointed out,[38] the question of which human features are essential (and thus to be retained in the "original position") and which are contingent (and so to be stripped away) is highly debatable. Rawls removes precisely those features—economic and social class, embeddedness in a particular political or social tradition, religious affiliation or faith—that are incongruent with his own views of what is relevant to justice, and he retains qualities conducive to his ethical and political predispositions. Thus, we might easily say of Rawls and his followers what Becker said of the philosophes—that "the principles they are bound to find are the very ones they start out with."

But these are hasty comparisons—and contestable ones, no doubt. It may be helpful to examine a contemporary instance in more leisurely fashion.

Where to turn for an instance worthy of our study? One of the highest honors in legal academia—an honor conferred on only one legal scholar each year—is an invitation to write the "Harvard Foreword," which is an article reflecting on the current state of American constitutional law that is published as the lead article of the most current volume of the *Harvard Law Review.* Most recently (as of the time I am writing), the honor went to the prolific philosopher, classicist, and legal scholar Martha Nussbaum.[39] Nussbaum uses the Foreword to explain and apply something called the "capabilities approach"—an approach that she has elsewhere described as "the most important theoretical development in human rights during the past two decades."[40] The description, even if oversanguine, suggests that there is something of significance here. So with Becker's discussion of the philosophes freshly in mind, let us consider Nussbaum and the capabilities approach.[41]

The central idea is commonly associated with the economist and social theorist Amartya Sen, who has argued that *capabilities,* rather than *resources* or *utility*, should be the object of efforts to promote human equality.[42] For her part, Nussbaum has adopted and developed the approach and turned it to different uses. Although she has expounded the approach in various books, articles, and lectures over the last decade or so, perhaps the most deliberate and systematic presentation of the core proposal occurs in a lengthy essay called "In Defense of Universal Values";[43] later works, while refining the approach in various respects, mostly extend and apply the capabilities approach to particular problems such as the treatment of nonhuman animals and of persons suffering from disabilities (or, in the case of the Harvard Foreword, to sundry issues of constitutional law). So Nussbaum's "Universal Values" essay provides a convenient subject for our examination (although I will make occasional reference as well to her other writings on the subject).

Nussbaum among the Philosophes

The parallels between Nussbaum's program and the project of Becker's philosophes are manifold. Like the philosophes, Nussbaum is not simply a detached theoretician; her thoughts are offered in service of a program of sweeping, and indeed global, reform. Although her political goals are not expressed in exactly the terms of the four articles that Becker used to describe the eighteenth-century program, a point-by-point comparison reveals the similarities.

First, far from believing that humans are "natively depraved," Nussbaum repeatedly affirms a view of inherent human dignity, and she expresses considerable confidence in the ability of individuals to live in accordance with "practical reason."[44] Second, she takes for granted the notion that, in Becker's phrasing, "the end of life is . . . the good life on earth"; a worldview or politics grounded in the assumption that life should aim at "the beatific life after death" never rises to the level of a possibility to be considered—not in this essay, anyway.[45] Like Becker's philosophes, Nussbaum also believes that "reason and experience" are the faculties to be used for achieving "the good life on earth"; her writings on the capabilities approach are in fact a performative affirmation of that assumption. Finally, the objective of "freeing . . . men's minds from the bonds of ignorance and superstition, and . . . their bodies from the arbitrary oppression of the constituted social authorities" pervades Nussbaum's essay (albeit with a more gender-inclusive emphasis). Her stated ambition is to "free [people] from tyrannies imposed by politics and tradition."[46]

If Nussbaum's political program closely resembles that of the philosophes, her accompanying philosophical objectives appear to be similar as well. Becker observed, as noted, that the philosophes wanted "to replace the old morality by a new and more solidly based one," and Nussbaum manifests a similar aspiration. More specifically, she is concerned to supply a justification for "human rights" that, unlike traditional or classical approaches, is "independent of any particular metaphysical or religious view."[47] The task is an important one because, as Nussbaum points out, "difficult theoretical questions are frequently obscured by the use of rights language, which can give the illusion of agreement where there is deep philosophical disagreement."[48] Nussbaum lists some of these questions and disagreements:

> People differ about what the *basis* of a rights claim is: rationality, sentience, and mere life have all had their defenders. They differ, too, about whether rights are prepolitical or artifacts of laws

and institutions. . . . They differ about whether rights belong only to individual persons, or also to groups. They differ about whether rights are to be regarded as side-constraints on goal-promoting action, or rather as one part of the social goal that is being promoted. They differ, again, about the relationship between rights and duties. . . . They differ, finally, about what rights are to be understood as rights to.[49]

In view of such questions, without a more secure justification than has been offered to date, "the appeal to rights is quite mysterious."[50] Nussbaum aims to dispel this mystery by "providing the philosophical underpinning for basic constitutional principles,"[51] including principles that support rights.

In meeting this philosophical challenge, moreover, Nussbaum faces the same challenge that Becker detected in the eighteenth-century program. Having dismissed the possibility of any more transcendent ethical standard, independent of humanity, that is, Nussbaum has nothing to appeal to except humanity and human experience itself. If Pope's demoralizing dictum that "whatever is, is right" is to be avoided, human experience must somehow be made into a standard for evaluating and criticizing human experience. This would seem to mean that some parts or layers of human experience must be selected and refined into normative criteria by which other parts or layers of human experience can be assessed. So, what subset of the comprehensive set of human experience can perform this normative function?

Human "Capabilities" as Political-Moral Justification

Here we reach the philosophical core of Nussbaum's position. She argues that human *capabilities* can provide a universal normative standard for evaluating political practices and arrangements. With reference to Vasanti, an Indian woman who serves as a central character throughout the essay for exploring issues and illustrating claims, Nussbaum explains the difference between a utilitarian approach (which she criticizes as inadequate[52]) and a political morality focusing on capabilities:

> The central question asked by the capabilities approach is not, "How satisfied is Vasanti?" or even "How much in the way of resources is she able to command?" It is, instead, "What is Vasanti *able to do and to be?*"[53]

Pursuing this question, Nussbaum goes on to elaborate ten central human capabilities that a just political system must secure. These include capabilities for (1) life; (2) bodily health; (3) bodily integrity; (4) the use of senses, imagination, and thought; (5) emotions; (6) practical reason; (7) affiliation (which includes "[h]aving the social bases of self-respect and non-humiliation" and thus entails a nondiscrimination principle); (8) living with other species; (9) play; and (10) control over one's environment.[54]

The terms in which Nussbaum recommends this "capabilities approach" are again powerfully reminiscent of the claim made by Becker's philosophes. As noted, the philosophes presented their views as the outcome of historical research covering a variety of periods and societies directed at distinguishing what was "universal" from what was merely local. In a similar spirit, Nussbaum describes her list of capabilities as "the result of years of cross-cultural discussion"[55] seeking to identify capabilities—the "Universal Values" mentioned in her title—that are or at least can be universally recognized. "Ideas of activity and ability are everywhere," she asserts, "and there is no culture in which people do not ask themselves what they are able to do, what opportunities they have for functioning."[56]

But if Nussbaum's cross-cultural "capabilities approach" is parallel to the eighteenth-century thinkers' philosophical history, does her more modern strategy also suffer from the same deep philosophical flaw? From quasi-factual observations about what humans "are able to do and to be," does Nussbaum succeed in articulating "philosophical underpinnings" for "universal values"?

There are from the outset powerful deterrents to even asking that question. In the first place, Nussbaum's proposal contains so much to argue about—and so many specific prescriptions of immediate practical significance—that we are likely to look past the question of underlying philosophical justification. For example, is Nussbaum's particular list of the relevant capabilities the best possible list? Or, assuming the list itself is acceptable in the abstract, what should the different capabilities be understood to include? To mention a current controversy, do the capacities for "affiliation" and "bodily integrity" (which, Nussbaum explains, entails "having opportunities for sexual satisfaction"[57]) mean that governments act unjustly if they decline to authorize same-sex marriage? And how far must the state go to ensure that the central capabilities can actually be developed and exercised? Nussbaum stresses that mere "negative" liberties are not enough.[58] But how much affirmative support must a just government provide to guarantee that individuals can enjoy good health, nutrition, and shelter (ingredients of "bodily health"), or "opportunities for sexual satisfaction" (as noted, a corollary of "bodily integrity"), or opportunities for "experiencing and producing self-expressive works" (a component of "senses, imagination, and thought")?[59]

Nussbaum's recent Harvard Foreword raises even more such contentious questions of application. The American constitutional system is obviously an intricate one, and it presents complex and contested questions concerning the judicial role vis-à-vis other branches and the proper mode of interpreting a distinctive legal text. Even a reader entirely sympathetic to Nussbaum's general approach might well wonder whether a highly abstract list of human "capabilities," however admirable, can be neatly laid onto this constitutional system and, within the space of a few pages, generate concrete answers to a wide range of specific and often highly technical constitutional questions. In a complex legal system, for example, can the claim that "conscience" is an important human capability really answer the technical question of which parties should have legal "standing" to litigate the constitutionality of particular government expenditures?[60]

These and similar questions are so immediate and provocative that it may seem almost pedantic to look beyond them and ask whether the capabilities approach itself (as opposed to Nussbaum's particular, highly debatable elaboration of that approach) is theoretically secure. In addition, there is a strong incentive *not* to raise that question. The incentive derives from the specter of moral nihilism—the nihilism implied in Becker's amoralist rendering of Pope's line that "whatever is, is right"—that lurks in the corners of modern philosophical discussions of the nature of morality. As Nussbaum herself argues, other approaches to problems of morality, justice, and rights have often been shown to be seriously deficient at the "meta" level. Their deficiencies can provoke the worry that all of our talk about morality and justice and rights might be a sort of elaborate sham—a species of "self-deceptive rationalizing," as Nussbaum puts it.[61] But this conclusion would be unacceptable to Nussbaum, and to many of us; we do not want to be—and we insist that we *are not*—nihilists.

So if the capabilities approach promises to avoid some of the pitfalls of other moral theories like utilitarianism, and if it also offers a fair amount of "cross-cultural consensus," as Nussbaum assures us, then perhaps we would be wise to leave well enough alone, and hence to refrain from asking troublesome questions. And indeed, some modern thinkers *have* advocated a course of cultivated silence on these questions. Proposing a "'silence is golden' policy" with regard to questions about the underlying truth or ontological status of moral statements, Jeffrey Stout explains that "[t]o search for such a something is to engage in a metaphysical quest, to enter the Serborian bog where whole armies have sunk." The solution to this difficulty, Stout suggests, is to "shun the question. Avoid the bog. Stop the cycle. Give up the idea that [moral] truth must be a substantial something."[62]

For better or worse, though, these questions are not easy to banish. In the present instance, Nussbaum's express purpose, as she repeatedly tells us, is not merely to offer an attractive political platform for people to sign onto, but rather to provide stronger "philosophical underpinnings" for treating the elements of that platform as normative. She offers the capabilities approach as a way of addressing at least some of the difficult philosophical questions that have made "the appeal to rights ... quite mysterious." So it seems licit to ask whether she succeeds at that level. Does Nussbaum manage to avoid the eighteenth-century error of simply smuggling her own set of values into her more empirical-looking claims without ever actually producing any justification for them? Or, conversely, does she provide simply one more instance of high-minded intellectual deception and self-deception of the kind so engagingly depicted by Becker?

The Resort to "Intuition"

An initial, fundamental doubt can be stated succinctly: Why should the fact that human beings are *capable of* doing something, or of being something, mean that the capability is *morally valuable?* Humans are capable of doing and being all sorts of things. They are capable of altruistic service or artistic creation, to be sure—but also of cruelty, violence, exploitation, masochism, and indifference. Humans are capable of being benefactors, artists, occasionally even saints; and they are capable of being cheats, thieves, rapists, and pederasts. Some capabilities seem admirable or praiseworthy—not surprisingly, these are the ones Nussbaum selects for her list—while others encompass behaviors or personal attributes that we deplore. So how can *capability* itself supply a governing normative criterion?

In response to this challenge, Nussbaum relies pervasively and at more than one level on an appeal to "intuition." "The argument in each case," she explains, "is based on imagining a form of life; it is intuitive and discursive."[63]

Thus, at the elementary level of justification for her approach, Nussbaum argues that we experience a "basic intuition" to the effect that "human abilities exert a moral claim that they should be developed."[64] Stated in this way, though, the argument seems frail. In the first place, it is hardly clear that people do in fact have the "basic intuition" described by Nussbaum. Whether people would report having such an intuition very likely depends on whether they happen to be thinking of admirable capabilities (like the capabilities for learning, perhaps, or for love) or more dubious capabilities (such as the ability to feel sadistic pleasure by inflicting gratuitous suffering): the less desirable capabilities almost surely do *not* generate any intuition supporting a "moral claim that they should be developed." We may indeed view it as a sort of "tragedy," as Nussbaum contends, when capabilities to learn and love are left unfulfilled, but we do not perceive anything tragic when a person's potential to develop an addiction to heroin or a proclivity for child molestation goes unrealized.

Indeed, Nussbaum herself quickly qualifies her initial, more sweeping contention. Noting that "the capacity for cruelty . . . does not figure on the list," she explains that "[n]ot *all* human abilities exert a moral claim, only the ones that have been evaluated as valuable from an ethical viewpoint."[65] Elsewhere she points out that we do not protect capabilities "*qua* capabilities," but only upon a "prior evaluation, deciding which [capabilities] are good, and, among the good, which are most central, most clearly involved in defining the minimum conditions for a life with human dignity."[66] The qualification is offered in passing and in an "of course" tone. Nussbaum seems not to notice that her caveat renders her position circular: it is morally valuable, the amended claim now asserts, to protect and cultivate *morally valuable* capabilities.

The circularity effectively negates Nussbaum's claim that "capabilities" can serve as source of "philosophical underpinnings" for "universal values." Instead, capabilities simply become one more item—along with actions, attitudes, emotions, dispositions, motives or intentions, personal traits or attributes, political arrangements, and various other things—that stand *in need of* moral evaluation; they do nothing to supply a *criterion or standard of moral evaluation.*

But let us suspend this doubt and suppose that people do have the "basic intuition" Nussbaum describes. Even so, might they not be asked to examine that intuition, and to attempt to give a supporting account of it? One possible account might invoke the sort of position often attributed to Aristotle of a natural teleology or "metaphysical biology": human beings have built-in normative ends or an innate "telos" (reflected, perhaps, in observable "capabilities"?), and the point of morality is to realize this telos.[67] But although a scholarly admirer of Aristotle,[68] Nussbaum explicitly declines to embrace any such teleological metaphysics; as noted, she disclaims reliance on *any* specific "metaphysical or religious" premises. Consequently, the nature and status of her claimed intuition remain murky.

In later work, Nussbaum offers a response to the criticism that she relies on mere intuitions, but the response is not so much an actual defense as an attempt—quite possibly a successful one—to pull other theorists into her plight. Thus, noting that John Rawls offered a sustained criticism of the use of intuition in normative political philosophy, Nussbaum argues that in reality Rawls's approach depends as much on intuition as her own does; his reliance on intuition is simply less conspicuous because his theory has "more moving parts."[69] In this respect, Nussbaum may well be right. But a deficiency is no less vitiating because other theorists suffer from the same deficiency.

In short, her pervasive reliance on "intuition" to do normative work leaves Nussbaum vulnerable to the criticism that she is not actually arguing or reasoning but merely stating her own opinions and hoping that readers will join her in those opinions. And perhaps that *is* all she is doing; perhaps I am mistaken (as one reader has suggested to me) in supposing that Nussbaum is attempting anything more ambitious than that. On this more modest reading, Nussbaum's list of ten basic capabilities would be merely a sort of laundry list of things that she happens to value, and that she hopes other people will value as well.

In that case, however, it seems that Nussbaum is not so much reasoning as merely reporting, to quote Becker, "truths already, in some fashion, revealed to [her]." (Or perhaps not even "truths," but merely "values" she happens to hold.) Moreover, it is hard to know what to make of her title—"In *Defense* of Universal Values"—or of her repeated assertions that the capabilities approach can provide "philosophical underpinnings" for "universal values" and "human rights," and that the approach can address and remedy in some fashion the philosophical difficulties that Nussbaum describes concerning what rights are and where they come from. It seems more plausible, therefore, and more charitable, to interpret Nussbaum as doing—or at least *trying* to do—what she says she is doing.

And indeed, Nussbaum attempts to supplement her appeals to intuition and to shore up her contentions about capabilities by appealing to several other fashionable notions: the ideas of a "really human life," of "human dignity," and of an "overlapping consensus." But these supplements fail to salvage the capabilities approach.

Capabilities and the "Really Human"

A large part of Nussbaum's argument emphasizes that the possibility of exercising the particular capabilities she has identified is essential to a "life that is really human," or to the ability "to live really humanly" or in "a truly human way."[70] Although these themes pervade Nussbaum's essay, however, her discussion leaves a good deal obscure.

To begin with, there is something a little odd about a claim that implies that virtually none of the Homo sapiens who have inhabited and indeed constituted human history have lived "really human" lives. Yet this seems to be the logical consequence of Nussbaum's contention that a "really human" life is unavailable without protection for the capabilities she identifies coupled with the fact that few if any societies have afforded anything approaching the level of support for these capabilities that Nussbaum views as "a basic social minimum."[71] Particularly with respect to women, Nussbaum asserts that even today "almost all world societies are very far from providing the basic minimum of truly human functioning, where many or even most women are concerned."[72] Women in such circumstances have surely been living lives less free and full than might be desirable. But is it cogent, or helpful, to suggest that these women's lives have not been "really human"?

The question prompts a closer look at the basic contention. What exactly does it mean to say that the frustration of particular capabilities makes a person's life less than "really human"? The claim might be understood in what we might call either a "descriptive" or a "normative" senses. In the first or descriptive sense, Nussbaum's contention simply observes that if a person is prevented from doing something that she is capable of doing (whatever that something might be), then for better or worse she will do less than she might have done. A possible human experience—an experience that humans in general and this individual in particular would be *capable* of having—will be denied her.

Taken in this straightforward sense, Nussbaum's contention seems correct, and indeed almost tautologous: if you are prevented from realizing or exercising some capability, then to be sure your life will be limited in the sense that you will not do something that you could have done, or experience something you could have experienced. In this nonjudgmental sense, the contention also seems normatively empty. Whether a legal or cultural restriction keeps you from worship or poetry, on the one hand, or from heroin addiction or the craving for "blood lust," on the other, it will still be true that you will have been prevented from having an experience that you could have had. Your life will to that extent be more limited—less "full"—than it might have been. But what is the normative content of this conclusion?

Clearly this cannot be what Nussbaum means. Instead, it seems, she means her argument to be taken in a more judgmental or normative sense. As noted already, her contention that the frustration of a capability denies a person a life that is "fully" or "really human" evidently refers only to capabilities for engaging in *morally valuable* functioning. So denial of the opportunity for artistic expression deprives people of a kind of experience—or of "functioning"—that would make their lives more "fully human." But denial of the opportunity to plunder, pillage, and rape, while admittedly depriving people of experiences they are *capable* of having (and that at least some of them would *choose* to have, given the option), does not take away anything that would contribute to living "in a truly human way."

In avoiding tautology and moral emptiness, however, this version of the claim renders the criterion of the "really human" purely conclusory, thereby creating overwhelming practical and theoretical problems. The practical problem is that the judgmental criterion of the "really human" life now becomes useless for the resolution of any genuinely contested moral question. Does government commit injustice by prohibiting, say, the use of cocaine, or the viewing of hard-core pornography? Such prohibitions surely limit a human capability; insofar as the prohibitions are effective they prevent people from doing things they are capable of doing, and that some people would choose to do. But supporters and opponents of such prohibitions obviously disagree about whether those particular capabilities contribute to a life that is morally valuable. And the notion of a "really human" life in the judgmental or normative sense now does nothing to ease that disagreement; it merely provides a different, potentially deceptive route back to the question of whether the use of cocaine may be morally acceptable.

This observation points to the underlying theoretical problem: Nussbaum's normative conception of the "really human" life produces the same circularity we noticed earlier with respect to the notion of "capabilities," and thereby drains the idea of the "really human" life of any independent substantive content. It is morally valuable to live the "really human" life, and the "really human" life is one devoted to "functioning" that is morally valuable. The circularity simply ensures that once again, as Becker put it, "the principles they are bound to find are the very ones they start out with." Or, to use our terms from earlier chapters, the appealing rhetoric of the "really human" becomes a convenient vehicle for smuggling in the advocate's preestablished values and commitments.

"Human Dignity"

Similar difficulties surround Nussbaum's use of the language of "human dignity," an appeal that occurs in the "Universal Values" essay[73] but becomes even more conspicuous and pervasive in her more recent writings about the capabilities approach.[74] The capabilities that ought to be recognized and protected, she suggests, are those that contribute to a life worthy of "human dignity." In invoking human dignity, Nussbaum joins—or perhaps incorporates by reference—a venerable enterprise: "human dignity" is a central notion in much modern human rights thinking, and it is crucial as well in Catholic social teaching. Moreover, as she notes, the term has older and respectable roots, figuring in the writings of thinkers like Aristotle, Locke, and Kant.[75]

Despite its impressive pedigree, however, the appeal to human dignity raises questions that the uninitiated may be impertinent enough to ask. What *is* "human dignity," exactly, and how is it that human beings come to have it? Obviously, normative theorists who rely on the notion are not using "dignity" in the everyday sense of the term. In ordinary speech, we talk of "dignity" as a quality that some people have and others do not, or that people have on some occasions but not others. A grave, calm, soft-spoken gentleman may be described as having "dignity," but it would seem odd or even laughable to use the word with respect to a rambunctious child, or a vulgar, clownish teenager. The theorists of human rights are plainly using the term to refer to some quite different quality. But what exactly is that quality?

Sometimes the term is used as a window into a more religious or metaphysically ambitious account of human personhood. In religious writings, for example, the claim that humans have "dignity" is closely associated with the belief that humans are made "in the image of God."[76] In a similar vein, Michael Perry argues that some such religious assumption is necessary to any claim that humans have the sort of dignity that makes us inherently bearers of rights.[77] But in the more secular framework in which theorists like Nussbaum work and speak—in the cage of modern secular discourse—"dignity" cannot be elaborated in this religious sense. So, can "dignity" be redeemed in a purely secular worldview?

Some of the more aggressive defenders of a naturalistic, secular framework insist that it cannot: notions like "dignity" and "intrinsic moral worth" are no longer meaningful, and they should be abandoned. As noted, Becker himself thought that in the modern worldview, human beings must be viewed as "little more than a chance deposit on the surface of the world, carelessly thrown up between two ice ages by the same forces that rust iron and ripen corn."[78] Stephen Hawking, explaining the implications of the prevailing scientific view for human beings, observes that "[t]he human race is just a chemical scum on a moderate-sized planet."[79] Nobel Prize-winning biologist Jacques Monod includes "belief in the natural rights of man" among those "disgusting" archaic beliefs that "afflict[] and rend[] the conscience of anyone provided with . . . a little intelligence."[80] John Gray excoriates what he views as the hypocrisy and self-deception of those who purport to embrace both science and the pieties of liberal humanism. We ought to give up such sentimental nonsense, Gray contends, and admit that on modern assumptions we are "straw dogs."[81] Steven Pinker recently published an essay revealingly entitled "The Stupidity of Dignity."[82]

In this climate, we are left wondering. What is "dignity," exactly, and how (on secular assumptions) do we come to have it?

The claim that all humans have "dignity" is closely related to the claim that all humans have "equal moral worth"—a point on which Nussbaum likewise insists.[83] At least to all appearances, however, humans differ vastly in their virtues and abilities. So what is it that gives us "equal moral worth"? Louis Pojman argues that as a historical matter, the idea of human equality descends from religious rationales.[84] But those rationales are excluded from the cage of modern secular discourse. How, then, can the claim be understood, and justified?

Pojman examines ten leading secular arguments advanced by theorists such as Ronald Dworkin, John Rawls, Kai Nielsen, Joel Feinberg, Thomas Nagel, and Alan Gewirth, and he finds all of these arguments wanting. Sometimes the arguments turn on demonstrable fallacies or on flagrant and unsupported discursive leaps; more often they do not actually offer any justification for equal worth at all but instead simply assert or assume it, or else posit that in the absence of any persuasive objection we should adopt a "presumption" of equal worth.[85] Pojman concludes that egalitarian commitments are "simply a leftover from a religious world view now rejected by all of the philosophers discussed in this essay."[86] Secular egalitarians are free riders, living off an inheritance they view with disdain. And he wonders whether "perhaps we should abandon egalitarianism and devise political philosophies that reflect naturalistic assumptions, theories which are forthright in viewing humans as differentially talented animals who must get on together."[87]

In a similar vein, Jeremy Waldron argues that John Locke's commitment to equality was firmly grounded in religious assumptions, and that modern efforts to support the commitment have not to this point succeeded.[88] Waldron's concluding observations sound faintly ominous:

> [M]aybe the notion of humans as one another's equals will begin to fall apart, under pressure, without the presence of the religious conception that shaped it. . . . Locke believed this general acceptance [of equality] was impossible apart from the principle's foundation in religious teaching. We believe otherwise. Locke, I suspect, would have thought we were taking a risk. And I am

afraid it is not entirely clear, given our experience of a world and a century in which politics and public reason have cut loose from these foundations, that his cautions and suspicions were unjustified.[89]

Suppose, though, that the claim that all persons have "dignity" (or "equal moral worth") is somehow established—or at least assumed for purposes of argument. Even so, the project of deriving particular normative conclusions from that claim remains perilous. Is "human dignity" offended or violated by the imposition of capital punishment, for example? Some theorists think it is; at the far extreme, others think that the imposition of capital punishment in cases of especially egregious crimes acknowledges the moral responsibility, and hence respects the dignity, of the perpetrator.

In the end, it is hard to resist the suspicion that the language of "dignity" provides not so much a useable standard from which to argue or reason as a way of dressing up different people's earnest intuitions approving or disapproving some particular law or practice. Instead of saying "I find corporal punishment of children offensive," we can say "Corporal punishment of children is an offense against human dignity." The second formulation looks more substantial, more serious, less purely personal. But unless the nature and source of "human dignity" can be elaborated, it adds nothing of substance to the first formulation.

If one harbors such a suspicion, Nussbaum's appeals to "human dignity" will do nothing to allay it. Indeed, and perhaps to her credit, Nussbaum sometimes appears to concede that "dignity" is a conclusory or merely clarifying term that can do no actual argumentative work. Thus, she explains that the capabilities approach "considers the account of entitlements not as *derived from* the ideas of dignity and respect but rather as ways of *fleshing out* those ideas."[90] The statement suggests that dignity is not an inherent quality that humans have and from which particular rights or entitlements derive, but rather a sort of encompassing honorific label for the kind of life that humans would enjoy if our basic entitlements (which, once again, are based on what?) were recognized and realized.

I hasten to add that I am not at all sure that this is an accurate interpretation of Nussbaum's use of the idea of dignity. More often she talks of the capabilities approach as "informed by an intuitive idea of a life that is worthy of the dignity of a human being."[91] In this description, it sounds as if "dignity" is some quality that humans inherently enjoy or possess, and of which different forms of life may be "worthy" or not; and it might seem to follow that dignity would supply a sort of abstract standard for judging whether particular entitlements should be recognized. In arguing about some particular claimed entitlement or right (freedom from capital punishment, perhaps, or a right to minimum welfare), we would ask: "Would a life without that right be worthy of human dignity?"

But however Nussbaum's appeals to "human dignity" are understood, it seems clear that the connections between dignity (whatever it is) and particular conclusions about rights or valuable capabilities will have to be drawn, as Nussbaum repeatedly acknowledges, by "intuition." And thus vanishes any hope that the deficiencies of intuition, already discussed, will be remedied by the invocation of the standard of "dignity." We are, it seems, right back where we started.

Capabilities and Consensus

Nussbaum also attempts to support her particular list of valuable capabilities by arguing that the list reflects, or at least is capable of achieving, a sort of cross-cultural "overlapping consensus."[92] But this contention does little to shore up her "capabilities approach" as a way of providing "philosophical underpinnings" for "universal values," for at least two reasons.

In the first place, the contention is dubious as an empirical matter. At present, it is clear that much in Nussbaum's political program is controversial, even in Western nations committed to liberal democracy; and the program would surely be even more in tension with dominant views held in other cultures, such as in India or in predominantly Muslim regions. Nussbaum understands this; indeed, she devotes much of her essay to defending her views against critics of various kinds, thus making it clear that at least many of the specifics in her program are far from commanding any consensus at present.

Is there nonetheless a consensus at some more general level, though, supporting at least the basic capabilities that Nussbaum lists? This is a harder question, in part because Nussbaum describes her favored capabilities in very abstract and favorable terms—"life," "bodily integrity," and so forth. But even in its general, carefully crafted form, Nussbaum's list may not enjoy anything approaching a global consensus. Her program is very much in the Western "liberal" tradition, as she acknowledges, so naturally it resonates with Western "liberal" values. But would the proposal elicit the same support in non-Western nations?

Nussbaum addresses this doubt at some length, arguing that there are people who support the values and principles she favors even in countries such as India.[93] No doubt there are—just as there are surely people even in Western countries who *reject* those liberal values and principles. But how does this conflicted state of affairs support the claim of *consensus,* except perhaps through a sort of cross-cultural gerrymandering? And of course, as Democrats and Republicans both know perfectly well, gerrymandering is a strategy that is not limited to one party. If it is possible to splice together a dominant liberal tradition in the West with incipient or minority liberal traditions in, say, the Arab world to produce an "overlapping consensus" *supporting* Nussbaum's values, then why is it not equally possible to combine a dominant nonliberal position in the Muslim world, say, with minority nonliberal traditions in the West to produce an overlapping consensus *opposing* those values?[94]

But suppose Nussbaum's claims about consensus are correct as an empirical matter. A second problem now arises: namely, the existence or nonexistence of consensus has no obvious relevance to the question of "philosophical underpinnings," or justification— which, once again, is what Nussbaum purports to be providing. Whether or not a consensus currently exists, or will soon emerge, it seems clear (as Nussbaum herself indicates) that her position has not enjoyed any consensus in most cultures through most of history. Does it follow that the "universal values" were not truly values in those times and places?

The standard example is pertinent here: if a global consensus through much of the world's history regarded slavery as acceptable, was the consensus correct? *Was* slavery then permissible? Nussbaum rejects such conclusions, and she criticizes the "cultural relativism" implicit in this view.[95] But this rejection renders problematic her reliance on (ostensible or hoped for) present or achievable consensuses—unless, once again, she is simply speculating about the political prospects of her program.

Enlightenment All Over Again?

In sum, Martha Nussbaum purports to have offered a philosophical basis, or at least "philosophical underpinnings," for "universal values" and for rights of the liberal sort. But the key components in her account—capabilities, the "really human" life, present or potential consensuses—combine to supply not a cogent justification for universal values, but rather a rhetorical framework for artful question-begging, and thus for smuggling. Human "capabilities" are not a *standard* of moral evaluation, but rather a part of human life *in need of* moral evaluation. The "really human" life also provides no substantive standard for moral evaluation, but instead operates as a conclusory label to be applied to the sort of life judged to be morally valuable on other (perhaps unstated) grounds. Sanguine claims about or hopes for an "overlapping consensus" seem both empirically dubious and, more importantly, philosophically irrelevant to the question of justification.

Nussbaum, of course, is far from being idiosyncratic in these respects. On the contrary, her views merely reflect one particular, skillful interweaving of some standard threads of modern political-moral thought. With some adjustments, therefore, criticisms of Nussbaum's "capabilities approach" will be applicable to many such mainstream efforts to justify morality or justice or rights in an Enlightenment or post-Enlightenment world.

The spectacle puts one in mind of Becker's wry comment on the philosophes; with only minor adjustments, Becker might be describing many of today's political-moral theorists. Their political faith, Becker observed,

> assumes everything that most needs to be proved, and begs every question we could think of asking. These skeptics who eagerly assent to so much strike [us] as overcredulous. We feel that they are too easily persuaded, that they are naive souls after all, duped by their humane sympathies, on every occasion hastening to the gate to meet and welcome platitudes and thin panaceas.[96]

6

SCIENCE, HUMANITY,
AND ATROCITY

Just over a half century ago, researchers in occupied Manchuria conducted scientific experiments on logs. The project sounds innocuous enough—until we learn that "logs" was the researchers' term for the human beings on whom they were experimenting.

The term arose, possibly, from research on frostbite. "Those seized for medical experiments," a later report explained, "were taken outside in freezing weather and left with exposed arms, periodically drenched with water, until a guard decided that frostbite had set in.... [T]his was determined after the 'frozen arms, when struck with a short stick, emitted a sound resembling that which a board gives when it is struck.'"[1]

In one such experiment, the "log" was a three-day old baby. Experimenting on a baby can pose difficulties, of course, because the baby may decline to cooperate. The researchers explained how they overcame one obstacle in this case. "Usually a hand of a three-day-old infant is clenched into a fist... but by sticking the needle in [the baby's finger], the middle finger could be kept straight to make the experiment easier."[2]

In *The Song Sparrow and the Child,* Joseph Vining's reflection on the claims of science and humanity begins with a terse, eerie recitation of these and similar incidents of scientific experiments conducted on human beings during the twentieth century in Manchuria, Nazi Germany, and Pol Pot's Cambodia. The incidents are conveyed through quotations, sometimes of the coldly clinical prose that the researchers themselves chose as most suitable for their purposes. These quotations are juxtaposed against others from an array of distinguished scientists and philosophers explaining the naturalistic cosmology that, in the view of these luminaries, modern science has conferred on us. We live, it seems, in a stark, cold cosmos devoid of any inherent meaning, purpose, or value. "The more the universe seems comprehensible," Nobel Prize–winning physicist Steven Weinberg remarks, "the more it also seems pointless."[3] In this pointless universe, "living creatures just are very complicated physico-chemical mechanisms," J. J. C. Smart explains.[4]

And what of ourselves—of human beings? Another Nobel Prize winner, Francois Jacob, instructs us:

> Biology has demonstrated that there is no metaphysical entity hidden behind the word "life." . . . From particles to man, there is a whole series of integration, of levels, of discontinuities. But there is no breach either in the composition of the objects or in the reactions that take place in them; no change in "essence."[5]

So, what are we supposed to make of this pairing up of descriptions of moral atrocities with statements of a scientific worldview? Is Vining trying to do to science what critics sometimes do to Christianity when they give descriptions highlighting, say, the sexual abuses of clergy, or the Inquisition—thereby implicitly condemning a whole movement of life and thought by equating it with the enormities that any large-scale human enterprise will occasionally produce? If so, readers might well toss Vining's book aside as a cranky manifestation of the "antiscience" that is one of the book's abiding concerns. To be sure, scientists have sometimes behaved unfeelingly, even monstrously—just as other humans have done. But surely there is nothing inherent in the scientific method or worldview that leads to the atrocities of Manchuria or the Third Reich.

Or is there?

The question runs through Vining's multifaceted meditation, and the answers that gradually, tentatively emerge are complicated, provocative, and counter to the culture that prevails in much of academia today. In that and other respects, *The Song Sparrow and the Child* is continuous with earlier writings[6] that have established Vining among the more profoundly challenging—and, yes, idiosyncratic—legal thinkers in recent decades. *Song Sparrow* is a short, but not an easy, book, and even after reading it more than once we may not be sure that we have discerned its meaning. But let us try.

Science, Antiscience, and Totalistic Science

To begin with, we should take note that *Song Sparrow* is a book by a law professor writing about science: that is an unusual and risky, and, some might think, audacious project. No one will doubt the subject's significance, though. Of the various influences that over the last several centuries have shaped and reshaped the way we live and think, science is surely among the most powerful. But has science's overall influence, on balance, been healthy—or destructive? The question is one that all of us, even lawyers, are entitled to ask.

Taking passages out of context, one might suppose that Vining views science as pernicious, and that he himself is a partisan of what he calls "antiscience"—the wholesale Luddite or fundamentalist condemnation of science along with its methods and conclusions. But an even moderately careful reading shows the error of this interpretation. Far from disparaging science, Vining is effusive in paying his respects. He speaks of "the deep necessity of science, the scientist in each of us."[7] Much of what is good in modern life, he says, we owe to science.[8] Science is "a gift . . . , as music is a gift."[9] And Vining elaborates: "science brings gifts, of fascination, of beauty, of relief from pain, gifts of unclouded thought, of freedom to love; and in fact these gifts and their effects are enjoyed even by those who live in a world whose material constitution they deny."[10]

Still, Vining is obviously concerned, even alarmed, about *something*. So if science is not the object of that concern, what is? The book's first paragraph proposes the answer that is repeated throughout: what Vining finds threatening is not *science,* exactly, but rather "total claims" made in the name of science, or "total theory," or "total vision." It is the reductionist insistence that there is ultimately "nothing but" or "merely" (phrases that Vining finds ominous, like symptoms of a cancer) the objective "systems" and "processes" that scientists study—and hence that the kinds of impersonal explanations given by science and immensely valuable for explaining *some* things can ultimately account for *everything* (including ourselves, and including the scientists among us).

Vining's principal target is thus the sort of worldview endorsed by John Searle, who declares that the world "consists entirely of physical particles in fields of force, and . . . some of these particles are organized into systems that are conscious biological beasts, such as ourselves." Searle goes on to explain that "the simple intuitive idea is that systems are collections of the particles where the spatio-temporal boundaries of the system are set by causal relations. . . . Babies, elephants, and mountain ranges are . . . examples of systems."[11] It is this totalistic view, and not science itself, that Vining sees not merely as mistaken but as a profound threat to humanity—and even, paradoxically perhaps, to science itself (which in Vining's view appears to be the sort of healthy "golden mean" threatened on one side by "antiscience" and on the other by "total vision"). Much of the book is thus devoted to describing and understanding this "total vision"—not only its substance but also its mind-set, and its tone.

The affirmative substance and tone of "total vision" are conveyed in part through quotations, such as that from Searle given above. The book provides numerous similar instances and expressions. "The brain," as one scientist puts it, "is merely a meat machine":[12] again, that ominous word "merely." In the same vein, Vining quotes neurobiologist Jean-Pierre Changeaux, who explains that "[t]he brain secretes thought as the liver does bile."[13] Changeaux adds that beliefs—which can be "defined as a specific state of nerve cell activity"—are comparable to diseases: "they can propagate from one brain to another, and spread 'infection' much as viral attacks do."[14]

More generally, Vining says, the gaze of total science looks out upon

a world of swirling flux . . . in which all, including mathematics and the mathematician, becomes processes and processes of processes. . . . Things merely happen and nothing can be more important than anything else because it is merely something happening. There is no such thing as catastrophe. The raging

fire that caught up with the smoke jumpers in Norman MacLean's
Young Men and Fire is grass burning. Grass burning is just something happening. Flesh burning is no different. The wind rises, the
fuel changes, the temperature escalates, the spread accelerates,
process builds on process, the organization of the fire replaces the
organization of a tree, of a human body, and then the fire is gone.[15]

But the nature of total theory is not fully captured by such imagery. Nor can total theory be adequately understood merely in terms
of affirmative claims dispassionately presented in propositional
form. On the contrary, Vining suggests that total theory has the
qualities of a "creed" or faith—or an antifaith.[16] And just as Christian creeds developed largely in response to perceived heresies, the
character of the naturalistic creed is as clearly manifest in what
it aggressively *denies* as in what it *affirms.*

Thus, total theory conspicuously leaves some elements out of its
account of the world: purpose, spirit, transcendence, divinity.[17] But
it does not merely omit or forget to mention these elements; it mili-
tantly opposes them.[18] It seeks to root them out with a kind of censorious zeal.[19] For Nobel Prize–winner Jacques Monod, for example,
"Judeo-Christian religiosity" is not merely false; it is (along with, by
the way, "scientistic progressism, belief in the natural rights of man,
and utilitarian pragmatism") "disgusting." Such notions, Monod
insists, "afflict[] and rend[] the conscience of anyone provided with
some element of culture, a little intelligence."[20] (*Song Sparrow* was
written just before the onslaught of recent books sometimes described as the "new atheism,"[21] but surely those writings could be
added to the evidence Vining gives for these descriptions.)

Pondering such denunciations, Vining wonders whether what is
called "'science' . . . is molded by and is inseparable from the enemy

it constructs to hate."[22] And he detects in "late twentieth-century cosmological speculation...the psychology of the adolescent who doesn't understand, and who destroys."[23]

With totalistic science, as with other encompassing faiths, heresy and error are always cropping up not only among the unenlightened but within the congregation of the (anti-)faithful as well, and they must above all be weeded out from that field. Thus, with a sort of monastic severity, Changeaux exhorts mathematician Alain Connes that "[t]he materialist program" involves "an act of self-discipline" through which even the scientifically converted must "eliminate" within themselves "all remaining traces of transcendence."[24] And as if to allay suspicions of heretical tendencies, Connes hastens to concur: "I grant that the brain . . . has nothing of the divine about it, that it owes nothing to transcendence whatsoever."[25] Philosopher Daniel Dennett pronounces that if progress is to be made in artificial intelligence, "we must give up our awe of living things."[26] And Vining sorrowfully describes one of his favorite science authors, Lewis Thomas ("He was a wonderful man and I keep his books on a special shelf"[27]), who in Vining's view struggled to rein in his gift for seeing beauty and meaning in the world in order to conform to the censorious demands of totalistic science. Hence the wonderful, sometimes troubled, quality of Thomas's writings—tossing out but then hastily disowning insights and intuitions and hypotheses that " '[m]y scientist friends will not be liking,' "[28] alluding to the irrepressible likelihood of something in the universe that transcends material processes but then quickly passing off such allusions as mere playfulness or jokes. "Jokes," Vining observes sadly, "being the freedom of the oppressed."[29]

Central to Vining's discussion is an ostensible distinction between science itself, which he admires, and totalistic science, which chills and appalls him. But is this distinction an illusory one? Or do the assumptions on which science is conducted necessarily commit its devotees to making totalistic claims?

Vining thinks not. "There are great scientists," he reminds us, "from Newton to Einstein who are not troubled by divinity, nor driven by a desire to eliminate it from the thought and speech of all."[30] But maybe the religious or poetic flourishes of a Newton or an Einstein were a sort of holiday in which they took temporary leave of their scientific vocation? Maybe the more mundane colleagues of these giants of science are in fact being more rigorously, ploddingly faithful to the logic of the scientific enterprise? Vining's perception is that over the course of the twentieth century, totalistic claims from scientists and science-admiring philosophers seemed to grow more insistent and aggressive—and more censorious: the assertions quoted earlier from Weinberg, Searle, Dennett, and Changeaux constitute just part of the evidence that he compiles.

These are thinkers whose intellectual credentials may be intimidating to most of us. So their apparently total confidence in asserting a totalistic view has force. How might such assertions be resisted? And *should* they be resisted? Like Vining, some of us might find the comprehensively naturalistic worldview unappealing: so what? Since when did theories get accepted or rejected based on whether we find them edifying, or flattering, or spiritually uplifting?

What Do We Believe, Really?

Rather than confronting such questions and doubts head-on, Vining offers instead a more oblique and measured (and, perhaps, frustrating) response—one constituted by an apparently meandering meditation that circles around and around recurring themes. To appreciate this response, we need to consider Vining's somewhat unusual understanding of the character of believing and, hence, of the function and limits of reflective reasoning.

Most of us probably think of our beliefs as being at our beck and call—as being immediately transparent to us. Asked what you believe about something, you can simply look inside yourself, so to speak, and then report whatever belief you find there. The belief might be false, of course. But your sincere statement that it *is* your belief (at least as of the time of the report) seems unassailable. If you say you believe X and someone says, "No, you don't," the objector will seem merely boorish and obtuse.

Vining has a different conception. In his view, a belief is not simply a readily observable propositional piece on our cognitive chessboard: it is something less on the surface and instead more rooted in the depths of our being. Discovering what we believe—what we really, genuinely believe—involves not a simple introspection and report but a more serious and searching investigation of . . . well, of what we *think* we believe, yes, but also of how we live, what we desire, what we would and would not be willing to do. It may turn out, upon close examination, that people do not really believe some of what they casually thought they believed—and vice versa. "We may think we believe something here, or do not believe something there, but we do not have the last word on what we believe unless we read ourselves as a whole, in the same way we read others to determine what it is they are really saying and what it is they actually believe."[31]

Hence, someone might be mistaken not only *in* his beliefs, but also *about* them—about what his own beliefs actually are. To assert this possibility is not to insult. Rather, "an inquiry into actual belief, asking for candor ... is according a dignity to the one of whom the demand is made."[32]

The point is not simply to demonstrate (or purport to demonstrate) an inconsistency in someone's professed beliefs and then quickly to conclude that he does not really believe what he insists he *does* believe, as Ronald Dworkin does when he argues that hardly anyone really believes that abortion is murder.[33] It is not that sort of surface consistency that interests Vining, but rather the deep resonance of genuine belief with and within a person's most central commitments—with and within her life. Wittgenstein once observed that "[v]irtually in the same way as there is a difference between *deep* and shallow sleep, there are thoughts which occur deep down and thoughts which bustle about on the surface."[34] Vining's earnest inquiry is directed to those deeper-down thoughts and beliefs.

Consistent with this personal and holistic conception of belief, the function of reasoning and reflection is not, for Vining, merely to marshal arguments—to "move from proposition to proposition"—so as to construct a proof or demonstration, or to compel someone to accept a proposition that she initially opposed. That sort of exercise hardly ever succeeds, and it would be quite pointless even if it did succeed, because the underlying beliefs might well remain unaffected by the dialectical exercise. No genuine assent would result. "Binding you to me by successful moves of my mind would lose all that can be hoped for."[35]

Instead, Vining conceives the function of reasoning and reflection to be that of enlisting us in the enterprise of examining our actions, assumptions, commitments, and ways of talking in order to determine what we *really* believe. Reflection for him should serve the purpose that Michael Polanyi described:

I believe that the function of philosophic reflection consists in bringing to light, and affirming as my own, the beliefs implied in such of my thoughts and practices as I believe to be valid; that I must aim at discovering what I truly believe in and at formulating the convictions which I find myself holding; that I must conquer my self-doubts, so as to retain a firm hold on this programme of self-identification.[36]

This project of determining what we really believe must be a cooperative enterprise, Vining thinks[37]—and one that aims to achieve self-understanding, candor (a virtue on which Vining places great emphasis), and genuine assent. We may well change our opinions during the course of the project. But the change will typically come not because we are coerced by argument or evidence into repudiating our previous convictions, but because we become able to acknowledge beliefs that at some level we have held all along without being wholly conscious of them, or perhaps without being willing to own up to them.

Song Sparrow is Vining's attempt to engage in such mutual reflection with respect to science and the claims of total theory. And his conception of the enterprise points to one reason why he thinks that lawyers—not just those who are officially licensed by the state, but others as well, because "[t]here is the lawyer and law in all of us"[38]—have a valuable role to play in debates about total claims involving science. That is because the question as he conceives it is not so much whether some scientific explanation of some particular fact or phenomenon is correct, but whether anyone—you, me, the scientists themselves—actually believes in the totalistic worldview that so many modern scientists and other thinkers publicly sponsor. It is lawyers, after all, who examine and cross-examine and reexamine, and who probe for inauthenticity and suppression of truth. So in trying to discern what you and I—and Steven Weinberg, and John Searle—really believe, we must "[d]o what lawyers do with witnesses' testimony," treating even the "doctors or scientists or mathematicians [as] witnesses."[39] Do we and they believe, all things considered, that we are "nothing but" or "merely" complicated material systems and processes? We may *say* we believe this, but do we *really*?

That is Vining's question. A critic might object that this is not the only question, or the most cogent one. It might be, after all, that the reductively naturalistic worldview is true even if hardly any of us can bring ourselves entirely to embrace it—or, for that matter, that this worldview is not true even if many of us do sincerely believe it. Shouldn't the question be *what the truth is,* not *what we believe?* Shouldn't the latter question be wholly subordinated to the former one?

Perhaps. But Vining would reply, I suspect, that we deceive ourselves with this distinction. There is no escaping the fact that it is *we*—we finite, fallible, alternately credulous and skeptical human beings—who are posing the questions, and we are posing them for ourselves and for our purposes. Separated from the question of *what we believe,* the question of *what the truth is* can mean nothing to us.

So the question posed, for better or worse, is whether we—scientists included—really believe in the totalistic claims sometimes emanating from scientists. Vining adopts a variety of strategies for pursuing that question.

Science as a Human Enterprise

One strategy is to examine closely the scientific enterprise itself to see whether *it* can be reduced to the sorts of objective, impersonal "systems" and "processes" into which it characteristically attempts to reduce its own subjects of study. And in Vining's examination, it turns out that science itself is a deeply human and personal enterprise. Consequently, and ironically, if the totalistic, person-reducing claims sometimes asserted by scientists were actually true, and were fully accepted, the scientific enterprise would be impossible.

In conducting this examination, Vining stresses the dependence of science on assent. The objective conclusions of a scientific experiment are not self-validating and self-executing, as it were: they must win the assent of *persons*—of the community of scientists and, for that matter, of nonscientists.[40] Science is a cooperative enterprise. No single scientist can personally verify or vouch for more than an infinitesimal fraction of the sum of scientific knowledge; each must rely on the work and reports of others, and in order to do that each scientist must be able to assume that other scientists are working in good faith.[41] These qualities—"assent," "good faith"—are irreducibly personal in nature.

And what exactly is the significance of these observations? In some respects they may seem to resemble a familiar argument made by, among others, C. S. Lewis, in a famous debate with the philosopher Elizabeth Anscombe. Lewis argued in essence that a comprehensively naturalistic worldview cancels itself out. That is because if that wholly naturalistic worldview were correct, it would follow that all of our beliefs—including our belief in a naturalistic worldview—are the product of nonrational natural causes, such as chemical processes in the brain. But there is no epistemic efficacy in chemical processes, and we put no stock in beliefs determined by merely natural causes. So if you believe in the naturalistic worldview, the logic of your own belief should cause you to abandon this belief: naturalism "cuts its own throat."

Every particular thought (whether it is a judgment of fact or a judgment of value) is always and by all men discounted the moment they believe that it can be explained, without remainder, as the result of irrational causes. Whenever you know that what the other man is saying is wholly due to his complexes or to a bit of bone pressing on his brain, you cease to attach any importance of it. But if naturalism were true then all thoughts whatever would be wholly the result of irrational causes. Therefore, all thoughts would be equally worthless. Therefore, naturalism is worthless. If it is true, then we can know no truths. It cuts its own throat.[42]

Lewis thought this criticism was compelling; Anscombe didn't.[43] At the very least, Lewis's argument points to a paradoxical quality in comprehensive naturalism—one that manifests itself in debates not only about epistemology but about free will as well.[44]

Vining's reflections resemble Lewis's argument insofar as Vining suggests that if the claims of totalistic science were true, science itself would be subverted. In this sense, total theory may appear to be self-cancelling. But it seems that Vining's point is not the rationalistic one that totalist science has somehow been *refuted* by a demonstration of internal inconsistency. That conclusion might or might not be justified, but even if it is, what would be gained by the demonstration? The confirmed naturalist might respond, "Okay, you've identified a difficulty in my argument—a sort of paradox. I commend you for your cleverness. But you haven't shown—or even purported to show—that the naturalist position is *false*. Nor have you said anything that compels me to abandon my belief in naturalism. And in fact, I still believe it."

It is precisely at this point, I think, that Vining's reflections become relevant. His goal is not so much to demonstrate that totalistic science is self-refuting on a merely analytical level, but rather to show that even the scientists themselves who make totalistic claims do not and cannot fully believe in those claims. So in response to the defiant assertion that "I still believe it," Vining's message seems to be: "No, actually you don't. You believe in science and the natural world, of course. We all do. But if you reflect candidly on your actions and commitments as a whole, even including your commitments *to science,* you will see that you do not and never did believe in naturalism—not as the whole story."

Atrocities and the Morality of Scientists

But it is not only reflection on the scientific enterprise and its methods that leads Vining to this understanding. He is led there as well (and he seeks to lead us there) by pondering the significance of the moral atrocities, large and small, that were so conspicuous in the last century—in Manchuria, Germany, and Cambodia, to mention some flagrant examples. From start to finish, these atrocities loom over Vining's discussion.

The claim is not exactly that scientific research leads to atrocities (although it can, sometimes), or that scientists are moral monsters (although no doubt some have been). On the contrary. Though he worries about the potentially destructive consequences of total theory,[45] Vining thinks that, by and large, people who devote themselves to science are admirable, moral beings. In their most truly scientific work they are "driven by love and awe,"[46] by a "passion for truth,"[47] and by the "fascination," "beauty," and aspiration to "unclouded thought" that science can give us.[48] And both their work itself and their writings about their work reflect admirable, and deeply moral, commitments—to each other, to humanity and future generations, to the pursuit of truth.

But now comes the troubling question: How do the partisans of science explain and justify these moral values and commitments? Or more precisely, how do they explain and justify them *within the framework and on the impersonal assumptions of totalistic science?* For example, commenting on Lewis Thomas's profound concern that deforestation or nuclear holocaust might produce a world that would not "see fit" to permit the continued existence of creatures "like us," Vining asks:

> Why should we care at all . . . ? If we are the random product
> of a billion years of evolution, and the system does not "see fit"
> (though those would be forbidden words) to bring forth a product
> "like us" in another billion years, what concern is that of ours?
> The dice roll six, the dice roll two. The six does not care whether
> a two or a six is rolled next. The dice themselves do not care.
> Only if there is some identification with future creatures, crea-
> tures after our individual death, creatures after the passing of
> every body that is in material existence at the time of our own
> death, identification, real, through a connection other than near
> succession in time in the products of the processes of the material
> world, can there be any claim of the distant future on our present
> desires.[49]

This is the central incongruity explored throughout the book: the frequent and apparently sincere expression of moral commitments and aspirations by people who purport to hold a worldview within which, in Vining's estimation, these commitments and aspirations seem alien and indeed come close to being unintelligible.

Thus, most people (scientists included) react with outrage upon learning of the experiments on human beings conducted in occupied Manchuria or Nazi Germany. But why? We routinely perform scientific experiments on animals, after all, and though the practices can be controversial we do not typically experience the same moral indignation as we do in the cases of experimentation on humans. Suppose that humans are "merely" complex natural "systems," as total theory tells us they are, and that there is no difference in "essence" between humans and animals, as Francois Jacob declares. Suppose we are, in John Gray's phrase, "straw dogs."[50] Then why do we draw such a drastic distinction here? How do we account for our conviction that experimenting on *the sparrow* is so radically different from experimenting on *the child?* This is the central question that Vining presses over and over throughout the book. (Though, as we will see, from a different direction he himself doubts the solidity of the line between sparrow and child, and seeks to draw the sparrow over to the child's side of the line.)

Nor is it merely our condemnation (and the scientists') of large-scale moral enormities that is in tension with the totalistic worldview so frequently professed. In fact, the writings even of scientists who assert totalistic claims teem with assertions of value, obligation, caring, and moral commitment. These assertions seem to be sincere, Vining suggests, but once again, they are hard to place within the naturalistic framework that these writers purport to embrace.[51]

Once again, we can question the significance of these incongruities, if that is what they are. Do they show that the partisans of totalistic science are guilty of inconsistency, or of a so-called per-formative contradiction? Maybe or maybe not, but in any case this is not quite Vining's point. Analytical philosophers would likely respond to such a charge with conceptual distinctions and explanations calculated to dissolve or deflate or deflect the apparent contradiction, while scientists themselves—evolutionary psychologists, for example—might respond with explanations of how a species might evolve so as to favor, say, the carriers of its own genetic materials and thus to support what at least looks like a sort of altruistic behavior. But Vining's inquiry is subtly different. The question is not whether a satisfactory philosophical defense of the moral distinction between the sparrow and the child could be developed (a defense that, if persuasive, might operate to exonerate, against a charge of inconsistency, people to whom the defense would never have occurred). Nor is it whether our embrace of the distinction can be scientifically *explained*.

The question, rather, is what our words and actions in this matter tell us about what, in fact, we *really believe*. And Vining thinks (though it is, of course, hard to be certain, especially for others) that despite some protestations to the contrary, most of us really believe in a realm of value that cannot be adequately accounted for in purely naturalist terms. He thinks that if we exert ourselves to reflection and candor, and if we work up the courage to speak in good faith, we will acknowledge such beliefs. Theorists may *say* they believe in a merely naturalistic universe. But their genuine beliefs are better than their theory-driven professions.[52]

So John Searle may declare that babies and animals are merely complex systems of "physical particles in fields of force." "But Searle would stay his hand from vivisecting a human being or pulling out

SCIENCE, HUMANITY, AND ATROCITY

a dog's nails with pliers and then burning it alive. . . . In staying his hand, he would reveal much."[53]

Openings into "Spirit"

Vining's examination is not limited, however, to showing tensions between what we say we believe in some contexts and what we say and do in other contexts. In a more direct and affirming vein, he asks us to contemplate what he calls "openings"—realms of experience through which, if we pay close attention, we can sense the reality of something beyond the reductionistic world of material systems and can look into the world of what Vining calls, with misgivings, "spirit."[54]

The same openings will not present themselves to everyone. For some, *music* will provide this sort of insight.[55] I recall in this respect a former colleague who by his own account was incapable of religious faith but was deeply sensitive to art and music, and who confided to me that he was troubled by a naturalistic worldview because he could find no real home in it (as opposed to unsatisfying, tone-deaf evolutionary *explanations*) for Mozart's lofty compositions. The sublimity of the "Jupiter" symphony or the *Requiem* are undeniably real. So if evolutionary naturalism cannot adequately account for this sublimity, then . . . , well, my colleague honestly wasn't sure what conclusion to draw.

For other people, *language* with its intricacies and subtleties and poetry provides an opening. For still others, *land*—fields, mountains, forests—can offer a glimpse. *Death* can be yet another source of insight: "Speak of death, stand up and uncover the head in respect for death, and you have stepped through the opening, something has come to you through the opening."[56]

Still another opening, Vining suggests, can be discovered by careful reflection on "the large fact of law"[57]—and on our long-standing insistence in law on a distinction between the "authoritative" and the "authoritarian." The latter—or the exertion of physical power to force others to do what one wants—might be rendered intelligible in purely naturalistic terms. But real "authority," as Vining understands it, is a different and more mysterious matter: "authority" is something that we understand not as coercing us, exactly, but as having an authentic claim on our attention and respect. So, what is it that might have such a quality? The question cannot be answered in purely naturalistic and impersonal terms. Even so, we search for and believe in authority. The fact that we do this, Vining suggests, indicates again a belief in something beyond the naturalistic.[58]

On a more intimate level, perhaps the most pervasive and important opening is simply the presence of other people—of human beings. Speaking under the constraint of theory, of course, we might assert that humans are merely complex systems of particles. Or, in Hawking's words, "chemical scum on a moderate-sized planet." But we do not believe this. Or at least we do not believe it when we have the "direct experience . . . of seeing a person and being seen as a person," or of actually "looking into the eyes of others." In those moments we perceive "the extraordinariness of our individuality," so that a "sense of life springs within us" and we know that there is more to a person than system and process and particles in motion.[59]

Elsewhere, Vining quotes a biologist who explains "love" as a "temporary chemical imbalance of the brain induced by sensory stimuli." Vining goes on to reflect:

When presented in law with this sentence about love, there would be interest in what this same individual said at home, what he meant when heard to say "I love you" to his wife, child, friend, or sister. Putting the two statements together, the one made at home and the one made professionally, as would be done in cross-examination on a witness stand, a lawyer or jury would conclude, I think, either that the word "love" in the one statement, made in class when teaching the penguin's love as a textbook example of a system operating in an adaptive way, means something different from "love" in the other statement at home; or, if the two words are meant to convey the same, that he does not believe what he is saying in class.[60]

Holding the Line, Hopefully

When we are being reflective and candid we know these things, Vining suggests. But under the pressure of a theory or ideology, we may be induced to tell ourselves otherwise, and we may also be induced to act on those inauthentic doctrines. The moral atrocities of the twentieth century were grotesque manifestations of this possibility. (Or of this "capability"?) Dehumanizing racism and slavery are manifestations of the same possibility.

Horrendous as they are, however, these enormities are in a sense still confined. In the scientific experimentation on humans conducted under the Third Reich, and in the slavery of the antebellum South, only particular classes were relegated to nonperson status. The claims of naturalistic total theory, by contrast, have sterner and more unrelenting implications: the person is—*all* persons are—negated entirely. Vining more than once makes the point that the view of persons advocated by the proponents of total theory is a sort of universalization of the view taken of Jews and blacks in anti-Semitic fascist and slave regimes. In total theory, "[a]ll humanity is the target."[61]

Actually, Vining's concern is not confined to humanity. Though much of the discussion works from what he takes to be a common distinction between humans and other animals—between the child and the sparrow—Vining himself doubts that, viewed as a *moral distinction,* this line can hold. We react with moral outrage—or at least we do if we have not been morally mutilated by corrupt culture or heartless and hubristic theory—when we learn of experimentation on humans. Most of us may not instinctively react in the same way to experimentation on nonhuman animals. But our different attitudes may merely show that we are under the same kinds of reflective disabilities with respect to animals from which the researchers in Manchuria and Germany suffered with respect to humans. Vining suggests that if we look at an animal "eye to eye"[62]—if we really look, and reflect—we will see that the categorical moral divide we often draw between humans and other animals is unsustainable. "The strictest 'rationalist,' most fastidious in his arguments, who has a dog, who nuzzles it and cares for it, and weeps when it dies, may not be a strict rationalist in actual belief."[63]

The point is powerfully made, I think, in an incident recounted by Timothy Jackson:

Walking dully along Temple Street in New Haven, one March day in 1979, I awoke from a rationalist's dream. I heard over my right shoulder the screeching of tires, then a loud "Thump!" followed by horrific howling. I turned to see a beautiful black Labrador retriever staggering along the side of the road with blood dripping from its nose and mouth. It was instantly clear, to me and the other pedestrians transfixed on the sidewalk, that this dog was doomed. Its internal injuries from being hit by the car, which did not stop, were so severe that nothing could be done. It was only a matter of time . . . and time seemed to clot more and more slowly with each high-pitched "Yelp!" from the beast. It obviously did not know how to die, because it came up to two of us in front of Timothy Dwight College and seemed to look imploringly into our eyes for some sort of explanation. I suddenly felt the need to beg pardon.

Partly inspired by Kant's speculation that animal subjectivity is "less even than a dream," I had just two months before written a graduate seminar paper arguing that animals don't feel morally significant pain. . . . Now, confronted by the Lab's agony, I saw how absurdly callous and callow this opinion was. I did not go through any elaborate process of reasoning; I simply felt for the dying dog so obviously in pain and so needlessly undone. As it slumped down in a patch of grass, I was touched by its misery and ashamed of myself. . . . [64]

Vining's questioning of the line between song sparrow and child does not lead him to any particular recommendations for terminating research involving experimentation on animals. On the contrary, he acknowledges that such research will often be warranted—just as there are situations in which *human* lives must be sacrificed for the benefit of other humans. More generally, Vining acknowledges that economics—the "dismal science" of making trade-offs—has its necessary jurisdiction. Even so, we will make the trade-offs differently, he suggests, if we do not indulge in the false comfort of denying the moral status of the subjects we are sacrificing.[65]

Nor is the point merely that nonhuman animals should be included along with humans in the class presumptively entitled to concern and protection. That sort of agenda would immediately raise boundary questions. What kinds of animals should be included in the class deserving of respect and concern? Dogs, cats, and dolphins? Snails? Amoeba? *Only* animals? Why not plants? Vining notes the boundary issue, which is real enough, but he does not dwell on it: he simply says that where to draw the line between what is and is not morally valuable—between "spirit" and mere particles in motion—requires ongoing reflection.[66] We might draw the line in a variety of ways or places: Vining does not pretend to tell us exactly where to draw it. That is not this book's purpose.

Its central purpose, rather, is to prevent the line itself from being obliterated by the claims of "total theory" in the way so many theorists and scientists do, at least if we take their statements at face value. Everything is particles and force fields, process and system. So say the theorists. But Vining's reflection is a powerful affirmation that we—and they, the theorists themselves—do not really believe this. To assent to this creed would be "a form of death, a giving up, a farewell."[67] Conversely, by resisting the claims of "total theory" we can hold onto the hope with which Vining's book ends— for an eventual "convergence of scientific and other forms of thought" in which "the scientist in all [is] no longer overshadowed by the antiscientist in any."[68]

7

OPENING UP THE CAGE?

Contemporary public discourse in this country, the critics say, is impoverished—even to the point of being "appalling,"[1] as Ronald Dworkin puts it. This book has offered a somewhat unconventional diagnosis of this situation: public discourse is impoverished because the constraints of secular rationalism prevent us from openly presenting, examining, and debating the sources and substance of our most fundamental normative commitments. Unable to acknowledge its deeper, determining strata, our discourse is condemned to superficiality.

This embarrassment is not uniformly debilitating, to be sure. Many public issues turn on straightforward economic or utilitarian considerations, for example, about which most citizens can agree with respect to basic premises, or *ends*. Disagreements in these cases can turn on different—but fully debatable—assessments of competing *means*. Thus, most people agree that, other things being equal, economic prosperity is good and unemployment is bad, and we can have meaningful discussions about which tax or monetary or trade policies are most conducive to these goals. But on a host of other issues—the sorts of issues often associated with the so-called "culture wars," the sorts of issues discussed in this book—competing positions seem to reflect more deep-seated divergences in normative commitments. And on these issues, the secular cage works to close out meaningful and authentic discussion.

Even with respect to these issues, discussion and debate stagger along anyway, as they must, and somehow stumble their way to conclusions. We manage to argue for conclusions by, among other things, smuggling. Under the benign auspices of more respectable notions like liberty and equality, we sneak in normative values and premises that are suspect or officially inadmissible. The practice of smuggling enables our deliberations to function in semirational fashion; the fact that our most fundamental commitments have to be smuggled, and hence are not fully and forthrightly acknowledged and interrogated, ensures that our discourse will be thin, unsatisfying, and often unseemly.

This diagnosis of our malaise naturally provokes demands for prescriptions, or at least for predictions. If our current ways of talking are unseemly and unsatisfying, how *should* we talk? What sort of public discourse *should* we practice? And can our current discourse, dependent as it is on illicit importation, persist in its present form? If not, what sort of discourse will replace it?

Such questions are natural enough—inevitable, probably—and I have a short answer and a somewhat longer answer to them. The short answer is . . . I don't know. The most sensible response to such questions, probably, is to plead the Fifth. It seems unlikely that anything as sprawling and multifaceted and magnificently polycentric as a form of discourse can be scripted according to anyone's prescription. Moreover, even the most acute thinkers have usually been less than adept at predicting what shape or substance a discourse is likely to take. For over a century, for example, prominent legal thinkers have been predicting how legal discourse is destined to evolve: pretty much without exception these thinkers have proven to be false prophets—sometimes comically false.[2] I have no particularly pressing desire to immerse myself in the general embarrassment.

So then, is there nothing to be said in response to the "what is to be done?" question? Actually, there is something, I believe, and again it can be said briefly and then elaborated. (The elaboration will be my slightly longer answer to the initial set of questions.) It comes down to this: we ought to be more open. Although we cannot either prescribe or predict how discourse will evolve, we can be more open to alternative possibilities. We can call off the cultural border patrol agents who police the boundaries of discourse (with varying degrees of vigilance) to keep out would-be entrants who lack a certified secular passport. In short, we can open the door—and the windows, if there are any—of Weber's cage.

Admittedly, counseling greater *openness* sounds like one of those exquisitely innocuous nostrums that is at once difficult to refuse—who after all wants to come out in opposition to "openness"?—and utterly useless. But in fact, the counsel is somewhat less innocuous, and consequently less manifestly useless, than it may seem.

Circles of Discourse

One can imagine a situation in which belief in Nature (in the classical sense) and God and cosmic meaning has simply become extinct, but in which people (or at least *some* people) come to think that this condition is lamentable and hence undertake a project of reconstructing meaning and belief. Probably some people *do* find themselves in such a situation: the characters in some of Woody Allen's movies sometimes portray such a predicament. If the prophets of secularization had been more prescient, and if the world thus had truly become as "disenchanted" as thinkers like Weber (or, from Chapter 5, Carl Becker) seemed to think it was, then it is conceivable that our society as a whole might face just this sort of challenge—a challenge to fabricate "reenchantment."

It would be a daunting and perhaps impossible challenge. If you really, truly do not believe there is any inherent meaning or purpose or value in the cosmos, then even if you wish there were, is it actually possible (perhaps through some sort of refined system of induced self-delusion) to lift yourself into genuine belief? Once you've watched Mommy and Daddy putting out the presents, can you really get yourself to believe in Santa Claus again?

It is a hypothetical question, though, at least on the societal or political level, because in fact this is not the world we live in. Not in the United States anyway. Set aside the question raised in the previous chapter by Joseph Vining about whether even people who profess to believe in a purely materialistic nature devoid of inherent meaning actually at bottom hold that grim view. Let us accept that such people—and if you are reading a book like this you may well be one of them—do in fact believe what they say they believe. Even so, as is widely appreciated by now, Americans generally do not find the world to be so rigorously disenchanted. On the contrary, the overwhelming majority of Americans embrace a wide variety of less reductionistically materialistic systems of belief. Most believe in God in some sense.[3] Many adhere to one or another version of traditional religion. Others gravitate to less conventional forms of "spirituality."[4]

Nor is the divide as simple as that between those constituencies who are educated and intellectual and those who are not. To be sure, commitment to something like scientific naturalism is likely higher, and belief in something like "Intelligent Design" is likely lower, among the intelligentsia than among the laity. Nonetheless, James Lindgren, who studies such things (and who describes himself as agnostic), tells me that the best data show remarkably high levels of religious belief for people with graduate degrees—far higher than "secularization" predictions would anticipate.

Consequently, outside the sphere of secular public discourse, or of Rawlsian "public reason," there are circles of discourse that are metaphysically and theologically much thicker than the more insubstantial talk that critics like Dworkin and Susan Jacoby lament. So the challenge, it seems, is not so much to create deeper belief ex nihilo, but rather to figure out whether and how and on what terms to admit such thicker belief into public discourse.

We might picture the issue in terms of a Venn diagram, with circles representing the various families of belief and conversation that flourish to differing degrees in contemporary society. The basic recommendation of secular liberalism as articulated by theorists like Rawls is that "public reason" would confine itself to a small area of overlap—the famous though perhaps illusory "overlapping consensus"—where these circles intersect. By contrast, the burden of this book has been that the area of overlapping consensus (if there even is such an area) is too cramped. The secular liberal recommendation leaves our discourse with resources too meager to function effectively, and as a consequence conversations depend on smuggling in normative contraband from the outside—from the larger, denser circles. Which suggests the possibility that we might expand the circle of acceptable public discourse beyond the area of overlap—to decriminalize smuggling, so to speak—so that participants in public discourse might openly draw upon the beliefs and resources of the thicker conversations and families of belief that some but not all participants accept.

Even now, of course, the constraints on public discourse are for the most part enforced culturally, not legally.[5] And the cultural enforcement is uneven—more rigorous in the academic domain than in the political one. But it could be that this sort of rigor is exactly what we do not need at the moment. Maybe the cultural enforcers should become more latitudinarian in their attitudes— more inclusive. Maybe some of them should be retired altogether.

Many of those denser families of belief that might thereby become eligible for public participation are, of course, "religious" in one sense or another. Hence, even to notice the possibility of opening up public discourse to such beliefs is immediately to raise the venerable, vexed question of the role of "religion in the public square"—a question that has been debated by now at excruciating length in countless books, articles, editorials, and symposia and on various levels (constitutional law, political morality, pragmatic politics, "constitutional etiquette"[6]). It would be foolhardy for me to plunge into that turbulent and often turbid debate this late in the day, and this late in the book.[7] So I will limit myself to making a single point—one that most obviously and directly flows from the discussion of the preceding chapters.

Shutting Down Conversation

Perhaps the most common objection (though hardly the only one) to admitting religious views into public discourse maintains that religion is a "conversation-stopper." Richard Rorty made the point with characteristic directness. "[T]he Enlightenment's central achievement," Rorty thought, was "the secularization of public life."[8] This secularization entails the privatization of religion. And "[t]he main reason religion needs to be privatized is that, in political discussion with those outside the relevant religious community, it is a conversation-stopper." If someone speaks to an issue by invoking the will of God, Rorty maintained, there is simply nothing that anyone else can say. Rorty thought that the often expressed concern that religious expression will cause division and argument misperceives the problem. In fact, the invocation of God's will in public debate "is far more likely to end a conversation than to start an argument."[9]

If indeed religion silences conversation, then it is understandable why those who favor a liberal democracy based on deliberation—on conversation about public matters—would be wary of admitting religion into public discourse. It is understandable as well that critics of contemporary discourse like Susan Jacoby or Ronald Dworkin would list the resurgence of religion in politics among the causes of what they perceive as a degraded public conversation.[10]

In their turn, proponents of religion in the public square respond that the sort of objection raised by Rorty and others exhibits misunderstanding—or simply ignorance about what religion is—on the part of those who make it. There is nothing inherent in religion, they say, and nothing distinctive to religious believers, that is more peremptorily preclusive of discussion than there is in other, more secular perspectives and believers.[11] Proponents may point to an earlier era's overtly theological analyses of public concerns by people like Martin Luther King, Jr.,[12] Reinhold Niebuhr,[13] John Courtney Murray,[14] and Abraham Joshua Heschel[15]—reflective analyses displaying a depth of wisdom and insight that compare favorably (to put the point gently) with those of more contemporary and secular political thinkers—as evidence that religious perspectives can enliven and deepen public deliberation rather than truncating or silencing it.

This again is not the place to enter into this clash of claims. For now, what ought to emerge from this book's earlier chapters is the overwhelming irony—irony in the standard sense, not in Rorty's specialized sense[16]—in the "conversation-stopping" objection. After all, who is it that is trying to stifle or regulate conversation? Rorty's opponents are not telling him: "Stop talking secular." Rather it is Rorty and like-minded thinkers who issue the injunction: "Don't talk religion."

More generally, earlier chapters have suggested that in considering concrete issues such as assisted suicide, church–state separation, or human rights and the "capabilities approach," it is the requirement that public discourse be confined to the secular that leaves participants with . . . well, with nothing very probing or substantial to say, and that thereby forces them to smuggle more muscular considerations into the conversation under the cloak of "liberty," "equality," or associated notions. Conversely, relaxing the constraints on discourse, far from stifling the conversation, would at least open up the possibility of a richer and more searching discussion.

The "conversation-stopper" objection seems particularly ironic coming from someone like Rorty. Think back to Henry Steele Commager's effusive description, reported in Chapter 1, of the Enlightenment's faith in the power of "Reason" to address and resolve fundamental problems about the nature of the cosmos, the rights of man, and the meaning and point of life. Rorty celebrated the "secularization" that he associated with the Enlightenment, but he admitted—insisted, even—that Enlightenment "Reason" has not lived up to expectations. Thus, even as he inveighed against religion in public discourse, Rorty condemned as well those who claim to be speaking with and for "reason." "The claim that . . . we [secular atheists] are appealing to reason, whereas the religious are being irrational, is hokum."[17] Rorty went on to criticize those who speak with "voices claiming to be God's, or reason's, or science's." These voices should be demoted—"put on a par with everybody else's."[18]

But then, who *is* "everybody else," exactly? And how is "everybody else" supposed to talk? Aren't the messages that Rorty would demote precisely the sorts of things we want and need to be able to say in order to have a meaningful discussion at all? "The Bible is God's word, and the Bible teaches. . . ." Or, "Reason should rule, and reason supports the conclusion that. . . ." Or, "In these matters science must be our guide, and science shows that. . . ." If you are not supposed to say any of these things in public discourse, what exactly *can* you say? (Maybe "I really, *really* want . . . [whatever]"?) And what can anyone else say to you? Rorty insisted that "the epistemology suitable for . . . a democracy is one in which the only test of a political proposal is its ability to gain assent from people who retain radically diverse ideas about the point and meaning of human life."[19] Okay. But then, how are we—any of us—supposed to try to gain that assent if both the invocation and the criticism of those "radically diverse ideas about the point and meaning of human life" have been ruled out of bounds by the constraints of secular public discourse?

Given Rorty's doubts about the efficacy of reason, his insistence on excluding religion from public discourse begins to look merely arbitrary—an inherited commitment derived from assumptions he no longer accepted, and which has hence degenerated into a mere prejudice. More generally, his prescription looks like a recipe for a discourse that is assured in advance of being shallow, empty, and pointless.

Why would anyone want to waste precious time and energy in that sort of predictably futile and boring conversation? Contrary to Rorty, it appears that it is not religion after all, but rather the imposition of artificial constraints on discourse, that is the "conversation-stopper."

Conversation, or Babel?

Even so, it is easy enough to appreciate Rorty's concern. Suppose your neighbor says, "The nation should ban abortions [or pull out of Iraq immediately, or open the borders to unrestricted immigration, or . . .] because this is the will of God." We can indulge this supposition, though it is a caricature: even devout religious believers who are at all thoughtful hardly ever say *that* sort of thing, exactly. One wonders how many actual religious believers Rorty and like-minded critics have actually talked with. But let that pass: let us suppose that your neighbor simply and unblushingly invokes the "will of God" as the ground for his position. Suppose as well that you do not believe in any sort of god. How can you have a conversation with your theistic neighbor?

True, in theory you *could* try to interrogate your neighbor about why he believes in God, and also about why he is so confident that God's will is as he supposes. But that sort of conversation is unlikely to go very far. So, isn't religion in fact a conversation-stopper here?

More generally, how can people with very different "comprehensive doctrines" about God or the cosmos or "the point and meaning of human life" have productive conversations about public issues? Their starting points are so different, it seems, that they will have no common ground on which to engage with each other. So wouldn't opening up public discourse to all of the various beliefs held by Americans be a device for bringing about, not meaningful conversation, but rather Babel?

I admit it: this is a hard question. And once again, I offer no confident predictions. In criticizing prescriptions coming from the likes of Rawls and Rorty, I do not mean to imply that they were not struggling with a difficult challenge. Nor do I dismiss the possibility that what we have now—basically, a generally secular but unevenly policed public discourse supplemented by sporadic incursions of religion and by rampant smuggling—is the best we can do in a society as pluralistic as ours.

This *might* be the best we can do. Still, it is not settled that we are foreordained to remain in this less-than-happy condition. Let us consider some more cheerful possibilities.

In the first place, it is true that genuine conversation can indeed be difficult (and is perhaps rare) among people whose basic worldviews differ. For that matter, genuine conversation can be difficult even among people—spouses, for example, or siblings—who share a great deal in common. Even so, no one really believes that if people disagree they cannot engage in productive conversation. Or at least this is surely not the claim made by Rawls, Rorty, and others. Anyone this pessimistic might as well give up on the idea of public deliberation and public discourse altogether. The fact is that discussion has its point, and its value, precisely when it involves people who see things differently, at least initially and perhaps continuously.

Why then should the proponents of secular discourse be so gloomy about the possibility of genuine conversation among people who have different "comprehensive doctrines" and who do not agree to bracket those doctrines for purposes of public discussion? The assumption seems to be that people who disagree about *particulars*, or conclusions, can nonetheless engage in productive discussion as long as they agree on *basic premises*. Conversely, people who disagree about basic premises will not enjoy any similarly meaningful discussion.

But why should that be so? The view seems to reflect what we might call a "geometry model" of discourse (meaning standard Euclidean geometry—the kind we learned in high school). We agree on basic definitions and axioms ("Parallel lines never meet"), and if we disagree on conclusions (on the Pythagorean theorem, say), that is because someone has done the proofs incorrectly. So the purpose of discussion is to retrace the steps in our reasoning and see how we have done those proofs—to show how and where someone has made a mistake in getting from axioms to conclusions. Conversely, if we do *not* share the axioms—if you think parallel lines can never meet but I think they can—then this sort of discussion will not work. Our discussion will have no traction, nothing to get hold of to move it along.

A more attentive inspection ought to show, however, that in reality our thinking and conversations, whether public or private, rarely work in this way. Sometimes, it is true, we reason from axiom or basic premise to conclusion. But other times we reverse directions: we are more convinced of our conclusions than of our premises,[20] and hence reason from conclusion backward to premises. (Rawls's influential notion of a "reflective equilibrium"[21] should serve to illustrate this multidirectional movement.)

And even this picture is too tidy. In fact, the very effort to classify our beliefs into basic assumptions and more particular conclusions misdescribes the way we think and talk. It would be more accurate to say that we have a whole assortment of beliefs (and not only "beliefs" but also experiences and impressions and memories and feelings and images, and also needs and yearnings, and also traditions and practices), some more general and some more particular, of which we are conscious to varying degrees, and which we are convinced or committed to in varying degrees, and which relate to and act upon each other in varying and unpredictable and often invisible or surreptitious ways. (Quine's metaphor of a "web of belief"[22] or Wittgenstein's notion of a "form of life"[23] might serve to illustrate this complex set of relationships.) Consequently, it is always possible that, however much we may disagree with another person's worldview, something in that view will connect with something in our own that will result in constructive engagement.

Which leads to a further observation: whether conversation among differently minded people will occur and what form it will take are matters impossible to predict in the abstract. The fact of difference—even of "radical divers[ity in] ideas about the point and meaning of human life"—in no way precludes the possibility of conversation. But whether conversation will actually occur, and if so what it will look like, cannot be known in advance. The only thing is to try and see.

In this vein, in a short essay called "Religion as conversation-starter," Andrew Koppelman notes that under "the norms of civility that developed in the United States during the twentieth century," it is now "well settled that it is impolite to challenge someone else's religious beliefs. Religion is private."[24] This norm has been affirmed and elaborated, Koppelman notes, by a host of leading political philosophers, including John Rawls, Bruce Ackerman, Ronald Dworkin, Thomas Nagel, Amy Gutmann, Dennis Thompson, Stephen Macedo, David Richards, Charles Larmore, Samuel Freeman, Richard Rorty, and Robert Audi.

But the strategy has been "a disaster." So Koppelman concludes that "the norm of politeness needs to be revisited."

As soon as A invokes religious reasons for his political position, then it has to be OK for B to challenge those reasons. It may be acrimonious, but at least we'll be talking about what really divides us (and we'll avoid the strange theoretical pathologies that have plagued modern liberal theory, though that seems to be a disease mainly confined to the academy). It's more respectful to just tell each other what we think and talk about it.[25]

Koppelman accurately describes the stakes. There *is* a risk that a more open conversation may be acrimonious. Even so, that sort of conversation is ultimately more respectful of the participants. More respectful and also, potentially, more productive and substantial: that is because we will be talking about what we really believe. In this spirit, Paul Horwitz remarks that "if we are to have discussions that are worth our time," then we need to "begin the task of attempting to develop and encourage some set of meaningful rules, or etiquette, for talking about religion in a useful way in the public square." If we do this, Horwitz predicts, "[o]ur discussions will be less anodyne but also less antiseptic, less polite but richer and more honest."[26]

Nor is it foreordained that such discussions must be acrimonious or impolite. Christopher Eberle examines the familiar claim of Rawls and like-minded theorists that "respect" for our fellow citizens demands that we practice "restraint" in our public discourse— that we refrain in political decision making from relying on convictions, and in particular religious convictions, that do not satisfy all of the aspirations of "public" reason or justification. Eberle finds the claim unwarranted. On the contrary, he argues that an insistence on such restraint can itself be disrespectful: it is like allowing someone to be part of your social group as long as they agree not to talk about the things that matter most to them. Conversely, sharing what you most deeply believe, and submitting yourself to criticism and instruction by your fellow citizens on the basis of what *they* most deeply believe, can be a profound expression of respect.[27]

Eberle thus proposes to replace the common liberal insistence on "restraint" in public discourse with an ideal of "conscientious engagement." He outlines and explains the various requirements and aspirations that such an ideal would entail.[28] But of course Eberle cannot forecast the exact form or content of discourse conducted under this ideal. One would hope, he says, that citizens practicing "conscientious engagement" would eventually satisfy even the liberal ambition for a politics in which important decisions are made on the basis of public justifications that are acceptable even to diversely minded citizens. But there are no guarantees.

And so, in the end, it seems that the only general prescription that can be offered is, once again, the seemingly bland recommendation of . . . openness. It may turn out that in our pluralistic society, the sort of thin, desiccated public discourse we have today—a discourse haphazardly policed in politics and more rigorously regimented in the academy by the constraints of secularism—is the best we can do. But we will only know if we open up the cage and see what happens.

Notes

I. THE WAY WE TALK NOW

1. Susan Jacoby, *The Age of American Unreason* (2008).
2. Id. at 283, xi–xii.
3. Ronald Dworkin, *Is Democracy Possible Here? Principles for a New Political Debate* 4 (2006).
4. Id. at 22.
5. Jacoby, *Age of American Unreason*, at 3–30.
6. Dworkin, *Is Democracy Possible?* at 5.
7. Id. at 1.
8. Id. at 127.
9. Id. at 130.
10. Danny Priel, "In Search of Argument," 86 *Tex. L. Rev.* 141, 144 (2007) (reviewing Dworkin, *Is Democracy Possible?*).
11. Id. at 143.
12. See, e.g., Jacoby, *Age of American Unreason*, at xvii (alluding to a "stunning failure of American public schooling at the elementary and secondary levels"); at 282 (describing a "massive failure of American education at both the high school and college levels"); Dworkin, *Is Democracy Possible?* at 128 (asserting that "Americans are horribly misinformed and ignorant about the most important issues").
13. Dworkin, *Is Democracy Democracy?* at 129.

14. Jacoby, *Age of American Unreason,* at 242–278.

15. Dworkin argues that for politicians, "a punchy sound bite on the evening news is political gold, [while] anything remotely resembling an actual argument is death." Dworkin, *Is Democracy Possible?* at 128. See also Jacoby, *Age of American Unreason,* at xx: "America is now ill with a powerful mutant strain of intertwined ignorance, anti-rationalism, and anti-intellectualism. . . . This condition is aggressively promoted by everyone, from politicians to media executives, whose livelihood depends on a public that derives its opinions from sound bites and blogs, and is passively accepted by a public in thrall to the serpent promising effortless enjoyment from the fruit of the tree of infotainment."

16. Jacoby, *Age of American Unreason,* at 183–209. Dworkin attempts to treat religion in a more respectful way while still arguing that it ought to remain a private matter. Dworkin, *Is Democracy Possible?* at 50–89. For more virulent expressions of this concern, see Christopher Hitchens, *God Is Not Great: How Religion Poisons Everything* (2007); Kevin Phillips, *American Theocracy* (2006).

17. See, e.g., Owen M. Fiss, "Reason in All Its Splendor," 56 *Brook. L. Rev.* 789 (1990).

18. Mary Ann Glendon's *A Nation under Lawyers* 294 (1994).

19. See John Rawls, *Political Liberalism* 231–240 (paperback ed. 1996).

20. See, e.g., Michael J. Perry, *The Constitution in the Courts* 102–110 (1994); Alexander Bickel, *The Least Dangerous Branch* 24–26 (1962).

21. See, e.g., Ronald Dworkin, *A Matter of Principle* 69–71 (1985).

22. Dworkin, *Is Democracy Possible?* at 157, 156.

23. Daniel A. Farber, "Missing the 'Play of Intelligence,'" 36 *Wm. & Mary L. Rev.* 147, 147, 157 (1994).

24. Robert F. Nagel, "Name-Calling and the Clear Error Rule," 88 *Nw. U. L. Rev.* 193, 199 (1993).

25. Dworkin, *Is Democracy Possible?* at 157.

26. Jeremy Waldron, "Public Reason and 'Justification,'" 1 *J. Law, Phil. & Culture* 107, 131 (2007).

27. Id. at 133.
28. Deborah L. Rhode, "Legal Scholarship," 115 *Harv. L. Rev.* 1327, 1327, 1336, 1339 (2002).
29. Id. n. 64.
30. Henry Steele Commager, *The Empire of Reason* 40 (1977).
31. Id. at 42.
32. James Q. Whitman, "Reason or Hermeticism?" 5 *S. Cal. Interdisc. L.J.* 193, 195 (1997).
33. See Rawls, *Political Liberalism,* 212–254 (1996 ed.)
34. Quoted in David L. Holmes, *The Faiths of the Founding Fathers* 88 (2006).
35. Rawls, *Political Liberalism,* at xviii.
36. Id. at 37.
37. Id. at 133–172, 223–227.
38. Id. at 49.
39. Id. at 51.
40. Waldron, "Public Reason," at 115.
41. Rawls's notorious abortion footnote, in which he disposes of a deeply controversial issue in an (admittedly long) paragraph by simply *declaring* that any "reasonable" balance of competing values will support a position close to that of *Roe v. Wade,* is a stark manifestation of the kind of discourse that such "public reason" is able to support. See Rawls, *Political Liberalism,* at 243 n.32: "Suppose further that we consider the question [of abortion] in terms of these three important political values: the due respect for human life, the ordered reproduction of political society over time, including the family in some form, and finally the equality of women as equal citizens. (There are, of course, other important political values besides these.) Now I believe that any reasonable balance of these three values will give a woman a duly qualified right to decide whether or not to end her pregnancy during the first trimester. The reason for this is that at this early stage of pregnancy the political value of the equality of women is overriding, and this

right is required to give it substance and force. Other political values, I think, would not affect this conclusion. . . . [A]ny comprehensive doctrine that leads to a balance of political values excluding that duly qualified right in the first trimester is to that extent unreasonable."

42. John Rawls, "The Idea of Public Reason Revisited," in *The Law of Peoples* 144–145 (1999).

43. See, e.g., Suzanna Sherry, "The Sleep of Reason," 84 *Geo. L.J.* 453 (1996).

44. Peter Gay, *The Enlightenment: An Interpretation: The Science of Freedom* 16 (1969).

45. See generally Henry May, *The Enlightenment in America* (1976).

46. See Holmes, *Faiths of the Founding Fathers,* at 87.

47. For this and similar sanguine assessments from the time, see Steven D. Smith, *The Constitution and the Pride of Reason* 3–4 (1998).

48. See generally, Sidney E. Mead, *The Lively Experiment: The Shaping of Christianity in America* (paperback ed. 2007).

49. Jose Casanova explains: "In one form or another, with the possible exception of Alexis de Tocqueville, Vilfredo Pareto, and William James, the thesis of secularization was shared by all the founding fathers: from Karl Marx to John Stuart Mill, from Auguste Comte to Herbert Spencer, from E. B. Tylor to James Frazer, from Ferdinand Toennies to Georg Simmel, from Emile Durkheim to Max Weber, from Wilhelm Wundt to Sigmund Freud, from Lester Ward to William G. Sumner, from Robert Park to George H. Mead. Indeed, the consensus was such that not only did the theory remain uncontested but apparently it was not even necessary to test it, since everybody took it for granted." Jose Casanova, *Public Religion in the Modern World* 17 (1994).

50. See generally George M. Marsden, *The Soul of the American University: From Protestant Establishment to Established Nonbelief* (1996).

51. *Lemon v. Kurtzman,* 403 U.S. 602, 612–613 (1971).

52. See generally William P. Marshall, "The Limits of Secularism: Public Religious Expression in Moments of National Crisis and Tragedy," 78 *Notre Dame L. Rev.* 11 (2002).

53. See, e.g., Susan Jacoby, *Free Thinkers: A History of American Secularism* 317–65 (2004).

54. *New York Times,* November 4, 2004, section A, p. 1.

55. Louis Dupre, *Passage to Modernity: An Essay in the Hermeneutics of Nature and Culture* 17 (1993).

56. Remi Brague, *The Law of God: The Philosophical History of an Idea* vii (Lydia Cochrane tr., 2007).

57. Overwhelming evidence for this assertion is marshaled in Daniel Boorstin, *The Lost World of Thomas Jefferson* (1993) (first published 1948). I give a succinct summary of the evidence from Boorstin and a few other sources in Steven D. Smith, "Nonsense and Natural Law," in Paul Campos et al., *Against the Law* 100 (1996). For a recent study highlighting the religious themes and thinkers of the Enlightenment, see David Sorkin, *The Religious Enlightenment* (2008).

58. Owen Chadwick, *The Secularization of the European Mind in the Nineteenth Century* 17 (1975), is a masterful exploration of the variety of causes, both social and intellectual, that contributed to modern secularization.

59. For a magisterial study of such developments, see Louis Dupre, *Passage to Modernity* (1993). For a more recent study in a similar vein, see Michael Allen Gillespie, *The Theological Origins of Modernity* (2008).

60. See Charles Taylor, "Modes of Secularism," in *Secularism and Its Critics* 32 (Rajeev Bhargava ed., 1998) ("The origin point of modern Western secularism was the wars of religion; or rather, the search in battle-fatigue and horror for a way out of them.").

61. See Chadwick, *Secularization of the European Mind,* at 161–188; Mark Lilla, *The Stillborn God: Religion, Politics, and the Modern West* 58–65 (2007).

62. See, e.g., Christian Smith, "Introduction: Rethinking the Secularization of American Public Life," in *The Secular Revolution* 1 (Christian Smith ed., 2003). Smith stresses the collaborative efforts of "waves of networks of activities who were largely skeptical, freethinking, agnostic, atheist, or theologically liberal; who were well educated and socially located mainly in knowledge-production occupations; and who generally espoused materialism, naturalism, positivism, and the privatization or extinction of religion." Id.

63. See Casanova, *Public Religion in the Modern World*.

64. Peter Berger, *The Desecularization of the World* 10 (1999).

65. See, e.g., From *Max Weber: Essays in Sociology* 155 (H. H. Gerth and C. Wright Mills eds. and trs., 1946) ("The fate of our times is characterized by rationalization and intellectualization and, above all, by the 'disenchantment of the world'").

66. More specifically, Weber used the metaphor of an "iron cage" to refer to the initially Protestant form of discipline which, gradually losing its religious content, evolved into the condition of secular and bureaucratic rationalization that has generated and supported modern capitalism. Max Weber, *The Protestant Ethic and the Spirit of Capitalism* 181–182 (Talcott Parsons tr., 1958).

67. See generally Elizabeth Anderson, *Value in Ethics and Economics* (1993).

68. See, e.g., Martha C. Nussbaum, "Foreword: Constitutions and Capabilities: 'Perception' against Lofty Formalism," 121 *Harv. L. Rev.* 4, 18–20 (2007); John Rawls, *A Theory of Justice* 183–192 (1971).

69. F. H. Bradley, *Appearance and Reality* xiv (1897) (quoted in Michael S. Moore, *Causation and Responsibility* 24 (2009).

70. Michael J. Klarman, "Rethinking the History of American Freedom," 42 *Wm. & Mary L. Rev.* 265, 270 (2000).

71. Id. at 270–271 (footnote omitted).

72. Peter Westen, "The Empty Idea of Equality," 95 *Harv. L. Rev.* 537 (1982).

73. Id. at 547 (footnotes omitted).

74. See, e.g., Andrew Koppelman, "The Fluidity of Neutrality," 66 *Rev. Politics* 633 (2004); Kent Greenawalt, "How Empty Is the Idea of Equality?" 83 *Colum. L. Rev.* 1167 (1983).

75. Jürgen Habermas, Intolerance and Discrimination, 1 I.CON 2, 5 (2003).

76. Rawls, *Political Liberalism*, at 16–18; Rawls, *Idea of Public Reason*, at 168.

77. See Charles Taylor, *A Secular Age* (2007); Charles Taylor, *Sources of the Self* (1989); Alasdair MacIntyre, *Whose Justice? Which Rationality?* (1988); Alasdair MacIntyre, *After Virtue* (2d ed. 1985).

78. Martha Nussbaum, "Human Rights and Human Capabilities," 20 *Harv. Hum. Rts. J.* 21, 21 (2007).

2. LIVING AND DYING IN THE "COURSE OF NATURE"

1. 497 U.S. 261 (1990).

2. A federal judge in New York upheld that state's prohibition; a federal judge in Washington struck down a similar law. The cases then went to federal courts of appeals, which ruled that terminally ill patients have a constitutional right to what was then typically called "physician-assisted suicide." *Quill v. Vacco,* 80 F.3d 716 (2d Cir. 1996); *Compassion in Dying v. Washington,* 79 F.3d 790 (9th Cir. 1996). (Initially, a three-judge panel on the Ninth Circuit reversed the lower court and upheld the Washington prohibition. But that panel decision was overturned by a larger body of Ninth Circuit judges sitting en banc.)

3. 521 U.S. 702 (1997).

4. 521 U.S. 793 (1997).

5. See, e.g., "Symposium on *Glucksberg* and *Quill* at Ten: Death, Dying, and the Constitution," 106 *Mich. L. Rev.* 1453–1667 (2008).

6. *Baxter v. State of Montana,* http://www.internationaltaskforce.org/pdf/Baxter_v_State.pdf (December 8, 2008).

7. Ronald Dworkin, *Sovereign Virtue* 465 (2000).

8. Michael J. Sandel, *Public Philosophy* 113 (2005).

9. Reprinted at http://www.nybooks.com/articles/1237.

10. 521 U.S. at 728–732.

11. For example, the asserted interest in protecting life may seem wholly unobjectionable when we are thinking about protecting the lives of people who desire to remain alive, as with a homicide law. But does the state have a legitimate interest in compelling individuals to remain alive if they do not wish to do so? Justice Stevens has argued that the claimed interest in preserving life for those who do not desire it is impermissibly "theological." See *Cruzan v. Director, Missouri Dep't of Health,* 497 U.S. 261, 346–351 (1990) (Stevens, J., dissenting). Justice Souter, though concurring in the judgment in *Glucksberg,* declined to embrace the "preserving life" rationale because he believed it reflected a "moral judgment contrary to [the patients']." 521 U.S. at 782.

12. In particular, the interest in preventing undue influence seemed persuasive even to justices like Souter, who were dubious about the state's more general interest in preserving life. 521 U.S. at 782–788.

13. See David P. T. Price, "Assisted Suicide and Refusing Medical Treatment: Linguistics, Morals, and Legal Contortions," 4 *Medical L. Rev.* 270, 272–273 (1996) ("Jurisdictions throughout the world have almost invariably declined to view refusals to competent patients of medical treatment which could prolong life as physician-assisted suicide.").

14. Judith Jarvis Thomson, "Killing and Letting Die: Some Comments," in *Intending Death: The Ethics of Assisted Suicide and Euthanasia* 104, 107 (Tom L. Beauchamp ed., 1995).

15. *Compassion in Dying v. Washington,* 79 F.3d 790, 824(9th Cir. 1996).

16. Philosophers' Brief, at II.B.

17. 521 U.S. at 801.

18. Thomson, "Killing and Let Die," at 106.

19. 521 U.S. at 801–802 (citations omitted).

20. For a helpful presentation of the doctrine, see Allison MacIntyre, "Doctrine of Double Effect," in *Stanford Encyclopedia of Philosophy*, http://plato.stanford.edu/entries/double-effect/ (2004).

21. 79 F.3d 790, 858 (Kleinfeld, J., dissenting).

22. See, e.g., Jonathan Bennett, *The Act Itself* 194–225 (1995).

23. Cf. MacIntyre, "Doctrine of Double Effect," at 2. ("Many morally reflective people have been persuaded that something along the lines of double effect must be correct.").

24. The Second Circuit ruled that in prohibiting assisted suicide while permitting assistance in the refusal of life-sustaining treatment, New York law irrationally discriminated among similarly situated persons, thus offending equal protection requirements. The Ninth Circuit en banc court spoke in "substantive due process" terms, ruling that Washington's prohibition on assisted suicide restricted liberty without any rational basis. The court discounted the interests asserted by the state, suggesting that since these interests would apply equally to situations in which patients chose to refuse life-sustaining treatment but the state did not attempt to vindicate the interests in those situations, these interests could not in fact be very important. 79 F.3d at 822–824.

25. 870 F. Supp. at 84 (emphasis added).

26. Ronald Dworkin, *Life's Dominion* 88 (1993) (emphasis added).

27. Id. at 89.

28. Id. at 13 (emphasis added). However, Dworkin argues that the harm is "less if it occurs after any investment [in life] has been substantially fulfilled, or as substantially fulfilled as is anyway likely." Id. at 88.

29. *Compassion in Dying v. Washington*, 850 F. Supp. 1454, 1464 (W.D. Wash. 1994) (emphasis added).

30. *Compassion in Dying v. Washington*, 49 F.3d 586, 594 n.2 (9th Cir. 1995) (emphasis added).

31. 80 F.2d at 729 ("Surely, the state's interest [in preserving life] lessens as the potential for life diminishes").

32. 79 F.2d at 820 (emphasis added), 821 (emphasis added).

33. Cf. Albert R. Jonsen, "Criteria that Make Intentional Killing Unjustified," in *Intending Death,* at 42, 50–52 (arguing that although most proponents of a "right to die" would limit the right to terminally ill persons, this limit cannot be squared with the professed commitment to self-determination as the decisive value).

34. Leon Kass, *A More Natural Science: Biology and Human Affairs* 259 (1985).

35. Michael J. Seidler, "Kant and the Stoics on Suicide," 44 *J. Hist. Ideas* 429, 432 (1983).

36. John Locke, *Second Treatise on Government* 9 (C. B. Macpherson ed., 1980) (emphasis in original). Cf. Sandel, *Public Philosophy,* at 114–115 (observing that the autonomy-based argument for a right to suicide "is at odds with a wide range of moral outlooks that view life as a gift, of which we are custodians with certain duties").

37. For a particularly salient example, see John Paul II, *The Gospel of Life (Evangelium Vitae)* at secs. 64–67 (1995).

38. Steven Weinberg, *The First Three Minutes: A Modern View of the Origin of the Universe* 154 (1977).

39. Bertrand Russell, "A Free Man's Worship," in *Why I Am Not a Christian* 104, 107 (1957).

40. See Ludwig Wittgenstein, *On Certainty* 29e (para. 211) (G. E. M. Anscombe and G. H. Wright eds., 1969).

41. For discussion, see Steven D. Smith, *Law's Quandary* 33–37 (2004).

42. See *Lemon v. Kurtzman,* 403 U.S. 602, 612 (1971).

43. See *Cruzan v. Director, Missouri Dep't of Health,* 497 U.S. 261, 346–351 (1990) (Stevens, J., dissenting); *Webster v. Reproductive Services,* 492 U.S. 490, 565–572 (1989) (Stevens, J., dissenting and concurring).

44. A revealing sample of such opinions is provided in Richard Posner's Holmes lecture of a few years ago and the various passionate reactions to that lecture. See Richard A. Posner, *The Problematics of Moral and Legal Theory,* and responses by Ronald Dworkin, Charles

Fried, Anthony Kronman, John T. Noonan, Jr., and Martha Nussbaum, in III *Harv. L. Rev.* 1637 (Issue 7, 1998).

45. Martha C. Nussbaum, "Skepticism about Practical Reason in Literature and the Law," 107 *Harv. L. Rev.* 714, 740 (1994).

46. See, e.g., Richard Posner, *The Problematics of Moral and Legal Theory* 3-90 (1999).

47. J. S. Mill, *Utilitarianism* 97 (Roger Crisp ed., 1998).

48. Alasdair MacIntyre, *After Virtue* (2d ed. 1985).

49. G. E. M. Anscombe, "Modern Moral Philosophy," in A. Martinich and David Sosa, *Analytic Philosophy: An Anthology* 381-392 (2001). In a similar vein, see W. T. Stace, *Man against Darkness and Other Essays* 10 (1967).

50. I encountered this quotation in Michael J. Perry, "Morality and Normativity," 13 *Legal Theory* 211 (2008). Perry quotes and discusses a number of other philosophers who make similar claims. Id. at 234-236.

51. John M. Rist, *Real Ethics: Rethinking the Foundations of Morality* 44 (2002).

52. Richard Joyce, *The Myth of Morality* (2001); J. L. Mackie, *Ethics: Inventing Right and Wrong* (1978).

53. See, e.g., Francis Kamm, 1 *Morality, Mortality* 7 (1993): "We present hypothetical cases for consideration and seek judgments about what may and may not be done in them. The fact that these cases are hypothetical and often fantastic distinguishes this enterprise from straightforward applied ethics."

54. Judith Jarvis Thomson, "A Defense of Abortion," 1 *Phil. & Pub. Aff.* 47, 59-61 (1971).

55. The problem, by now discussed in countless articles and books, is said to have been introduced in Philippa Foot, *The Problem of Abortion and the Doctrine of the Double Effect in Virtues and Vices* (1978).

56. For a careful attempt to defend ethical intuitionism by attaching it to Kant's moral imperatives, see Robert Audi, *The Good in the Right* (2004). Even if an account such as Audi's is persuasive, however,

that account would not necessarily provide a good justification for the way intuitions are routinely used in moral philosophizing today. Audi notes that "[a]ppeals to intuitions in resolving moral questions are a pervasive strategy in contemporary ethical discourse," but that "only a small proportion of the many who appeal to intuitions . . . as evidence in ethical theorizing would espouse ethical intuitionism." Id. at 24.

57. For a discussion of the difficulty of saying what a "moral" judgment, feeling, or intuition is, see Alexander Miller, *An Introduction to Contemporary Metaethics* 43–46 (2003).

58. MacIntyre, *After Virtue,* at 253.

59. For a critical discussion, see Larry Alexander and Maimon Scharzschild, "Grutter or Otherwise: Racial Preferences and Higher Education," 21 *Const. Comm.* 3 (2004).

3. TRAFFICKING IN HARM

1. John Stuart Mill, "On Liberty" 13, in J. S. Mill, *On Liberty and Other Writings* (Stefan Collini ed., 1989) (emphasis added).

2. In *Commonwealth v. Bonadio,* 415 A.2d 47, 50–51 (Pa. Sup. Ct. 1980), for example, the Pennsylvania Supreme Court stated that the "concepts underlying our view of the police power . . . were once summarized . . . by the great philosopher, John Stuart Mill, in his eminent and apposite work, *On Liberty* (1859)"; and the court proceeded to quote extensively from Mill, beginning with his statement of the harm principle. In the state court decision affirmed by the Supreme Court in the *Cruzan* case, discussed in the previous chapter, the Missouri Supreme Court noted that "courts regularly turn to J. S. Mill for inspiration" and went on to quote with approval Mill's formulation of the harm principle. *Cruzan v. Harmon,* 760 S.W.2d 408, 417 n.11 (Mo. Sup. Ct. 1988), aff'd in *Cruzan v. Missouri Dept of Health,* 497 U.S. 261 (1990). See also *Armstrong v. State,* 989 P.2d 364, 373 (Mont. Sup. Ct. 1999) (quoting Mill's harm principle, and sug-

gesting that the principle is embodied in both the Montana and United States constitutions).

3. Andrew Koppelman, "Drug Policy and the Liberal Self," 100 *Nw. U. L. Rev.* 279, 279 (2006).

4. See Randy E. Barnett, "The Proper Scope of the Police Power," 79 *Notre Dame L. Rev.* 429, 486–491 (2004) (discussing view that police power extends only to activities that cause harm).

5. Bernard Harcourt, "The Collapse of the Harm Principle," 90 *J. Crim. L. & Criminology* 109, 131 (1999).

6. Joel Feinberg, *Harm to Others* (1984); Joel Feinberg, *Offense to Others* (1985); Joel Feinberg, *Harm to Self* (1986); Joel Feinberg, *Harmless Wrongdoing* (1990).

7. See Mill, "On Liberty," at 98 (observing that "there are many acts which, . . . if done publicly, are a violation of good manners, and coming thus within the category of offences against others, may rightfully be prohibited"). See generally Joel Feinberg, *Offense to Others* (1985).

8. Vincent Blasi described Feinberg's opus as "[a]mong the most balanced, comprehensive, and rigorous treatises of recent times." Vincent Blasi, "Six Conservatives in Search of the First Amendment: The Revealing Case of Nude Dancing," 33 *Wm. & Mary L. Rev.* 611, 619 (1992). Kent Greenawalt appraised the project as a "nuanced and exhaustive treatment of the subject." Kent Greenawalt, "Legal Enforcement of Morality," 85 *J. Crim. L. & Criminology* 710, 711 (1995). See also Richard J. Arneson, "Liberalism, Freedom, and Community," 100 *Ethics* 368, 368 (1990) (Feinberg "argues brilliantly" for his positions and his work is characterized by "sensitive and precise conceptual analysis"); Robert P. George, "Moralistic Liberalism and Legal Moralism," 88 *Mich. L. Rev.* 1415, 1415 (1990) (review essay) (Feinberg's work "a model of clear, rigorous, and fairminded philosophical argument").

9. See Patrick Devlin, *The Enforcement of Morals* (1965).

10. See James Fitzjames Stephen, *Liberty, Equality, Fraternity* (Liberty Fund ed. 1993).

11. See, e.g., H. L. A. Hart, *Law, Liberty, and Morality* 32–33 (1963).

12. Harcourt, "Collapse of the Harm Principle," at 138.

13. See Mill, "On Liberty," at 76.

14. See, e.g., Mill, "On Liberty," at 86 (arguing that "with the personal tastes and self regarding concerns of individuals the public has no business to interfere"); id. at 87 ("intrusively pious" persons should "mind their own business"); Feinberg, *Harm to Others*, at 9 (conduct not covered by coercion-legitimating principles is *"not the business of the state"*) (emphasis in original).

15. *State v. Parson,* 447 S.W.2d 543, 546 (W.V. Sup. Ct. App. 1994). See also *United States v. Joseph,* 37 M. J. 392, 397 (1993) ("According to ancient legal maxim, one's liberty to swing one's arms stops where another's nose begins."); *Boissonneault v. Mason,* 221 N.W.2d 393, 393 (Mich. Sup. Ct. 1974) (invoking "the now classic observation that your right to swing your arm ends at the tip of my nose").

16. Thomas Hobbes, *Leviathan* 104 (Am. ed., 1950) (1651).

17. See Mill, "On Liberty," at 75 (asserting that "society is not founded on a contract, and . . . no good purpose is answered by inventing a contract in order to deduce social obligations from it").

18. Harcourt, "Collapse of the Harm Principle," at 57 (emphasis added).

19. Feinberg, *Harm to Others*, at 227, 228, 245.

20. Mill, "On Liberty," at 14.

21. Jeremy Bentham, *The Principles of Morals and Legislation* 2, 1 (Prometheus Books 1988).

22. J. S. Mill, *Utilitarianism* 55 (Roger Crisp ed., 1998).

23. Id. at 56.

24. Id. at 57.

25. Id. at 58. Competent judges would consist of people "equally acquainted with, and equally capable of appreciating and enjoying, both [conditions]." Id. at 56–57. This standard permits the disqualification of many of those who might *think* they prefer the

lower pleasures—who prefer professional wrestling over opera and poetry—because such people arguably have not been acquainted with or at least are not "capable of appreciating and enjoying" the higher pleasures. In this way, Mill's expressed embrace of a preference version of utilitarianism allowed him to take the next step away from a straightforwardly subjective utilitarianism—to approval of "the *intrinsic superiority* of the higher [pleasures]." Id. at 58 (emphasis added).

26. Or, if we drop the paternalism restriction, on myself.

27. Arneson, "Liberalism, Freedom, and Community," at 377.

28. Id. at 378 (emphasis added).

29. For a similar though somewhat more elaborate example, see Feinberg, *Harmless Wrongdoing,* at 57–60.

30. See Restatement of Torts (2d) section 46 (recognizing claim for outrageous conduct causing severe emotional distress); section 905 (including "emotional distress" in the "nonpecuniary harm" for which compensatory damages are available).

31. Arneson, "Liberalism, Freedom, and Community," at 374 (emphasis added). Arneson ties this conclusion to a preference-utilitarian conception of harm. "The idea of harm that is invoked here is frustration of strong stable preference." Id.

32. Id. at 375.

33. Robert P. George, "The Concept of Public Morality," 45 *Am. J. Juris.* 17, 25 (2000).

34. Cf. id. at 30 (observing that "there are often compelling prudential reasons for law to tolerate vices, lest efforts to eradicate them produce worse evils still").

35. See, e.g., Ronald Dworkin, *A Matter of Principle* 349 (1985).

36. Feinberg, *Harm to Others,* at 12.

37. Mill, *Utilitarianism,* at 13–14 (emphasis added).

38. Id. at 35–36

39. Id. at 65–66.

40. Id. at 65 (emphasis added).

41. Id. at 64, 63.
42. Id. at 63, 67–68.
43. Id. at 64.
44. Id. at 70.
45. Id. at 63.
46. Id. at 75 (emphasis added).
47. Id. at 75 (emphasis added).
48. This of course would not be a necessary or even a very natural conclusion of saying that my business and I were "harmed" by your business. Causing "harm" would bring your business within government's and the law's "jurisdiction," as Mill puts it, id. at 76, but government obviously might decide that this sort of harm caused by free competition is no reason to prohibit you from operating your business in fair and competitive ways.
49. Feinberg, *Harmless Wrongdoing*, at 11.
50. Id. at 32.
51. Feinberg, *Harm to Others*, at 33–34.
52. Id. at 46, 45–51.
53. Id. at 47.
54. Id. at 46.
55. Id. at 34.
56. Feinberg, *Harmless Wrongdoing*, at 17–20.
57. Id. at 18.
58. Id. at 20.
59. Id. at 18.
60. Id. at 20–25.
61. Although Mill does make this claim, Mill, *Utilitarianism*, at 13, as noted, he arguably relaxes the requirement at times. See, e.g., id. at 98 (suggesting that public violations of "good manners" might be prohibited to avoid offense).
62. Feinberg, *Offense to Others*.
63. "[T]he liberal ... can grant ... that legal moralism is technically correct, or correct in the abstract, but insist that, in fact, non-

grievance evils can never (or hardly ever) have enough weight to justify the invasion of personal autonomy." Feinberg, *Harmless Wrongdoing,* at 38.

64. See, e.g., Feinberg, *Harm to Others,* at 65.

65. Id. at 109–114.

66. Id. at 111.

67. Id. at 111–112.

68. Feinberg, *Harmless Wrongdoing,* at 57.

69. Id. at 58.

70. Id.

71. Id. at 59–64.

72. See, e.g., Ronald Dworkin, *A Matter of Principle* 359–372 (1985), and the (in my view, at least) decisive criticism in John Hart Ely, "Professor Dworkin's External/Personal Preference Distinction," 1983 *Duke L.J.* 959. Richard Arneson explains: "[T]he distinction between external and personal interests tends to break down in genuine enforcement of morals cases. There, either the distinction cannot be drawn or it fails to mark a nonarbitrary line that matters. My desire to live my own life sometimes includes the desire to live in a certain kind of physical environment (no ticky-tacky apartments in the Cotswolds), or in certain relationships with others (a community of kindred spirits at the workplace), or in proximity to persons who share a minimal moral sensibility (no association with persons who are willing spectators at fight-to-the-death gladiatorial contests. . . . My desire to lead the life I want can, and often does, include the desire to live in certain relations with others, and this will necessarily mean wanting that others lead their own lives in certain ways (namely, related to me so my life flourishes)." Arneson, "Liberalism, Freedom, and Community," at 380.

73. Mill, "On Liberty," at 13 (emphasis added).

74. Id. at 56 ("But if he refrains from molesting others in what concerns them, and merely acts according to his own inclination and judgment in *things which concern himself.*"); at 61 ("in what concerns

only themselves"); id. at 80 ("the part of a person's life which *concerns only himself*"); at 94 ("so far as these concern the interests of no person but himself"); at 104 ("A person should be free to do as he likes in *his own concerns.*"); at 108 ("the freedom of the individual in *things which concern only himself*") (emphasis added).

75. Id. at 63.

76. Id. at 15 (emphasis added).

77. Id. at 87. See also id. at 76 (no jurisdiction "when a person's conduct affects the interests of no person besides himself, or needs not affect them unless they like.").

78. Id. at 77 (emphasis added).

79. Feinberg, *Harmless Wrongdoing,* at 67 (emphasis added).

80. Id. (emphasis added).

81. Id. at 79–80 (emphasis added).

82. Id. at 122 (emphasis added).

83. Feinberg, *Harm to Others,* at 118.

84. Id. at 46.

85. Id. (emphasis added).

86. Gerald Dworkin, "Devlin Was Right," 40 *Wm. & Mary L. Rev.* 927, 939 (1999).

87. See, e.g., John Rawls, "The Idea of Public Reason Revisited," in *The Law of Peoples* 131, 132 (1999) (noting, with respect to those with a "zeal to embody the whole truth in politics," that "[p]olitical liberalism does not engage those who think in this way").

88. Feinberg indicates early on that he hopes "to persuade the skeptical reader that liberalism is true doctrine." Feinberg, *Harm to Others,* at 15. This ambition might suggest that he is speaking at least in part to people who do not already share his liberal assumptions. Shortly thereafter, however, he explains that his methodology relies on the "coherence" or "ad hominem" method, which "presupposes a great deal of common ground between arguer and addressee (reader) to begin with." Id. at 18. Perhaps the clearest indication of intention explains that "I hope to convince many

who share my basic ideals and attitudinal outlook also to share less obvious specific judgments about the particular subject matter of the book." Id. at 19. Perhaps that somewhat select audience is presumed to accept in advance the harm principle more or less (though not completely) as Feinberg presents it?

89. Id. at 187.

90. See generally Robert George, *Making Men Moral* (1993).

91. Id. at 1426–1428.

92. Bernard Harcourt observes that "[o]nce non-trivial harm arguments have been made, we inevitably must look beyond the harm principle. We must look beyond the traditional structure of the debate over the legal enforcement of morality. We must access larger debates in ethics, law and politics—debates about power, autonomy, identity, human flourishing, equality, freedom and other interests and values that give meaning to the claim that an identifiable harm matters." Harcourt, "Collapse of the Harm Principle," at 183.

93. John Courtney Murray, S.J., *We Hold These Truths: Catholic Reflections on the American Proposition* 15 (1960).

4. DISORIENTED DISCOURSE

1. Brad Gregory, *Salvation at Stake: Christian Martyrdom in Early Modern Europe* (1999).

2. *Everson v. Board of Education,* 330 U.S. 1, 18 (1947).

3. In a prescient article published over a decade ago, Ira Lupu carefully reviewed developments supporting his conclusion that "[t]hough it may linger in the political and legal culture of constitutionalism, the image of separation of church and state is fading out." Ira C. Lupu, "The Lingering Death of Separationism," 62 *Geo. Wash. L. Rev.* 230, 279 (1994). More recently, John Witte notes that "the United State Supreme Court has, of late, abandoned much of its earlier separationism." John Witte, Jr., *God's Joust, God's Justice* 211 (2006). Thomas Colby asserts that over the past quarter century

Supreme Court decisions have been "driving notions of separation of church and state to the constitutional periphery." Thomas B. Colby, "A Constitutional Hierarchy of Religions? Justice Scalia, the Ten Commandments, and the Future of the Establishment Clause," 100 *Nw. U.L. Rev.* 1096 1115 (2006).

4. Stephen G. Gey, "Life after the Establishment Clause," 110 *W. Virg. L. Rev.* 1, 2 (2007).
5. See, e.g., Kevin Phillips, *American Theocracy* (2006).
6. See, e.g., *Wisconsin v. Yoder,* 406 U.S. 205 (1972); *Sherbert v. Verner,* 374 U.S. 398 (1963).
7. See, e.g., *Welsh v. United States,* 398 U.S. 333 (1970).
8. *Employment Division v. Smith,* 494 U.S. 872 (1990).
9. Id. at 888.
10. Steven G. Gey, "Vestiges of the Establishment Clause," 5 *First Amend. L. Rev.* 1, 4 (2006).
11. See notes 120–175 below and accompanying text.
12. Isaac Kramnick and R. Laurence Moore, *The Godless Constitution: A Moral Defense of the Secular State* 150–206 (2d ed., 2005). Susan Jacoby argues that "the Bush Administration could hardly have done more to demonstrate its commitment to pulverizing a constitutional wall that served both religion and government well for more than two hundred years." Susan Jacoby, *Freethinkers: A History of American Secularism* 353 (2004). "The Christian right," she asserts, has "financial power" and a "stranglehold on the Republican Party," and this combination "has produced decades of judicial appointments that have moved the entire federal bench to the right." Id. at 354–355. Kevin Phillips lays responsibility on religious conservatives, especially Southern Baptists, and the Republican Party. Phillips, *American Theocracy,* at 99–217. Cf. Martha C. Nussbaum, *Liberty of Conscience: In Defense of America's Tradition of Religious Equality* 4 (2008) (asserting that "[a]n organized, highly funded, and widespread political movement wants the values of a particu-

lar brand of conservative evangelical Christianity to define the United States").

13. Eric Claeys reports that "[e]vangelical Protestants and traditionalist Catholics became more politically active in the 1970s and 1980s in response to cultural debates about abortion, religion, sexual equality and other issues. From among these religious conservatives emerged religious academics who questioned important tenets of separationism." Eric R. Claeys, "Justice Scalia and the Religion Clauses," 21 *Wash. U.J.L. & Pol'y* 349, 359 (2006).

14. *Wallace v. Jaffree*, 472 U.S. 38, 91 (1985) (Rehnquist, J., dissenting) (criticizing at length the interpretation of the establishment clause in terms of a wall of separation). Perhaps surprisingly, in *Everson* itself no justice dissented from the proposition that the Constitution creates a "wall of separation": the four dissenting justices favored an even stricter separation than the majority did. Hence, Rehnquist's dissent in *Wallace* might be viewed as the dissent that one would have expected someone to write in *Everson*.

15. Leading manifestations would include Justice Thomas's plurality opinion, joined by Justice Scalia, in *Mitchell v. Helms*, 530 U.S. 793, 801 (2000), and Justice Scalia's dissenting opinion in *McCreary County v. ACLU*, 545 U.S. 844, 885 (2005).

16. See, e.g., Gey, "Vestiges of the Establishment Clause," at 9 ("The first and most important component of the separationist Establishment Clause paradigm is the proposition that the First Amendment mandates a secular government."); Jacoby, *Freethinkers*, at 359–360 (describing how "[i]mportant . . . separation of church and state is to American secularists"); Leo Pfeffer, *Creeds in Competition* 43 (1958) (equating "separation of church and state" with "the secular state").

17. See Nomi Stolzenberg, "The Profanity of Law," in *Law and the Sacred* 35 (Austin Sarat ed., 2007) (describing the "modern cultural deformity that finds expression in frightening levels of mutual

incomprehension between 'the religious' and 'the secular' that we see today").

18. See *Lemon v. Kurtzman,* 403 U.S. 602, 612–613 (1971); Kathleen M. Sullivan, "Religion and Liberal Democracy," 59 *U. Chi. L. Rev.* 195, 199 (1992) ("Secular governance of public affairs is simply an entailment of the settlement by the Establishment Clause of the war of all sects against all.").

19. Charles Taylor, "Modes of Secularism," in *Secularism and Its Critics* 31, 31 (Rajeev Bhargava ed., 1998). See also Bernard Lewis, *What Went Wrong? Western Impact and Middle Eastern Response* 96 (2002) ("Secularism in the modern political meaning . . . is, in a profound sense, Christian. Its origins may be traced in the teachings of Christ, confirmed by the experience of the first Christians; its later development was shaped and, in a sense, imposed by the subsequent history of Christendom.").

20. See, e.g., Matthew 5:34–35 (KJV) (heaven is God's throne, earth is God's footstool); Matthew 12:32 ("this world" contrasted with "the world to come"); John 8:23 ("[Y]e are of this world; I am not of this world"); John 12:25 ("life in this world" contrasted with "life eternal").

21. John 18:36.

22. Revelation 11:15.

23. Luke 20:25.

24. St. Augustine, *The City of God* (written 413–426).

25. See Brian Tierney, *The Crisis of Church and State* 1050–1300, at p. 8 (1964). See also Witte, *God's Joust,* at 214–215.

26. See John Witte, Jr., *Law and Protestantism: The Legal Teachings of the Lutheran Reformation* 87–117 (2002).

27. Cf. 2 Corinthians 4:18 ("for the things which are seen are temporal; but the things which are not seen are eternal").

28. Taylor, "Modes of Secularism," at 32. For Taylor's more detailed explanation of the relation of spiritual and secular time in premodern sensibilities, see Charles Taylor, *A Secular Age* 54–59 (2007).

29. Stolzenberg, "The Profanity of Law," at 51.
30. Id. at 30–31.
31. Matthew 6:10.
32. Jose Casanova, *Public Religion in the Modern World* 13 (1994).
33. Jose Casanova suggests that the two-realm view oversimplifies. In fact, "premodern Western European Christendom was structured through a double dualist system of classification. There was, on the one hand, the dualism between 'this world' and 'the other world.' There was, on the other hand, the dualism within 'this world' between a 'religious' and a 'secular' sphere." Id. at 15. Casanova's classification no doubt has advantages, but in addition to being slightly more unwieldy, it may tend to obscure the sense in which the church, though in "this world," was a sort of representative of the other or spiritual sphere. For present purposes, therefore, I will follow the more familiar and frugal usage and hence will talk of two realms.
34. Cf. Stolzenberg, "The Profanity of Law," at 38 (classical view "conceives of the secular sphere as subject to the will of god and divine law, while being nonetheless 'nonreligious' and outside the jurisdiction of religious law in another sense").
35. Bernard Lewis, *The Crisis of Islam* 20 (2003).
36. Id. at 6–7.
37. Cf. Jean Bethke Elshtain, *Sovereignty: God, State, and Self* 13 (2008) ("The saga of sorting . . . [spiritual and temporal authority] gave the history of the Western half of Christendom a distinctive dynamic that channeled cultural energy, conflict, and contestation.").
38. Brian Tierney, *The Idea of Natural Rights* 45, 54 (1997).
39. Id. at 55.
40. Whether kings derived their authority independently of or rather through the intermediary of the pope and the church from God was a fiercely contested issue. See Ernst H. Kantorowicz, *The King's Two Bodies* 456–458 (paperback ed. 1981). Not surprisingly, the more forceful popes such as Gregory VII, Innocent III, and Boniface VIII

maintained that secular authority, though in some sense separate, was received through the church. See Tierney, *Idea of Natural Rights,* at 68–69, 135–136, 189. Emperors such as Henry IV, Frederick Barbarossa, and Frederick II insisted that their power, though from God, was not bestowed through the church; Aquinas agreed. See id. at 59–60, 108, 139, 167.

41. Hugh of St. Victor, *De Sacramentis Christianae Fidei* (c. 1134), reprinted in Tierney, *Crisis* at 94–95.

42. John Witte explains that during the twelfth and thirteenth centuries, "the Church came to claim a vast new jurisdiction—literally the power 'to speak the law' *(jus dicere).* The church claimed personal jurisdiction over clerics, pilgrims, students, the poor, heretics, Jews, and Muslims. It claimed subject matter jurisdiction over doctrine and liturgy; ecclesiastical property, polity, patronage; sex, marriage, and family life; education, charity, and inheritance; oral promises, oaths, and various contracts; and all manner of moral, ideological, and sexual crimes. The church also claimed temporal jurisdiction over subjects and persons that also fell within the concurrent jurisdiction of one or more civil authorities." Witte, *God's Joust* at 12 (footnote omitted).

43. For a helpful collection of such arguments, see Tierney, *Crisis.*

44. The thirteenth-century canon lawyer and cardinal Hostiensis argued that "just as the moon receives its light from the sun and not the sun from the moon, so too the royal power receives its light from the priestly and not vice versa. Again, just as the sun illuminates the world by means of the moon when it cannot do so by itself, that is at night, so too the priestly dignity enlightens the world by means of the royal when it cannot do so by itself, that is when it is a question of inflicting a blood penalty." Tierney, *Crisis,* at 156.

45. Id. at 2.

46. See Mark Lilla, *The Stillborn God: Religion, Politics, and the Modern West* 58–65 (2007).

47. In the original, the primarily theological and scriptural section of the book begins on page 195 and continues for approximately 200 pages to the end of the book. Thomas Hobbes, *Leviathan* 78-79 (Penguin ed., C. B. MacPherson ed., 1968). Criticizing the common depiction of Hobbes as a purely secular thinker, Joshua Mitchell explains: "The central feature of Hobbes's system of political order is the *unity* of sovereignty, political and religious, from which derives, among other things, the Leviathan's right to command obedience . . . ; while reason can conclude for the unity of *political* sovereignty, it cannot conclude for the unity of political and religious sovereignty. Of religious sovereignty, as Hobbes insists again and again, reason must be silent; consequently, the unity of political and religious sovereignty must be established on the basis of Scripture." Joshua Mitchell, "Luther and Hobbes on the Question: Who Was Moses, Who Was Christ?" 53 *J. Politics* 676, 677 (1991). Jean Bethke Elshtain observes that "Hobbes's project was a political theology, but the theology fell out of the picture as the 'canon' or Western political thought got 'normalized'." Elshtain, *Sovereignty,* at xiv–xv.

48. The episode is described in Tierney, *Crisis,* at 53-55.

49. For an extensive presentation of the conflict, see Frank Barlow, *Thomas Becket* (1986), chs. 6-11.

50. For a recounting of the incident, see Steven D. Smith, "Interrogating Thomas More: The Conundrums of Conscience," 1 *St. Thomas L. Rev.* 580 (2003).

51. Taylor, *A Secular Age,* at 32.

52. William C. Placher, *A History of Christian Theology* 136 (1983)

53. See Timothy L. Hall, *Separating Church and State* 9-10, 70-91 (1998).

54. See generally the numerous selections in Tierney, *Crisis.*

55. See Witte, *God's Joust,* at 160-166. See also Hall, *Separating Church and State,* 65 at 62.

56. For a helpful survey that attempts to distill the various positions into four main "models," see Witte, *God's Joust,* at 210-224.

57. See Brian Tierney, "Religious Rights: A Historical Perspective," in *Religious Liberty in Western Thought* 29, 36–37 (Noel B. Reynolds and W. Cole Durham, Jr. eds., 1996).

58. See Smith, *Thomas More.*

59. *The Last Letters of Thomas More* 87 (Alvaro de Silva ed., 2001).

60. Casanova, *Public Religion,* at 22.

61. In fact, the Reformers differed significantly among themselves in their conceptions of the church, and Luther's own notions changed over time as he tried to distinguish his views of the church from those of Catholicism on one side and of more radical Reformers on the other. For a helpful overview, see Alister E. McGrath, *Reformation Thought: An Introduction* 130–138 (1988). See also Carl E. Braaten, *Principles of Lutheran Theology* 54–57 (2d ed. 2007) (discussing "the tension between the Protestant principle and Catholic substance" in Lutheran ecclesiology).

62. In Protestant thinking, John Witte explains, "[e]ach individual stands directly before God, seeks God's gracious forgiveness of sin, and conducts life in accordance with the Bible and Christian conscience." Witte, *God's Joust,* at 16. For a feisty assertion of this view in the context of a plea for freedom of conscience, see Elisha Williams, *The Essential Rights and Liberties of Protestants: A Seasonable Plea for the Liberty of Conscience, and the Right of Private Judgment, In Matters of Religion, Without any Controul from human Authority* (1744). Williams argued for "so clear and obvious a Truth, as may well pass for a self-evident Maxim, *That a Christian is to receive his Christianity from CHRIST alone.*" Id. at 11 (emphasis in original).

63. For a brief account of the incident (which may not have involved the exact famous words passed down in the legend), see Martin Marty, *Martin Luther* 67–70 (2004).

64. Heiko A. Oberman, *Luther: Man between God and the Devil* 204 (1989). Oberman qualifies the usual assessment, however: "Appealing to conscience was common medieval practice; appealing to a 'free' conscience that had liberated itself from all bonds would never

have occurred to Luther." Luther's innovation was to liberate the conscience "from papal decree and canon law." Id.

65. Thomas Paine, "Age of Reason" 6, in *The Theological Works of Thomas Paine* (1882).

66. Cf. Andrew R. Murphy, *Conscience and Community* 111 (2001) ("According to the orthodox view, conscience represented the voice of God within an individual.").

67. Cf. Tierney, *Religious Rights,* at 51.

68. See id. at 35–36. For a recent attempt to revisit and revive the idea, see Richard W. Garnett, "The Freedom of the Church," 4 *J. Cath. Soc. Thought* 59 (2007).

69. For a critical discussion of this development, see John Courtney Murray, S. J., *We Hold These Truths* 201–215 (1960).

70. Williams, *The Essential Rights,* at 12.

71. See generally Murphy, *Conscience and Community;* Noah Feldman, "The Intellectual Origins of the Establishment Clause," 77 *NYU L. Rev.* 346, 354–398 (2002).

72. See Sidney E. Mead, *The Lively Experiment* 60 (1963) (describing the American embrace of religious freedom as a "momentous revolution in the thinking and practice of Christendom" and as "one of the 'two most profound revolutions which have occurred in the entire history of the church'") (quoting Winfred E. Garrison).

73. Cf. Witte, *God's Joust,* at 211 ("Separation of Church and state is often regarded as a distinctly American and relatively modern invention. In reality, separationism is an ancient Western teaching rooted in the Bible.").

74. See generally Daniel J. Boorstin, *The Lost World of Thomas Jefferson* (1993 ed.). For a study emphasizing the continuities between founding era and medieval and classical thought, see also Ellis Sandoz, *A Government of Laws: Political Theory, Religion, and the American Founding* (2001).

75. See John T. Noonan, Jr., *The Lustre of Our Country: The American Experience of Religion Freedom* 86–89 (1998).

76. Virginia Act for Religious Freedom, reprinted in McClear, infra note at 63, 64.

77. For descriptions of the incident, see Philip Hamburger, *Separation of Church and State* 155–180 (2002); Daniel L. Dreisbach, *Thomas Jefferson and the Wall of Separation between Church and State* 25–54 (2002).

78. Cf. Witte, *God's Joust,* at 227 (observing that "the founders sometimes invoked the principle of separation of Church and state as a means to protect the individual's liberty of conscience from the intrusions of either Church or state, or both conspiring together"). In his famous letter to the Danbury Baptists, Jefferson likewise described "the wall of separation between church and State" as working "in behalf of the rights of conscience." Dreisbach, *Thomas Jefferson,* at 148. And Jefferson's letter and metaphor entered American constitutional law in *Reynolds v. United States,* 98 U.S. 145 (1878), a free exercise case.

79. See, e.g., James Madison, "Memorial and Remonstrance against Religious Assessments," reprinted in *Church and State in the Modern Age: A Documentary History* 59, 60 (J. F. McClear ed., 1995).

80. Id. at 60 (emphasis added). Cf. Vincent Blasi, "School Vouchers and Religious Liberty: Seven Questions from Madison's *Memorial and Remonstrance,*" 87 *Cornell L. Rev.* 783, 789 (2002) (observing that the term "cognizance" as used by Madison could not have meant "knowledge" or "awareness" but must rather be understood to mean "responsibility" or "jurisdiction").

81. See generally Peter D. Clarke, *The Interdict in the Thirteenth Century* (2007). Clarke explains that the effectiveness of papal interdicts was mixed: sometime rulers were brought into compliance, but sometimes the interdicts were counterproductive, arousing popular resentment against the papacy. Id. at 169–187.

82. See Tierney, *Idea of Natural Rights,* at 53–73.

83. Harold J. Berman, *Law and Revolution: The Formation of the Western Legal Tradition* 262 (1983).

84. See Edward Peters, *Inquisition* 67 (1988).

85. See *United States v. Ballard,* 322 U.S. 78, 86 (1944) ("The law knows no heresy, and is committed to the support of no dogma") (quoting Watson v. Jones). However, critics of "political correctness," hate speech regulation, or antidiscrimination laws sometimes suggest that there are modern secular equivalents. See generally David Bernstein, *You Can't Say That! The Growing Threat to Civil Liberties from Antidiscrimination Laws* (2003).

86. See Hamburger, *Separation of Church and State,* at 79–83. Laura Underkuffler explains that "[a]lthough these [clergy disqualification] provisions often purported to be efforts to 'encourage religion and religious teaching' or to ensure that religious teachers would 'not . . . be diverted from the great duties of their function,' the fact that such periods of disability often extended beyond the period of the actual holding of religious office indicates that they were motivated, at least in part, by a far greater concern—the danger of institutional merger of church and state." Laura Underkuffler-Freund, "The Separation of the Religious and the Secular," 36 *Wm & Mary L. Rev.* 837, 942 (1995) (footnotes omitted).

87. *McDaniel v. Paty,* 435 U.S. 618 (1978).

88. For a brief description, see Robert E. Rodes, Jr., *Ecclesiastical Administration in Medieval England* 56–59 (1977).

89. For a detailed account of the jurisdictional dispute, see Frank Barlow, *Thomas Becket,* 88–116 (1986).

90. See Rodes, *Ecclesiastical Administration,* at 54.

91. See *American Baptist Churches v. Meese,* 712 F. Supp. 756 (N.D. Cal. 1989).

92. Stolzenberg, "The Profanity of Law," at 31.

93. See Casanova, *Public Religion,* at 14 (describing how conflict between the realms generated "attempts to put an end to the dualism by subsuming one of the spheres under the other").

94. See Paul Johnson, *A History of Christianity* 141 (1976).

95. See Jaroslav Pelikan, 1 *The Christian Tradition: A History of the Development of Doctrine: 1 The Emergence of the Catholic Tradition (100–600)*

71-97 ((1971); Paul Tillich, *A History of Christian Thought* 33-36, 41-43 (1967).

96. See Casanova, *Public Religion,* at 15 ("But from now on, there will be only one single 'this world,' the secular one, within which religion will have to find its own place.").

97. Stolzenberg, "The Profanity of Law," at 35.

98. Cf. John Ayto, *Dictionary of Word Origins* 465 (1990): "**secular** Latin *saeculum,* a word of uncertain origin, meant 'generation, age.' It was used in early Christian texts for the 'temporal world' (as opposed to the 'spiritual world').... The more familiar modern English meaning 'non-religious' emerged in the 16th century."

99. Owen Chadwick, *The Secularization of the European Mind in the Nineteenth Century* 17 (1975).

100. Though this seems to be overwhelmingly the most common judicial usage, the older sense of the secular still appears from time to time even in the case law. See Steven D. Smith, "Nonestablishment 'Under God'? The Nonsectarian Principle," 50 *Vill. L. Rev.* 1, 4-6 (2005).

101. For a recent outstanding example, see 2 Kent Greenawalt, *Religion and the Constitution: Establishment and Fairness* (2008). Though not at all hostile to religion, Greenawalt treats it as axiomatic that government cannot make or act on theological judgments. Id. at 57, 195, 492-493, 523-524.

102. Stolzenberg, "The Profanity of Law," at 51.

103. See, e.g., Ira C. Lupu & Robert W. Tuttle, "Sexual Misconduct and Ecclesiastical Immunity," 2004 *BYU L. Rev.* 1789, 1805-1807.

104. Cf. Taylor, *Secular Age,* 40 at 427 ("And of course, no Pope or bishop could bring a ruler to beg penance on his knees, as happened to Henry II of England and Henry IV of the Empire."). See also Harold J. Berman, *Law and Revolution: The Formation of the Western Legal Tradition* 269 (1983): "When the church eventually became, in the secular mind, an association within the state, as contrasted with an association beyond and against the state, then the plural juris-

dictions in each country of the West were swallowed up by the one national jurisdiction, and the plural legal systems were absorbed more and more by the one national legal system."

105. For Christopher Eisgruber and Lawrence Sager, for instance, the central problem (which they think metaphors and slogans about "walls of separation" can only obscure), is that of "finding fair terms of cooperation for a religiously diverse people." Christopher L. Eisgruber and Lawrence G. Sager, *Religious Freedom and the Constitution* 4 (2007). See also id. at 53 (arguing that the challenge is not to keep church and state separate but rather to devise "terms of fair cooperation for a religiously diverse people"). Their formulation closely tracks John Rawls's description of "the problem of justice," which addresses this question: "How is it possible that there may exist over time a stable and just society of free and equal citizens profoundly divided by reasonable religious, philosophical, and moral doctrines?" John Rawls, *Political Liberalism* xxvii (paperback ed. 1996).

106. The Mexican government as depicted in Graham Greene's *The Power and the Glory* (1940) might be taken as an example.

107. This is roughly the position prescribed by current constitutional doctrine. See *Texas Monthly v. Bullock,* 489 U.S. 1 (1989).

108. See *Jones v. Wolf,* 443 U.S. 595 (1979).

109. See *Boy Scouts of America v. Dale,* 530 U.S. 640 (2000).

110. Kathleen Sullivan attributes this sort of view to Justice Scalia. See Kathleen M. Sullivan, "Justice Scalia and the Religion Clauses," 22 *U. Hawaii L. Rev.* 449, 461–465 (2000). On the "assimilationist" view espoused by Scalia, Sullivan maintains, "religious associations are not so different after all from other garden-variety interest groups"; consequently, "organized religion might as well be allowed to participate openly and freely in politics on a par with other groups and bring home its fair share of the spoil." Id. at 462.

111. Cf. Marci A. Hamilton, "Church Autonomy Is Not a Better Path to 'Truth,'" 22 *J. Law & Relig.* 215, 215–216 (2006–2007) (observing that

because they are "run by humans," churches "really are no different than large corporations").

112. Cf. Noah Feldman, "From Liberty to Equality: The Transformation of the Establishment Clause," 90 *Cal. L. Rev.* 694–706, 723–730 (2002) (arguing that modern Supreme Court jurisprudence has largely converted protection for religious freedom into equality terms and that the equality formulation offers no persuasive justification for a commitment to separation of church and state). "[T]he equality approach," Feldman argues, "just gives up the ghost and admits that there is no particular reason why church and state should remain separate, so long as conditions of equality are maintained." Id. at 730.

113. In this vein, Gerard Bradley asserts a "necessary relation between a Christian cultural matrix and 'separation of church and state.'" Gerard V. Bradley, "Church Autonomy in the Constitutional Order: The End of Church and State," 49 *La. L. Rev.* 1057, 1086 (1989). Operating outside such a matrix, "we constitutionalists are not constructively engaging with the church-state issue and have practically obliterated it." The constitutional commitment "has become opaque . . . , either because it has lost all meaning, or because it is an empty vessel into which one pours whatever meaning is desired." Id. at 1075.

114. Cf. Stolzenberg, "The Profanity of Law," at 74 ("Bereft of a religious sensibility, there is little to temper the confidence of secular liberals in their own judgments. . . . Lacking the religious mindset to function as a constant reminder and heightener of the awareness of the limits of the human mind, liberal secularism all too readily displays a hubris that galls religious believers and other critics of an overweening liberalism.").

115. See, e.g., William P. Marshall, "In Defense of *Smith* and Free Exercise Revisionism," 58 *U. Chi. L. Rev.* 308, 319 (1991) ("Granting exemptions only to religious claimants promotes its own form of in-

equality: a constitutional preference for religious over non-religious belief systems.").

116. For discussion of some of the complexities, see Steven D. Smith, *Law's Quandary* 34–36 (2004).

117. Frederick Mark Gedicks, *The Rhetoric of Church and State* 4–5 (1995).

118. William James, "Pragmatism," in *Pragmatism and Other Essays* 74 (Joseph L. Blau ed., 1963). See also id. at 112 ("We plunge forward into the field of experience with the beliefs our ancestors and we have made already; these determine what we notice, what we notice determines what we do; what we do again determines what we experience."). In a similar vein, Charles Taylor argues that our beliefs are the product not solely or even principally of the rational arguments we may on occasion offer for them as of the background assumptions, beliefs, and practices that he describes as the "social imaginary" and the "cosmic imaginary." Taylor, *Secular Age,* at 171–176, 346–351.

119. Stephen Gey observes that "the Court's repeated avowal of separationist values has created a culture in which the separation of church and state has entered the popular consciousness as a defining ideal of American constitutionalism." Gey, "Life after the Establishment Clause," at 7.

120. For valuable though quite different overview accounts of these various judicial and political developments, see Noah Feldman, *Divided by God* 150–234 (2005); John C. Jeffries, Jr. and James E. Ryan, "A Political History of the Establishment Clause," 100 *Mich. L. Rev.* 279 (2001).

121. *Everson v. Board of Educ.,* 330 U.S. 1 (1947). Of course, *Everson's* historical account has been much disputed. Noah Feldman observes that Everson "distorted the historical record by projecting the concerns of the post-World War II era back to the eighteenth century." Feldman, Equality, at 675. For my own effort to ascertain the original understanding of the establishment clause, see, e.g., Steven

D. Smith, *Foreordained Failure: The Quest for a Constitutional Principle of Religious Freedom* 17–54 (1995).

122. See, e.g., John H. Garvey, "Free Exercise and the Values of Religious Liberty," 18 *Conn. L. Rev.* 779, 779–782 (1986). Michael Smith noted that "[n]one of the Justices has written at length on the justification for the special constitutional place of religion. The Justices tend to be unreflective or reticent on the larger issues." Michael Smith, "The Special Place of Religion in the Constitution," 1983 Sup. Ct. Rev. 83, 88.

123. Feldman, *Equality,* at 674.

124. For thoughtful treatments from the 1960s, for example, see Alan Schwarz, "No Imposition of Religion: The Establishment Clause Value," 77 *Yale L.J.* 692 (1968); Paul Kauper, *Religion and the Constitution* (1964).

125. A list of a number of such works is provided in Alan Brownstein, "Taking Free Exercise Seriously," 57 *Case W. Res. L. Rev.* 55, 61 n.16 (2006). I discuss possible contemporary justifications at greater length in Smith, *Foreordained Failure,* at 77–117; Steven D. Smith, "The Rise and Fall of Religious Freedom in Constitutional Discourse," 140 *U. Penn. L. Rev.* 149, 196–225 (1991).

126. For a recent critical discussion concluding that there is no satisfying reason for giving religion special legal treatment, see Anthony Ellis, "What Is Special about Religion?" 25 *Law & Phil.* 219 (2006).

127. Michael Smith provided a helpful survey of the rationales that justices had employed as of the early 1980s. See Smith, *Special Place of Religion.* For a more recent catalogue, see 2 Kent Greenawalt, *Religion and the Constitution: Establishment and Fairness* 6–13 (2008). For my criticism of Greenawalt's justifications, see Steven D. Smith, "Discourse in the Dusk: The Twilight of Religious Freedom?" 112 *Harv. L. Rev.* 1869 (2009).

128. See, e.g., *Van Orden v. Perry,* 125 Sup. Ct. 2854, 2868 (2005) (Breyer, J., concurring in the judgment).

129. See William P. Marshall, "The Limits of Secularism: Public Religious Expression in Moments of National Crisis and Tragedy," 78 *Notre Dame L. Rev.* 11 (2002). For my much lengthier discussion of religion's potential both to divide and to unify, see Steven D. Smith, "Our Agnostic Constitution," 83 *NYU L. Rev.* 120 (2008).

130. *Newdow v. Elk Grove School District,* 328 F.3d 466 (9th Cir. 2003), vacated in *Elk Grove School Dist. v. Newdow,* 542 U.S. 1 (2004).

131. For a thorough examination that finds the divisiveness rationale largely unpersuasive, see Richard W. Garnett, "Religion, Division, and the First Amendment," 94 *Geo. L.J.* 1667 (2006).

132. Garvey, "Free Exercise," at 794-796.

133. John H. Garvey, *What Are Freedoms For?* 42-57 (1996). Garvey's religious rationale has in turn been criticized by other scholars. See, e.g., Larry Alexander, "Good God, Garvey! The Inevitability and Impossibility of a Religious Justification of Free Exercise Exemptions," 47 *Drake L. Rev.* 35 (1998).

134. I myself occasionally attempt to contribute to the project. See, e.g., Steven D. Smith, "What Does Religion Have to Do with Freedom of Conscience?" 76 *U. Colorado L. Rev.* 910 (2005).

135. Douglas Laycock, "The Underlying Unity of Separation and Neutrality," 46 *Emory L.J.* 43 (1997).

136. See, e.g., Laycock, id.; Douglas Laycock, "Substantive Neutrality Revisited," 110 *W. Virg. L. Rev.* 51 (2007); Douglas Laycock, "Comment: Theology Scholarships, The Pledge of Allegiance, and Religious Liberty: Avoiding the Extremes but Missing the Liberty," 118 *Harv. L. Rev.* 155 (2004); Douglas Laycock, "Formal, Substantive, and Disaggregated Neutrality toward Religion," 39 *Depaul L. Rev.* 993 (1990).

137. Laycock, "Unity," at 69.

138. The logic here is clear: "Funding secular programs, but not religious equivalents that provide the same secular benefit, is rank discrimination." Laycock, "Theology Scholarships," at 199.

139. Laycock has also clarified that he never meant to deny that his interpretation of separation "is inconsistent with the goals of the legal and political movement that has most emphatically claimed the banner of separationism." Laycock, "Substantive Neutrality Revisited," at 65–66.

140. Douglas Laycock, "The Many Meanings of Separation," 70 *U. Chi. L. Rev.* 1667, 1700 (2003) (reviewing Philip Hamburger, *Separation of Church and State* (2002)).

141. For useful overviews of these developments, see Frederick Mark Gedicks, "Spirituality, Fundamentalism, Liberty: Religion at the End of Modernity," 54 *Depaul L. Rev.* 1197, 1209–1215, 1225–1232 (2005); Daniel O. Conkle, "The Path of American Religious Liberty: From the Original Theology to Formal Neutrality and an Uncertain Future," 75 *Ind. L.J.* 1, 6–24 (2000).

142. Although the notion of "separation" has been closely linked to the notion of "no aid to religion" in the American constitutional tradition, see especially Noah Feldman, *Divided by God* 33–42, 244–249 (2005), the relation between these ideas is complicated, both historically and analytically. For further discussion, see Steven D. Smith, "Taxes, Conscience, and the Constitution," 23 *Const. Comm.* 365 (2006).

143. See, e.g., *McCreary County v. ACLU*, 545 U.S. 844, 860 (2005); *Everson v. Board of Educ.*, 330 U.S. 1, 18 (1947).

144. See, e.g., *Wisconsin v. Yoder*, 406 U.S. 205 (1972); *Sherbert v. Verner*, 374 U.S. 398 (1963).

145. *Employment Division v. Smith*, 494 U.S. 872 (1990).

146. Frederick Mark Gedicks, "A Two Track Theory of the Establishment Clause," 43 *B.C. L. Rev.* 1071, 1073, 1074 (2002). While noting the tension, however, Gedicks attempts to develop a "two-track" doctrine that can accommodate both commitments.

147. In this vein, Alan Brownstein observes that "the growing acceptance of formal neutrality as a framework for protecting the free exercise of religion" represents "part of the evolving replacement

for Separatism," and he goes on to criticize this development as a regrettable departure from important constitutional commitments. Alan Brownstein, "Protecting Religious Liberty: The False Messiahs of Free Speech Doctrine and Formal Neutrality," 18 *J. Law & Politics* 119, 120, 186–213 (2002).

148. An insightful discussion of this and closely linked problems is provided in Ira C. Lupu and Robert Tuttle, "The Distinctive Place of Religious Entities in Our Constitutional Order," 47 *Vill. L. Rev.* 37 (2002).

149. A seminal article developing this theme was Douglas Laycock, "Towards a General Theory of the Religion Clauses: The Case of Church Labor Relations and the Right to Church Autonomy," 81 *Colum. L. Rev.* 1373 (1981). In a similar vein, see Frederick Mark Gedicks, "Toward a Constitutional Jurisprudence of Religious Group Rights," 1989 *Wisc. L. Rev.* 99.

150. *Employment Division v. Smith,* 494 U.S. 872 (1990).

151. Richard Garnett, "Religion and Group Rights: Are Churches (Just) Like the Boy Scouts?" 22 *St. John's J. Legal Comm.* 515, 521 (2007).

152. See, e.g., Marci A. Hamilton, *God vs. The Gavel* 189–198 (2005); Jane Rutherford, "Equality as the Primary Constitutional Value: The Case for Applying Employment Discrimination Laws to Religion," 81 *Cornell. L. Rev.* 1049 (1996).

153. For an instance as well as for discussion and a listing of similar decisions, see *Combs v. Central Texas Annual Conference,* 173 F.3d 343 (5th Cir. 1999).

154. The Third Circuit, adopting the exception, followed precedent but noted that "[a]lthough our sister circuits seem to agree that the ministerial exception is grounded in the First Amendment, their rationales for adopting the exception . . . is [sic] often less clear." *Petruska v. Gannon University,* 462 F.3d 294, 305 n.8 (3d Cir. 2006). Courts have distinguished *Smith* by saying that *Smith* eliminated mandatory free exercise exemptions for *individuals* but did not remove religious *institutions'* right to be free from governmental

interference in their internal affairs. See, e.g., *Combs,* 173 F.3d at 349–350. *Smith,* however, did not acknowledge any such limitation on its ruling. And before *Smith,* the case for institutional free exercise rights seemed even less clear or established than the case for individual free exercise rights; see generally Laycock, *Towards a General Theory,* so it is not clear why institutional rights would now be more extensive than individual rights.

155. Richard Garnett notes that the ministerial exception suffers from "the lack of a clear doctrine and textual home" and hence "has something of an imprecise emanations-and-penumbras air about it." Garnett, "Religion and Group Rights," at 526–527.

156. Cf. Bradley, "Church Autonomy," at 1076 ("Liberalism . . . joins the whole problem of religion to that of individual autonomy, so that the former is at best an aspect or accent of the latter.").

157. Marie Failinger, "Wondering after Babel," in *Law and Religion* 94 (Rex J. Adhar ed., 2000).

158. Ronald Beiner, *Philosophy in a Time of Lost Spirit* 30 (1997).

159. James W. Nickel, "Who Needs Freedom of Religion?" 76 *Colo. L. Rev.* 941, 943 (2005).

160. Id. at 951.

161. See Nussbaum, *Liberty of Conscience,* at 18–26.

162. See id. at 265–266 ("Harping on the words 'separation of church and state' has done a lot of harm to reasoned public debate in this area, because it obscures the underlying issues and alienates people from one another.").

163. Id. at 274.

164. Christopher L. Eisgruber and Lawrence G. Sager, *Religious Freedom and the Constitution* 6 (2007).

165. Id. at 22–23.

166. Id. at 29. See also id. at 282 ("From the moment of its inception in the Everson case, the separation-inspired 'no aid' principle has sown confusion and incoherence.").

167. Id. at 17–18, 22–50, 55, 283–284.

168. Id. at 17–18.

169. Id. at 24.

170. Id. at 283.

171. Id. at 13. A proposal to treat religion "equally" with other interests contains an important ambiguity that should be noted, though we need not pursue it here. In the American constitutional regime, most interests are subject to the vicissitudes of politics, qualified only by something like a "rational basis" limitation as protection against unfavorable laws, but a few concerns—race and sex, for example—give rise to so-called heightened scrutiny from the courts, meaning that unfavorable laws directed against them must be justified by something like a "compelling interest." Would treating religion "equally" with other interests mean that religion is thrown into the political pot along with most other interests? Or would religious matters still call for some sort of "heightened scrutiny" by the courts? Eisgruber and Sager give the latter answer. But (referring to their earlier writings), Noah Feldman argues that they fail to justify this choice, and that "there is no better reason to protect the political equality of religious minorities than the political equality of anyone else." Feldman, *Equality,* 143 at 677, 714–716. For a careful discussion of the issue, see Thomas C. Berg, "Can Religious Liberty Be Protected as Equality?" 85 *Tex. L. Rev.* 1185, 1194–1204 (2007).

172. For a careful development of this objection, see Berg, id.

173. Eisgruber and Sager, *Religious Freedom and the Constitution,* at 63–66.

174. For more detailed criticism, see Ira C. Lupu and Robert W. Tuttle, "The Limits of Equal Liberty as a Theory of Religious Freedom," 85 *Tex. L. Rev.* 1247, 1268–1270 (2007).

175. The point is developed in Lupu and Tuttle, at 1252–1254, 1263–1264.

176. Bradley, "Church Autonomy," at 1057.

177. Id.

178. Stolzenberg, "The Profanity of Law," at 35.

5. THE HEAVENLY CITY OF THE SECULAR PHILOSOPHERS

1. Carl L. Becker, *The Heavenly City of the Eighteenth-Century Philosophers* 50–51, 105 (1932).
2. Id. at 77–78, 80, 83.
3. Id. at 78.
4. Id. at 85.
5. Id. at 39–40.
6. Id. at 80–81.
7. Id. at 50–51.
8. Id. at 56–57.
9. See, e.g., David Sorkin, *The Religious Enlightenment* (2008); Daniel Boorstin, *The Lost World of Thomas Jefferson* (1948, rev. ed. 1993); Henry May, *The Enlightenment in America* (1977).
10. Becker, *The Heavenly City*, at 58.
11. Id. at 82.
12. Id. at 60.
13. Pope's poetic pronouncement is susceptible of different interpretations. Arthur Lovejoy, for example, argued on the basis of considerable evidence that Pope wrote in the more classical "Great Chain of Being" tradition. Arthur O. Lovejoy, *The Great Chain of Being* 60 (1936).
14. Becker, *The Heavenly City*, at 60.
15. Id. at 67, 105.
16. Id. at 86.
17. Id.
18. Id. at 87, 108.
19. Id. at 100.
20. Id. at 95.
21. Id. at 102.
22. Id. at 104.
23. Id. at 102.
24. Id. at 30.

25. Id. at 31.
26. Id. at 103.
27. Id. at 40.
28. Id. at 30.
29. Id. at 148.
30. Id. at 41.
31. For a chilling survey, see Jonathan Glover, *Humanity: A Moral History of the Twentieth Century* (1999).
32. See note 9 above.
33. Id. at 14.
34. Id. at 13.
35. Id. at 102.
36. Robin West praises Dewey's "pragmatic liberalism" for just this feature—its quest to derive values from "experience" rather than from "first principles." See, e.g., Robin West, "Liberalism Rediscovered: A Pragmatic Definition of the Liberal Vision," 46 *U. Pitt. L. Rev.* 763, 681–683, 693–701 (1985).
37. For development of this point, see Steven D. Smith, "The Pursuit of Pragmatism," 100 *Yale L.J.* 409, 440–444 (1990).
38. For criticism of Rawls along these lines, see James Boyle, "Is Subjectivity Possible? The Postmodern Subject in Legal Theory," 62 *U. Colo. L. Rev.* 489, 506–509 (1991). And see generally Michael J. Sandel, *Liberalism and the Limits of Justice* (1982).
39. Martha C. Nussbaum, "Foreword: Constitutions and Capabilities: 'Perception' against Lofty Formalism," 121 *Harv. L. Rev.* 4 (2007).
40. Martha C. Nussbaum, "Human Rights and Human Capabilities," 20 *Harv. Hum. Rts. J.* 21, 21 (2007).
41. It should be obvious, I hope, that this discussion will focus only on Nussbaum's use of the capabilities approach; it does not attempt to survey the overall corpus of her scholarly work, which is impressively large and wide-ranging.

42. See, e.g., Amartya K. Sen, "Equality of What?" in *The Tanner Lectures on Human Value* 185 (Sterling McMurrin ed., 1980). For a review of Sen's ideas and of various criticisms and developments, see David A. Clark, "The Capability Approach: Its Development, Critiques, and Recent Advances," http://www.gprg.org/pubs/workingpapers/pdfs/gprg-wps-032.pdf.

43. Martha Nussbaum, "In Defense of Universal Human Values," in *Women and Human Development: The Capabilities Approach* 34–110 (2000).

44. Nussbaum, "In Defense," at 79, 82.

45. Nussbaum has explained her reasons for rejecting such an approach elsewhere. See, e.g., Martha C. Nussbaum, "Judaism and the Love of Reason," in *Philosophy, Feminism, and Faith* 9, 31–34 (Ruth E. Groenhut and Marya Bower eds., 2003).

46. Nussbaum, "In Defense," at 69.

47. Id. at 101.

48. Id. at 97.

49. Id.

50. Id. at 100.

51. Id. at 97. See also id. at 74 (arguing that an appropriate list of capabilities "provides the underpinnings of basic political principles that can be embodied in constitutional guarantees"); Nussbaum, *Frontiers of Justice,* at 70 (capabilities approach provides "the philosophical underpinnings for an account of core human entitlements").

52. See Nussbaum, "In Defense," at 61–65. See also Nussbaum, *Frontiers of Justice,* at 71–73; Nussbaum, Harvard Foreword, at 18–20.

53. Nussbaum, "In Defense," at 71 (emphasis added).

54. Id. at 78–80.

55. Id. at 76.

56. Id. at 100.

57. Id. at 78.

58. See id. at 54–55.

59. Id. at 40.

60. Nussbaum, Harvard Foreword, at 94–95.

61. Nussbaum, "In Defense," at 36.

62. Jeffrey Stout, "Truth, Natural Law, and Ethical Theory," in *Natural Law Theory: Contemporary Essays* 71, 94 (Robert P. George ed., 1992).

63. Nussbaum, *Frontiers of Justice,* at 78. See also id. at 82 (capabilities approach "starts from the outcome: with an intuitive grasp of a particular content, as having a necessary connection to a life worthy of human dignity").

64. Nussbaum, "In Defense," at 83.

65. Id. (emphasis added). In other work, Nussbaum elaborates on the point, explaining that human capabilities can be important or trivial and good or bad. Nussbaum, *Frontiers of Justice,* at 166.

66. Id.

67. See Alasdair MacIntyre, *After Virtue* 52–54, 148 (2d ed. 1985). Nussbaum dissents. See Nussbaum, "In Defense," at 76 ("As I interpret Aristotle, he understood the core of his account of human functioning to be a freestanding moral conception, not one that is deduced from natural teleology or any non-moral source.").

68. See, e.g., Martha Nussbaum, *The Fragility of Goodness* 240–263 (1986).

69. Nussbaum, *Frontiers of Justice,* at 173–176.

70. Id. at 72–73.

71. Id. at 75.

72. Id. at 86.

73. Id. at 72.

74. See, e.g., *Frontiers of Justice,* at 70, 74, 82, 174; Harvard Foreword, at 6, 7, 10–11, 24, 39, 43, 44, 48, 49, 50.

75. See, e.g., Nussbaum, *Frontiers of Justice,* at 43–45, 159–160.

76. See, e.g., Gaudium et Spes, "The Pastoral Constitution of the Church," ch. 1, in *The Documents of Vatican II* 210 (Walter M. Abbott, S.J., 1966).

77. Michael J. Perry, *The Idea of Human Rights* 11–41 (1998).

78. Becker, *The Heavenly City,* at 14.

79. Quoted in Paul Davies, *Cosmic Jackpot: Why Our Universe Is Just Right for Life* 222 (2007).

80. Quoted in Joseph Vining, *The Song Sparrow and the Child* 50 (2004).

81. John Gray, *Straw Dogs: Thoughts on Humans and Other Animals* (2002).

82. Steven Pinker, "The Stupidity of Dignity," *The New Republic,* May 28, 2008, reprinted at http://www.tnr.com/story_print.html?id=d8731cf4-e87b-4d88-b7e7-f5059cd0bfbd.

83. E.g., Nussbaum, Harvard Foreword, at 24, 39–41.

84. Often the justification takes the form of a claim that all humans are made by, and in the image of, God. Louis Pojman, "On Equal Human Worth: A Critique of Contemporary Egalitarianism," in *Equality: Selected Readings* 295 (Louis P. Pojman and Robert Westmoreland eds., 1997) ("The argument implicit in the Judeo-Christian tradition seems to be that God is the ultimate value and that humans derive their value by being created in his image and likeness."). And that rationale can be given more analytical form: Pojman identifies two principal justifications in the religious tradition, which he calls "the Essentialist Argument" and "the Argument from Grace." The first argument holds that "God created all humans with an equal amount of some property P, which constitutes high value." The second argument suggests that "actual value may be different in different people but grace compensates the difference." Pojman, at 295.

85. Id. at 283–294.

86. Id. at 283.

87. Id. at 296.

88. See generally Jeremy Waldron, *God, Locke, and Equality* (2002).

89. Id. at 243.

90. Nussbaum, *Frontiers of Justice,* at 174 (emphasis added).

91. Nussbaum, "In Defense," at 5.

92. E.g., id. at 74. See also Nussbaum, *Frontiers of Justice,* at 78.

93. Id. at 35–41, 47, 99–100, 109.

94. Sometimes Nussbaum seems to be referring not to any currently existing consensus, but rather to one that she thinks can be achieved in the future. Id. at 104, 110. Accurate or not, such predictions seem irrelevant to the issue of philosophical *justification*, except perhaps insofar as Nussbaum thinks a consensus can be achieved *because* the capabilities she lists are in fact morally valuable. But at this point another circularity looms. A set of capabilities is morally valuable, the argument seems to say, if it is likely to achieve an overlapping consensus; and the set of capabilities is likely to achieve an overlapping consensus if it is morally valuable.

95. Nussbaum, "In Defense," at 49.

96. Becker, *The Heavenly City*, at 46.

6. SCIENCE, HUMANITY, AND ATROCITY

1. Quoted in Joseph Vining, *The Song Sparrow and the Child* 6–7 (2004).

2. Id. at 10.

3. Id. at 11.

4. Id. at 8.

5. Id. at 9.

6. See especially Joseph Vining, *From Newton's Sleep* (1994); Joseph Vining, *The Authoritative and the Authoritarian* (1985).

7. Vining, *Song Sparrow*, at 13.

8. Id. at 94.

9. Id. at 27.

10. Id. at 81.

11. Id. at 8.

12. Id. at 48.

13. Id. at 54.

14. Id. at 53.

15. Id. at 109.

16. Id. at 26, at 73 (noting that "'faith,' like 'belief,' becomes a negative term").

17. Id. at 3.

18. Commenting on Changeau's expression of "amazement" that mathematicians can still sometimes talk of divinity, Vining observes: "The use of the word 'astonish' or 'amaze' can be put down as just one of the pejoratives sprinkling late-twentieth-century discussion. . . . Stand back, and look again at the range of discussion in the essays, books, and popularizations that appeared in such great numbers in the second half of the twentieth century: the reaching to deny spirit—and reference to 'theism' as a counterdenial of scientific truth—is striking. It is constant and widespread. Anything to the contrary 'amazes' and 'astonishes.' Even Newton and Einstein astonish." Id. at 72–73.

19. Though he does not enter into the debates, or take sides, Vining does comment on the censorious quality of the campaign to exclude creationism or "intelligent design" from the schools: "Strange, this struggle over the minds of young children—one might think that the theory of evolution, appealing, simple, fertile, fascinating, like a beautiful equation in mathematics, could fend for itself when presented to curious young minds." Id. at 28.

20. Id. at 50.

21. See Christopher Hitchens, *God Is Not Great: How Religion Poisons Everything* (2007); Daniel C. Dennett, *Breaking the Spell: Religion as Natural Phenomenon* (2006); Sam Harris, *The End of Faith: Religion, Terror, and the Future of Reason* (2004).

22. Vining, *Song Sparrow*, at 23.

23. Id. at 76–77.

24. Id. at 81.

25. Id. at 52.

26. Id. at 48.

27. Id. at 23.

28. Id. at 25.

29. Id. at 31.

30. Id. at 27.

31. Id. at 16.

32. Id. at 27.
33. See Ronald Dworkin, *Life's Dominion* 10–24 (1993).
34. Ludwig Wittgenstein, *Culture and Value* 42c (G. H. Von Wright ed., Peter Winch tr., 1980).
35. Vining, *Song Sparrow*, at 2.
36. Michael Polanyi, *Personal Knowledge: Towards a Post-Critical Philosophy* 267 (1958).
37. "Belief is what attaches words to reality; and it is up to the listener to determine whether belief is there, and it is the listener who can help the speaker see whether belief is there." Vining, *Song Sparrow*, at 149.
38. Id. at 1.
39. Id. at 16–17. "Everyone moving to a position on what he or she believes in is something of the position of a lawyer. Everyone is attending to testimony: to her own testimony to herself, . . . and to the testimony of others." Id. at 17.
40. Id. at 85–91.
41. Id. at 93–101.
42. See, e.g., C. S. Lewis, "Religion without Dogma?" in *God in the Dock* 129, 137 (Walter Hooper ed., 1970).
43. For a synopsis of the debate between Lewis and Anscombe, see Walter Hooper, *C. S. Lewis: A Companion and Guide* 618–620 (1996). For a more recent and more technical version of Lewis's argument, see Alvin Plantinga, "Is Naturalism Irrational?" in *The Analytic Theist: An Alvin Plantinga Reader* 72 (James F. Sennett ed., 1998).
44. See, e.g., William James, "The Dilemma of Determinism," in *William James, The Will to Believe and Other Essays in Popular Philosophy and Human Immortality* 145 (1956).
45. "We know that conventional limits and restraints can change with belief about the ultimate nature of things. The twentieth century has its warning examples, most gruesome where total vision has appeared in social and political thought. The connection between what we think about the nature of the world, and what we allow

ourselves to do, is now widely felt, and, with good reason, widely feared." Vining, *Song Sparrow,* at 1–2.

46. Id. at 39.
47. Id. at 134.
48. Id. at 81.
49. Id. at 32.
50. John Gray, *Straw Dogs: Thoughts on Humans and Other Animals* (2002). Gray's book provides an interesting counterpoint to Vining's. There are obvious similarities and parallels: each perceives and probes the tension between the scientific worldview and the moral commitments and values so often professed by those who proclaim this worldview. Gray in particular is exercised by what he views as the hypocrisy and self-deception of those who purport to embrace both science and the values of liberal humanism. But while Vining seeks to save moral commitment and transcendence from the overreachings of science, Gray appears to call for a more candid capitulation.
51. Vining, *Song Sparrow,* at 30–38, 112–114.
52. "I do not think they believe what they seem to say. The scientist or mathematician speaking cosmologically does not cease to be a person speaking, and acting." Id. at 12.
53. Id. at 136.
54. "Let us use the word 'spirit' again until talk can go beyond it." Id. Vining wonders whether "life" might be a better term but tentatively decides against it. Id. at 143–145.
55. Id. at 116.
56. Id. at 115–116.
57. Id. at 108.
58. Id. at 67–70, 103–108. This particular line of reflection is developed more fully in Vining's earlier work.
59. Id. at 123–124.
60. Joseph Vining, "Legal Commitments and Religious Commitments," 44 *U. San Diego L. Rev.* 69, 74 (2007).

61. Vining, *Song Sparrow*, at 26–27. Though the nature of the presentation is quite different, the viewpoint here and through much of the book is reminiscent of C. S. Lewis's small classic, *The Abolition of Man* (1944). The similarities to Lewis are sufficiently strong that it is hard not to see in the book's title—*The Song Sparrow and the Child*—an allusion to the Oxford pub, known as "The Eagle and the Child" or "The Bird and the Baby"—in which Lewis regularly met with J. R. R. Tolkien and others to read and discuss each others' work.

62. Id. at 143.

63. Id. at 17.

64. Timothy Jackson, *The Priority of Love: Christian Charity and Social Justice* xii–xiii (2003).

65. Vining, *Song Sparrow*, at 146–148.

66. Id. at 142–143.

67. Id. at 20.

68. Id. at 148–152, 135.

7. OPENING UP THE CAGE?

1. Ronald Dworkin, *Is Democracy Possible Here?* 1 (2006).

2. See, e.g., Steven D. Smith, "The (Always) Imminent Death of the Law," 44 *U. San Diego L. Rev.* 47 (2007).

3. See, e.g., *American Piety in the 21st Century: New Insights into the Depth and Complexity of Religion in the US, 2006.* Baylor Inst. for Stud. of Religion (2006).

4. For discussion, see Frederick Mark Gedicks, "Spirituality, Fundamentalism, Liberty: Religion at the End of Modernity," 54 *DePaul L. Rev.* 1197 (2005).

5. Insofar as the First Amendment's establishment clause has been interpreted to require that governments act only for "secular purposes," the invocation of religion in public debate can in theory lead to invalidation of legislation or other measures adopted on the basis of that debate. Only rarely has the Supreme Court actually

invalidated laws or public policies on this ground, however. See, e.g., *McCreary County v. ACLU,* 545 U.S. 844 (2005) (invalidating Kentucky Ten Commandments display on the ground that the display served only a religious, not a secular purpose); *Wallace v. Jaffree,* 472 U.S. 38 (1985) (invalidating Alabama "moment of silence" law in part based on religious statements made in its support).

6. For a proposal for the development of a "constitutional etiquette" governing the use of religion in public discourse, see Paul Horwitz, "Religious Tests in the Mirror: The Constitutional Law and Constitutional Etiquette of Religion in Judicial Nominations," 15 *Wm. & Mary Bill of Rts. J.* 75, 133-144 (2006). Some of Kent Greenawalt's work can be viewed as an elaboration reflection about the etiquette governing such discourse. See, e.g., Kent Greenawalt, *Private Consciences and Public Reasons* (1995).

7. I have occasionally dallied in that debate elsewhere. See, e.g., Steven D. Smith, *Getting over Equality: A Critical Diagnosis of Religious Freedom in America* 27-44 (2001); Steven D. Smith, "Believing Persons, Personal Believings: The Neglected Center of the First Amendment," 2002 *U. Ill. L. Rev.* 1233; Steven D. Smith, "'The Religious,' 'the Secular,' and 'the Moral': What Are We Talking About?" 36 *Wake Forest Law Rev.* 487 (2001)

8. Richard Rorty, *Philosophy and Social Hope* 168 (1999).

9. Id. at 171.

10. See, e.g., Susan Jacoby, *The Age of American Unreason,* 183-209 (2008); Dworkin, *Is Democracy Possible?* at 50-89. For stronger statements, see Christopher Hitchens, *God Is Not Great: How Religion Poisons Everything* (2007); Kevin Phillips, *American Theocracy* (2006).

11. See, e.g., Michael W. McConnell, "Five Reasons to Reject the Claim that Religious Arguments Should Be Excluded from Democratic Deliberation," 1999 *Utah L. Rev.* 639.

12. The Letter from the Birmingham Jail would be an obvious instance.

13. See, e.g, Reinhold Niebuhr, *The Irony of American History* (1952).

14. See, e.g., John Courtney Murray, *We Hold These Truths: Catholic Reflections on the American Proposition* (1960).

15. E.g., Abraham Joshua Heschel, *The Insecurity of Freedom* (1963).

16. See Richard Rorty, *Contingency, Irony, and Solidarity* (1989).

17. Rorty, *Philosophy and Social Hope*, at 172.

18. Id.

19. Id. at 173.

20. Cf. Ludwig Wittgenstein, *On Certainty* 39e (para. 307) (G. E. M. Anscombe and G. H. von Wright eds., 1969) ("If I tried I could give a thousand [grounds for my way of going on], but none would be as certain as the very thing they were supposed to be grounds for").

21. John Rawls, *A Theory of Justice* 48-49 (1971).

22. See W. V. O. Quine and J. S. Ullian, *The Web of Belief* (1978).

23. See e.g., Wittgenstein, *On Certainty*, at 46e (para. 358).

24. Andrew Koppelman, "Religion as conversation-starter," http://balkin.blogspot.com/2007/07/religion-as-conversation-starter.html.

25. Id.

26. Horwitz, "Religious Tests," at 146.

27. Christopher J. Eberle, *Religious Convictions in Liberal Politics* 109-151 (2002).

28. Id. at 104-108.

Acknowledgments

Any book reflects the influence and assistance of many minds; but with this book, written in pieces over a period of years, the people to whom I am indebted are simply too numerous to list. I nonetheless owe special thanks to Larry Alexander, Paul Campos, Bill Edmundson, Rick Garnett, Andy Koppelman, Michael Perry, and Joe Vining, each of whom read the book as a whole and offered detailed and enormously valuable suggestions.

I benefited from presenting several of the chapters in workshops and a conference at several law schools: Arizona State, Columbia, Georgetown, Michigan, San Diego, and the Universidad Torcuato di Tella.

Several of the chapters are adapted from previous publications, and are used here with permission. Portions of Chapters 1 and 4 are adapted from "Discourse in the Dusk: The Twilight of Religious Freedom?" a review of Kent Greenawalt's *Religion and the Constitution, Volume 2: Establishment and Fairness* that I published in the May 2009 issue of the *Harvard Law Review* (Vol. 122, No. 7). Special thanks are owed to the editors of the *Harvard Law Review* for their work on the book review and for permitting portions of the book review to appear in the current effort.

Chapter 2 is adapted from an article called "De-Moralized: *Glucksberg* in the Malaise," reprinted from *Michigan Law Review*, June 2008, Vol. 106, No. 8. Copyright 2008 by Steven D. Smith.

Chapter 3 is adapted from an article called "Is the Harm Principle Illiberal?" published in the *American Journal of Jurisprudence,* Vol. 51, p. 1 (2006), and is used with the *Journal*'s permission.

Chapter 6 is adapted from a review essay called "Science, Humanity, and Atrocity: A Lawyerly Examination," reprinted from *Michigan Law Review,* May 2006, Vol. 104, No. 6. Copyright 2006 by Steven D. Smith.

As always, I owe special thanks to my wife, Merina, for her unfailing love and support.

Index

281